Contents

Acknowledgements

I would like to thank Tim Gregson-Williams for his support of this second edition and Greig Aitken for his tact and persistence in bringing it all together. My thanks also go to staff and students at Lipson Community College for help with photos, my students for their criticisms, Jo for ideas and expertise and, as always, Richard for his patience and humour.

The author and publisher would like to thank the following for permission to use photographs: Underwood & Underwood/CORBIS, Figure 5.3; Bubbles/ Loisjoy Thurstun, Figures 8.1, 8.6, 12.3; Bubbles/J Lamb, Figure 9.1; Angela Hampton Family Life Pictures, Figures 8.2, 17.2, 17.3, 19.4; Sally and Richard Greenhill, Figures 8.4, 10.4, 16.3; Mike Abrahams/Network, Figure 8.5; Range/Bettman/UPI, Figure 9.3; Bruno Barbey/Magnum Photos, Figure 9.6; Ric Ergenbright/CORBIS, Figure 10.2; J. Allan Cash, Figures 10.3, 19.1; Brenda Prince/Format, Figure 10.5; Associated Press/Topham Picture Point, Figure 11.1; Action-Plus Photographic/Chris Brown, Figure 11.2; Bubbles/Jacqui Farrow, Figure 11.3; Life File/Nicola Sutton, Figure 11.6, 12.2; Collections/Sandra Lousada, Figure 12.4; Paul Lowe/Network, Figure 11.7; Maggie Murray/Format, Figure 13.2; Ulrike Preuss/Format, Figure 14.1; Cyril Letourneur/GLMR/Colorific!, Figure 14.3; BBC, Figure 14.5; Empics/Neal Simpson, Figure 15.1 (left), Rex Features/London (right); Collections/Anthea Sieveking, Figures 15.3, 16.4, 18.1; Bubbles/Ian West, Figure 15.2; Gary John Norman/Impact, Figure 15.5; Ronald Grant Archive, Figure 15.6; Nathan Benn/CORBIS, Fig 15.4; Life File/Angela Maynard, Figure 16.1; NYT Pictures, Figure 16.2; Postman Pat Wins a Prize, illustrated by Jane Hickson, Scholastic Ltd., Figure 16.10; Sarah Lenton/Practical parenting/Robert Harding Syndication, Figure 17.1; Nick Kelsh/CORBIS, Figure 17.4; Associated Press, Figure 18.2; Bubbles, Figure 18.3; Arthur Jumper/Life File, Figure 18.4; The Kobal Collection, Figure 19.2; Hulton-Deutsch/CORBIS, Figure 19.6; Redferns/David Redfern, Figure 19.3.

The author and publisher would also like to thank the following: Les Éditions Albert René for the use of the illustrations in Figure 10.1; *Scientific American* for permission to reproduce the Fantz bar chart (Figure 16.6),

BASICS IN PSYCHOLOGY

2nd Edition

Barbara Woods

Hodder & Stoughton

A MEMBER OF THE HODDER HEADLINE GROUP

Orders: please contact Bookpoint Ltd, 78 Milton Park, Abingdon, Oxon OX14 4TD.
Telephone: (44) 01235 827720, Fax: (44) 01235 400454. Lines are open from 9.00–6.00, Monday to Saturday, with a 24 hour message answering service. Email address: orders@bookpoint.co.uk

British Library Cataloguing in Publication Data
A catalogue record for this title is available from The British Library

ISBN 0 340 753676

First published 2000
Impression number   10 9 8 7 6 5 4 3 2 1
Year   2005 2004 2003 2002 2001 2000

Typeset by Wearset, Boldon, Tyne and Wear.
Printed in Spain for Hodder & Stoughton Educational, a division of Hodder Headline Plc, 338 Euston Road, London NW1 3BH by Graphycems.

adapted from R. Fantz (1961) 'The origin of form perception', *Scientific American*, **204**(5), 66–72; Academic Press for permission to reproduce Tables 9.1 and 16.1, 'Completion times' from B. Schmidt (1986) 'Mere presence and social facilitation', *Journal of Experimental Psychology*, **22**(3) – Table 16.1 is a summary of the results from two studies: B. Schwarz, A. Campos and E. Baisel (1973) 'Heart rate results on the visual cliff', *Journal of Experimental Child Psychology*, **15**, 86–9 and J. Campos, A. Langer and A. Krowitz (1970) 'Heart rate results from the visual cliff', *Science*, 196–7; for Figure 15.8, the authors and publishers of R. Rosenthal and L. Jacobson (1966) 'Teachers' expectancies: determinations of pupils' IQ gains', *Psychological Reports*, **19**, 115–18, 1966 Southern Universities Press. While every effort has been made to trace copyright holders, this has not been possible in all cases; any omissions brought to our attention will be remedied in future printings.

Index compiled by Frank Merrett, Cheltenham, Gloucester.

Introduction

The first edition of *Basics in Psychology* was published in 1995 to meet the needs of students and teachers using the new GCSE Psychology syllabus. Since then teachers have been able to develop a clearer understanding of what the syllabus means and what the examiners are looking for. Now we know what our students find most difficult, as well as the areas of greatest weakness in their examination answers.

This second edition has used this knowledge to refine and clarify the original material, and to present it in a way which is attractive and accessible. Features which have been retained include sections and chapters which reflect the SEG syllabus, a chapter devoted to the planning and reporting of research to support student's work on the practical exercise, the use of bold type to highlight key terms and an extensive glossary.

New features include exercises based closely on examination questions, bullet points to aid understanding and revision, greater use of tabs to identify core topics and definitions, a practical exercise checklist and finally an extended reading list.

My aim has been to provide a textbook which is suitable for a wide range of abilities and yet includes sufficient information to achieve an A grade in GCSE Psychology. Whether you use *Basics in Psychology* as a textbook or out of general interest, my hope is that you will find it enjoyable and stimulating.

Barbara Woods

WAYS OF EXPLAINING HUMAN ACTION

SECTION

In Section A we look at some of the ways in which psychologists have explained what humans do and why they do it. The topics in this section appear again in other parts of the book because they are core topics. For example, instincts are briefly described in this section because they re-appear in explanations for aggression and for attachment. These core topics are grouped in four chapters and to help you recognise these core topics when they appear later in the book, you will find a tab in the margin to indicate which of the four chapters they are described in. The chapters, along with a brief description and an example of the tab, are all shown in Box 1.1 on page 2.

1.1

INBORN   Chapter 1   **The Influences of Inborn Characteristics**
                             This chapter describes some of the abilities we are born with

LEARNING   Chapter 2   **The Role of Learning in Shaping Behaviour**
                             This chapter describes theories which explain how humans
                             learn from their environment

SOCIAL   Chapter 3   **Social and Cultural Influences**
                             Here we look at some of the ways that other people affect us

COGNITION   Chapter 4   **The Influences of Thinking and Perception**
                             This chapter describes some aspects of cognition – how we
                             see and make sense of the world we live in

If you want to find examples of any of the material in these four chapters, just look for the related tab anywhere in Sections C, D or E (Chapters 8–19) and read the text which is alongside it.

The Influences of Inborn Characteristics

If characteristics are inborn, then we are born with them. Because we are born with these abilities or characteristics, we do not have to learn them. Many psychologists consider inborn characteristics to be at least a starting point for later behaviour. However, there is considerable disagreement about just how important inborn characteristics are, and how important *experience* is in a person's behaviour. This disagreement is often referred to as the nature/nurture debate in psychology. In this chapter we are going to focus on the nature side. We will look at such inborn characteristics as instincts and reflexes, genetics and what we inherit from our parents, and how development unfolds in a fixed pattern – maturation and the sensitive period.

Instincts

DEFINITION

An **instinct** is a need, and the drive to satisfy that need, which is inborn.

Examples of instincts are attachment behaviours (p. 74), the bonding instinct (p. 82), the fighting instinct (p. 133), the aggressive instinct (p. 134), the life-enhancing instinct (p. 134).

INSTINCTS AND BEHAVIOUR

Instincts affect behaviour in several ways:

- By **contributing to survival:** instinctive attachment behaviours ensure the infant is fed and cared for. Ethologists explain aggression by identifying the **fighting instinct** which contributes to survival because it enables members of a species to, for example, acquire food sources and protect the young. When a threat to survival occurs, the fighting instinct is triggered. In humans, threats to the individual's wellbeing or self-esteem may trigger the fighting instinct, or **aggression**.

- Instincts ensure that behaviours **persist**, because although a need may be satisfied this is only temporary. The need is still present, and the drive to satisfy it will build up again.
- Instincts must be **satisfied** or **released** in some way, otherwise the energy which drives them builds up and creates unbearable pressure in us. From the psychodynamic viewpoint, Freud (see p. 134) argues that the **aggressive instinct** is primarily aimed against the self. We have to release this aggression somehow but in order to preserve ourselves we direct it outwards.
- Freud also argued that we have **life-enhancing instincts** (for example, hunger, sex and creativity). The **libido** is the drive which tries to achieve satisfaction of these instincts. The need to satisfy the libido during the **phallic stage** causes conflict which is resolved when the child identifies with the same sex parent. It adopts the behaviours and attitudes of this parent, so according to psychodynamic theory the libido is the basis for our **moral behaviour**, **gender role behaviour** and **personality**.
- They may affect our behaviour in ways we are not conscious of, according to Freud – we may not be aware of them but much of our behaviour is actually aimed at satisfying these instincts.

Reflexes

DEFINITION

A **reflex** is an automatic physical response to a specific stimulus – it is outside of conscious control.

Examples of a reflex include:

- the **rooting** reflex – when you gently touch a baby's cheek it will turn its head towards your finger
- the **sucking** reflex – if you put something in a baby's lips it will start sucking the object
- the **eye blink** – when a puff of air is blown close to your open eye you blink
- **salivation** – certain glands produce saliva when you smell, see or taste food
- **fear response** – this occurs when something loud, or sudden, or threatening happens: you 'jump' (known as the 'startle reflex'), your breathing and heart rate increase, muscles respond so you feel 'weak at the knees' or have 'butterflies' in your stomach
- **arousal** – the effects are very similar to those for fear, listed above, but the cause is not necessarily threatening; it may be due to excitement or simply to the presence of other people.

REFLEXES AND LEARNING

Some psychologists take the view that reflexes are the basis for learning, two examples being:

- **Cognitive development** – according to Piaget (see p. 232), reflexes such as sucking and grasping are used by the baby to explore and understand its world. Each reflex is represented in the infant's mind as a basic schema, which develops as its understanding increases. Nevertheless the basis for such learning is, for example, the grasping reflex which develops to enable the child to grasp objects of various sizes.
- **Classical conditioning** – a reflex is an innate response to a specific stimulus, but according to the principles of classical conditioning we can learn to produce that same response to a *different* stimulus. Details of how 'Little Albert' learned the fear response to his pet rat are given in Chapter 2, p. 11. So through classical conditioning we can learn to be frightened of people or objects which do not actually pose a threat.

Maturation

DEFINITION   **Maturation** refers to the genetically programmed sequence of change which can be modified by experience.

Examples of changes which are due to maturation are:

- the onset of puberty
- probably some perceptual abilities such as depth perception – see **visual perception** (p. 241)
- cognitive abilities such as **object permanence** and **decentration**, because they appear at a similar age in most children and in the same order. Because research shows that children do not have these abilities before a certain age, this suggests they are due to maturation – see **cognitive development** (p. 226.)

MATURATION AND DEVELOPMENT

Changes due to maturation are 'programmed' into the genes, so they are innate. The *sequence* of changes, and the approximate age at which they happen, are the same for all humans.

However, although they are not *caused* by experience, these changes can only fully take place if certain **environmental** factors are present. For example, the child needs experience in order to develop the muscles and co-ordination necessary to walk effectively. The adolescent girl who is severely under-nourished may not menstruate.

Unfortunately in many areas of development it is not so straightforward to identify when and how change may be due to maturation. For example, in **visual perception** or **cognitive development**, psychologists have identified changes which occur at a similar age for most children. The inference is that these changes are dependent to some extent on maturation. But equally, certain environmental factors must be present for development to take place and so one difficulty is to decide whether the appearance of a new ability is simply due to learning or is due to maturation.

Sensitive period

DEFINITION
The **sensitive period** is a period during development when the individual is genetically prepared to take particular advantage of certain experiences.

Examples of the sensitive period occur in:

- **attachments** – research suggests that children may be particularly open to develop relationships with others during the first two or three years of life (see p. 82). Attachment behaviours, which we considered at the beginning of this chapter, encourage others to interact.
- **visual perception** – although the newborn has certain visual abilities, they need experience to develop. Without this experience they may not develop properly, although the extent to which this is the case is difficult to test (see p. 242).

SENSITIVE PERIODS AND DEVELOPMENT

The sensitive period plays a part in explaining development because it is a time when the individual is particularly open and responsive to certain experiences or influences. Knowledge of when the sensitive period occurs helps development because:

- the appropriate experiences can be provided so that the child will benefit from them when it is most able to. Bowlby claimed that a good **attachment** between a baby and its mother could only occur within the first two to three years of life, the sensitive period for the development of attachment.
- if the child does not have the opportunity of appropriate experiences during the sensitive period, there may be difficulties with development

which will need extra care. Bowlby argued that if no attachments had developed by three years of age, it would be almost impossible for the child to develop an attachment. Using the example of **visual perception**, it may be that if the eyes do not receive a range of stimuli such as light and dark, movement and so on, then perceptual abilities may not develop properly.

Heredity

DEFINITION

Heredity refers to inborn characteristics. In the nature/nurture debate, the hereditarian position is that most of the variation in human characteristics is due to innate factors.

Examples of heredity in the nature/nurture debate are:

- that **intelligence** is largely inherited (see p. 176)
- that **visual perception** is innate – humans are able to perceive at birth (see p. 237). However other abilities develop later but it is difficult to find out whether these are due largely to experience (suggesting the role of nurture) or to maturation (nature), or indeed a combination of both.

THE IMPORTANCE OF HEREDITY IN THE NATURE/NURTURE DEBATE

Heredity is important to psychologists because they want to find out what causes particular behaviour. Those on the nature side of the nature/nurture debate say that **inborn characteristics** have most influence in making us what we are.

Once psychologists know the probable basis for a characteristic, this affects what can, or cannot, be done about it. For example, if **intelligence** is largely inherited, then little can be done to change it so trying to do so is a wasted effort. However, if heredity plays a smaller part in intelligence, this means that the environment has considerable influence – the nurture side of the argument. As a consequence there is a much greater role for intervening to enhance abilities or to modify difficulties.

There are several reasons why the nature/nurture debate is likely to remain inconclusive. These relate to the ethical and methodological difficulties of separating the influences of nature and nurture and the evidence which suggests that *both* play an essential role. These points are discussed in greater detail as they relate to intelligence (p. 185) and visual perception (p. 247).

One way of trying to separate the influences of nature and nurture is by studying twins.

Twin research

Twins are people who are born of the same mother at the same time. There are two types of twins:

DEFINITION

- **identical** twins develop from a single egg which splits just after fertilisation: they are called **monozygotic twins (MZ)** because monozygotic means 'one egg'. MZs are genetically identical.

DEFINITION

- **fraternal** twins develop from two eggs which are fertilized at the same time: they are called **dizygotic twins (DZ)**, meaning 'two egg'. Genetically they are as similar as any two siblings, they share 50% of the same genes. However, because they share the womb at the same time and are the same age, they may have more similar experiences than two siblings who are different ages.

Examples of twin studies occur in:

- **intelligence** – to investigate the heritability of intelligence (see p. 176)
- **temperament** – to investigate whether temperament has a genetic basis (see p. 166).

THE IMPORTANCE OF TWIN RESEARCH

Twin research is important in psychology because identical twins are unique in that they are two people who share identical genes – an identical genetic inheritance. They represent a rare opportunity to try to separate the influence of heredity from that of the environment. Twins have been studied in two ways:

1 Comparison of MZ and DZ twins – identical twins have identical genes (they are genetically 100% alike) so they should be very similar in every way. In contrast, because fraternal twins are only 50% genetically alike, they should be less similar. If this is found to be the case, then the greater similarity between identical twins could be explained by their genes, which lends support to the hereditarian view.

2 Comparison of MZ twins reared apart – another way to separate the environmental effects from the effects of heredity is to search out identical twins who have been reared apart. If they grow up in a different family, in a different city, then we can see what effect this has on two people who are genetically identical. If, when tested as adults on measures such as intelligence and personality, they score quite differently, this suggests that environment is very influential because it has changed genetically identical people. However, if they show very similar scores this supports the view that heredity is the most important influence.

Summary

Each of the concepts described above relate to inborn (or innate) characteristics, which represent the nature side of the nature/nurture debate. Some of these characteristics may be very influential, such as the role of instincts in aggression, but the influence of inborn characteristics is hard to identify. An example of this is the effect of maturation on the development of visual perception.

Exercises

1 What is an instinct?
2 Give an example of an instinct from this book and describe how it might affect someone's behaviour.
3 Give two examples of human reflexes.
4 Give one example of how a reflex can play a part in learning.
5 What do psychologists mean by maturation?
6 Why is maturation important in explaining human development?
7 What is meant by a 'sensitive period'?
8 How does a sensitive period play a part in the explanation of human development?
9 Why is heredity important in the nature/nurture debate in psychology?
10 What is the difference between monozygotic and dizygotic twins?
11 Why do psychologists study twins?

The Role of Learning in Shaping Behaviour

2

In this chapter we are going to look at various proposals of how behaviour can be shaped by the environment. In the nature/nurture debate which runs through psychology, this is the chapter which considers some aspects of the nurture side in more detail because we look at people's experiences and how they affect behaviour. The theories described here are used throughout the book to explain various aspects of human behaviour.

Learning

DEFINITION

Learning is a relatively permanent change in behaviour which is due to experience.

The way in which psychologists test whether something has been learned is by looking at behaviour. For example, two boys watch a video of a boy damaging toys. Afterwards both boys are given the same type of toys to play with. One child does the same thing as the boy in the video – we say he has learned the behaviour. We know this because we can *see* him doing the same thing! However, the other child plays with the toys without damaging them. He may have remembered what he saw in the video, and may do the same thing himself in a few days time, but unless we see him performing the behaviour, we cannot be sure he has learned it.

We are going to look at three explanations for how we learn:

1 classical conditioning
2 operant conditioning
3 social learning.

Classical conditioning

DEFINITION **Classical conditioning** is a form of learning in which an automatic response is elicited by a previously neutral stimulus through its association with an unconditional stimulus.

PRINCIPLES OF CLASSICAL CONDITIONING

In classical conditioning the automatic response is one over which the individual (or animal) has no control. Examples are listed in Chapter 1 under reflexes, such as salivation, fear response, eye blink. It was salivation which interested Ivan Pavlov, who was studying digestion in dogs. He noted that they salivated even when they saw an empty food dish. Pavlov showed that after pairing food (which triggers salivation) with the dish on many occasions, the dog eventually salivated to the dish alone. The dog had learned to associate the dish with food.

John Watson and Rosalind Raynor (1920) demonstrated the process of classical conditioning in an 11-month old boy. While 'Little Albert' was playing happily with a white rat, a metal bar was struck close to him – this frightened him. After repeating this several times (this repetition is called 'trials'), Little Albert became frightened of the rat, and indeed of other white furry things.

The process of classical conditioning is shown in Figure. 2.1

	Stimulus		Response
• The situation before conditioning starts	rat	→	no response
	loud noise (UCS)	→	fear (UCR)
• During trials	rat + loud noise	→	fear
• When conditioning has occurred	rat (CS)	→	fear (CR)

FIGURE 2.1 The classical conditioning process

The innate response (fear) is called the **unconditional response** (UCR) because it is not learned. The stimulus which causes fear (the loud noise) is called the **unconditional stimulus** (UCS).

Initially the white rat does not trigger fear but after several trials an association between the rat and fear develops, so Little Albert had learned the fear response to the rat. The rat is the **conditional stimulus** (CS), and the fear response is now called the **conditional response** (CR). Further research on classical conditioning has shown that:

- **Generalisation** occurs when a *similar* stimulus also triggers a response, for example Watson and Rayner found that Little Albert was also fearful of a white rabbit and of cotton wool.
- **Extinction** occurs when the conditional stimulus is presented *without* the unconditional stimulus. If Little Albert was able to play with the rat and there was no loud noise, eventually his fear response would be extinguished. This principle operates with some automatic responses, such as salivation in dogs, but not necessarily in humans as we see below.

CLASSICAL CONDITIONING AND HUMAN BEHAVIOUR

If we have learned to associate a person, thing or situation with fear or anxiety, this may influence our behaviour. For example:

- **Phobias** – a phobia is an irrational fear of something. Little Albert developed a phobia about cotton wool. Someone who has been in a car accident may develop a phobia of cars, of being in small places or of the particular street where it happened.
- **Avoidance** – we avoid the experiences which we have learned to associate with fear or anxiety, so the victim of a car accident may avoid driving down that street because of it. However, by avoiding the cause of fear, there is no opportunity for fearful responses to become extinguished, as we shall see shortly under operant conditioning.
- **Discipline** – if a girl sees a parent being angry because she did something wrong, this creates anxiety. The child's anxiety may become conditioned to the parent's facial expression, so that just a *look* of anger may be sufficient to warn the child that she is doing something wrong.
- **The weapons effect** – Berkowitz proposed that we may learn to associate certain objects (such as a gun) or people with anger, which is psychologically painful and can lead to aggression. When we are angry, therefore, these stimuli can trigger an aggressive response (see aggression, p. 137).

Operant conditioning

THE LAW OF EFFECT

Edward Thorndike was one of the first psychologists to study how animals operated on their environments. He found that a cat could learn to open a latch in order to escape from a box and reach some fish which was outside. Thorndike noted that the cat opened the latch by accident, but that every time it was returned to the box there was less time before it opened the latch and escaped. From this he generated the following law:

DEFINITION **The Law of Effect** – responses are learned when they produce pleasant consequences. If there are *no* pleasant consequences then the response stops; it becomes extinguished.

This is the basic principle of operant conditioning – it is what happens *after* a particular behaviour which determines whether or not it is learned. B. F. Skinner, who wanted to make psychology much more scientific, became the leading figure in the behaviourist approach and claimed that 'behaviour is shaped and maintained by its consequences'. Skinner argued that behaviour is strengthened by positive and negative reinforcement, and weakened by punishment.

REINFORCEMENT

Reinforcement is any consequence which strengthens behaviour. There are two types of reinforcement, which operate in different ways:

- **positive reinforcement** strengthens behaviour by rewarding it (which is a pleasant consequence, as stated in the Law of Effect);
- **negative reinforcement** strengthens behaviour by removing or stopping an unpleasant experience (which is also a pleasant consequence).

Positive reinforcement and human behaviour

Positive reinforcement means providing something which the individual wants, something which is rewarding, as a consequence of their behaviour. Anything which satisfies a basic human need is called a **primary reinforcer** (such as food or drink). Some psychologists argue that praise is a primary reinforcer, because it satisfies a basic need for approval from others. A gold star, sweets, a hug, money – all are called **secondary reinforcers** because they do not satisfy basic instincts. If reinforcement stops, then the behaviour should become **extinguished**.

Positive reinforcement can affect human behaviour:

- by **strengthening** it, so that it is more likely to be repeated. Initially the behaviour is rewarded every time it occurs. The child is congratulated every time he or she carries some dishes carefully. After several times the child should only be congratulated intermittently (see next point).
- when it is **partial**, so it is not provided after every response, extinction takes much longer, and if you are trying to strengthen a desired behaviour it is less work! An example of partial reinforcement is in gambling, where

there is only the occasional win but the gambler keeps gambling because he or she knows that *at some point* there will be another win. This is one reason why slot machines have flashing lights and make lots of noise when a player wins – it acts as reinforcement for players at other machines.

- by **shaping** behaviour, so that if a reward is provided after behaviour which is only slightly similar to that which is desired, this behaviour will occur more frequently and the less desired behaviour will drop away. Within this narrower range of behaviour, rewards will then be applied to behaviour which is more similar to that desired, and reward will be withdrawn from less appropriate behaviour. In this way behaviour which is initially random can be shaped to be that which is desired.

To be effective we must ensure that the rewards are applied immediately after the desired behaviour so that a close relationship between the behaviour and the consequence is established. We must also ensure that the consequences *are* rewarding for the individual, for example if a child is embarassed by public praise from a teacher this is an unpleasant consequence and so acts as punishment and weakens behaviour.

Negative reinforcement and human behaviour

Negative reinforcement strengthens behaviour by the removal or avoidance of something unpleasant. Some examples of negative reinforcement are:

- **pro-social behaviour** – if we see someone in distress we experience arousal, which is unpleasant. One way of stopping this unpleasantness is to help the other person and so reduce their distress. Having done this, our arousal subsides (see p. 272). This is an example of negative reinforcement because an action (giving help) stops an unpleasant experience (arousal), so we are more likely to help someone else in the future.
- **bullying** – if a child is bullied at school for his dinner money, then he may give the money up to stop the bully. The next time the bully approaches, the child will give the money quickly – his behaviour has been strengthened because it brought an unpleasant experience (being bullied)to an end. In addition, the bully has been rewarded for his behaviour, so he too is likely to continue.
- **stopping bullying** – if the boy stands up to the bully, who then stops bullying, this boy is likely to stand up to a bully the next time it happens. This is another example of negative reinforcement because the behaviour (standing up to the bully) ends the boy's unpleasant experience (being bullied).

PUNISHMENT

DEFINITION Punishment is any consequence which weakens behaviour. As with reinforcement, we must look at what the consequence means to the individual

Punishment and human behaviour

Behaviour may be weakened because it brings unpleasant consequences or because something pleasant is withdrawn, for example

- **unpleasant consequences** – if you ask your teacher for help and he or she snaps back, you will be less likely to ask for help again because your action (asking for help) has brought unpleasant consequences (being 'snapped' at).
- **withdrawal of benefits** – this can be used as discipline in schools, for example a child who has been disruptive in class may be isolated from the rest of the pupils for a time. Misbehaving (the action) has brought unpleasant consequences (to be out of contact with friends) and should therefore weaken the disruptive behaviour.
- **discipline** – if parents wish to weaken behaviour they must ensure the consequences are unpleasant for the child. For example, if parents send a naughty child to its room as punishment, the child who loves being with others should find this an unpleasant experience and therefore it should make the naughty behaviour less likely to occur again. But for a child who is very happy alone, this may be a pleasant consequence and so it is unlikely to weaken behaviour. Sometimes a child wants attention from a parent and finds the way to get it is to be naughty. So, punishment is *rewarding* for the child because it brings attention.

Punishment has been found to have limited effect in weakening behaviour. This may be in part because insufficient attention is given to how the consequences are perceived by the person receiving the punishment. Another difficulty with punishment is that it only shows the behaviour which is *not* desirable. A two year old may *stop* hitting her newborn baby brother when she is punished, but may *start* hitting the dog. Punishment does not show what the undesirable behaviour should be replaced with. In contrast, **positive reinforcement** shows which behaviour *is* desirable. It is therefore better to concentrate on rewarding the right behaviour rather than on punishing the wrong behaviour.

To summarise the three consequences which affect behaviour:

- **positive reinforcement** strengthens behaviour – because it is pleasant
- **negative reinforcement** strengthens behaviour – because it stops something unpleasant
- **punishment** weakens behaviour – because it is unpleasant.

Social learning

DEFINITION   **Social learning** is learning by observing others.

FEATURES OF SOCIAL LEARNING

The key features of social learning are that people, children in particular, learn by:

- **observation** of other people, so the child notices what her father says when he tells her off for being rude
- **imitation** – the child imitates the behaviour of those he or she has observed, so the child reprimands her teddy bear for being rude, using the same words and tone as her father used earlier
- **modelling** – those who are imitated are called models because they are modelling behaviour which the child imitates; in this case the father is the model
- **reinforcement** – if the child imitates a model's behaviour and the consequences are rewarding, the child is likely to continue performing the behaviour. If a parent overhears the child telling off her teddy bear and shows approval, this is reinforcement.

Models may be parents, siblings, friends, TV characters, teachers and anyone else who can be observed. Bandura, a leading social learning theorist, proposed that children are more likely to imitate models who are:

- similar (perhaps the same sex, or age)
- powerful (such as a parent, a teacher, a pop star)
- caring (such as a parent, relative, teacher)
- rewarded for their behaviour (such as gaining approval for being aggressive): this is known as **vicarious reinforcement**.

As the child develops, different models will become more or less important: a three year old girl will imitate the behaviour of her mother (who is the same sex, powerful and nurturant) whereas a 14 year old girl might imitate a pop star (who is the same sex and powerful as a young woman).

In order to imitate behaviour the child has to see what is done, hear what is said, remember all of this and then be able to reproduce it some time later. So observational learning requires **cognitive** abilities. As the child gets older it is able to notice, remember and reproduce more complex behaviour. Gradually, the child will **internalise** a model's behaviours so that it will be able to act as the model would act in a situation it has never seen the model in.

We do not imitate everything we observe. This may be because:

- the models are not important to us – Bandura found that boys are less likely to imitate a female model showing aggression than a male model showing aggression
- the behaviour is not appropriate in that setting – we may have learned that certain behaviours are approved of by our friends but not by our parents
- the model's behaviour had unpleasant consequences – if a boy sees his football hero sent off the pitch amidst boos and jeers, he is unlikely to imitate the behaviour which got the player sent off.

Social learning ideas have played a powerful role in the explanation of many kinds of human behaviour, for instance in:

- **aggression** – social learning theory developed out of studies of aggression, namely which models were most likely to be imitated and why (p. 139). The part which the media play in providing models of aggressive behaviour has been the subject of considerable research.
- **personality** – which develops through the gradual internalisation of the behaviour of models (see p. 161).
- **gender** – the performance of gender-role behaviours develops as a result of observing same-sex models, and being rewarded for appropriate behaviour (see p. 191).
- **moral development** – this occurs as children observe adults, and the consequences of their moral behaviour (see p. 253).

Summary

We have seen that classical and operant conditioning were developed out of work with animals. The former proposes that an automatic behaviour can be conditioned to a previously neutral stimulus through association with an unconditional stimulus. Operant conditioning says that behaviour is shaped and maintained by its consequences, by what comes *after* the behaviour. Social learning theory uses these principles, but proposes that humans learn by observing others, noting the consequences of their behaviour and the consequences when they themselves imitate behaviour. Social learning theory, therefore, takes into account an element which is missing from the other two, namely that learning also involves cognitive processes.

Exercises

1 Explain how a conditional response is learned.
2 Give an example of how classical conditioning might influence a person's behaviour.
3 What is the Law of Effect?
4 How does reinforcement relate to the Law of Effect?
5 Describe, using examples, the difference between negative reinforcement and punishment.
6 Give one example of how positive reinforcement could be used to change a person's behaviour.
7 Give one example of how negative reinforcement could be used to change a person's behaviour.
8 Describe the process of modelling.
9 Why do humans not imitate everything they observe?
10 Give an example of one way in which one person may influence another's behaviour.

Social and Cultural Influences

3

From birth the human infant is able to distinguish between humans and non-humans and quickly develops the ability to recognise and respond to others. We spend much of our waking lives in the company of other people. They may be family members, friends, people we hardly know, or complete strangers. Nevertheless any one of them may affect our behaviour, even without intending to. In this chapter we identify why we need others, and how they may influence our development and behaviour.

Affiliation

DEFINITION **Affiliation** is the need to be in contact with others.

THE IMPORTANCE OF AFFILIATION

Psychologists say we have a high or low affiliative need depending on the extent to which we need others. Those with a high affiliative need will be more active in seeking out others. Nevertheless we all seem to need others some of the time. There are several reasons why this social contact is important. These include:

- **to relieve distress** – if we feel worried, fearful, shocked or distressed we tend to seek out human company. Being with others reduces anxiety and may provide support for interpreting our experiences. Children seek out others to relieve their distress (see attachments p. 76) and family and friends provide valuable support for adults and children during a divorce (see p. 94).
- **for comparison** – we seek out others so we can compare ourselves to them and this is one source of our self-esteem (see p. 207). For example, you may feel a little depressed because your homework seemed really difficult,

so you will try to find out whether everyone else had problems. If they struggled too, then you regain some self-esteem because this shows the work was difficult – it is not *you* who is incapable.

● **to make sense of our experiences** – when we are not sure what something means, or how we should behave, we look to others to see what their understanding is (see bystander behaviour p. 273). Children in particular use others to help them understand their experiences (see gender p. 191).

● **to provide approval** – we need to know that others think we are alright, that they like us, that they approve of who we are and what we do. This contributes to our self-esteem (see p. 209).

● **to give a sense of identity** – we need others to give us our identity. If people do not respond to us then it is as though we do not exist. The groups we belong to give us a sense of identity (see social identity theory p. 118). We need others for the social roles we play (see later in this chapter). If they respond to us in accordance with the role we are playing this contributes to our self-image (see p. 216).

● **providing a basis for closer relationships** – even the newborn infant responds to others and this is the basis for the development of attachments. As we grow up it is the basis for friendships and sexual relationships (see attachment p. 79).

THE INFLUENCE OF OTHERS ON OUR BEHAVIOUR

While we need others for the type of reasons we have noted above, they can also influence our behaviour in a number of ways, for example:

● **social facilitation** – the presence of other people can improve our performance on an easy task and damage performance of a difficult task (see p. 104).

● **conformity** – we conform to the norms of our society, or social group. We are not asked to conform; we do it in order to feel part of the group, to support the group or to be accepted by the group. This is one reason why peers are so influential (see conformity p. 107 and prejudice p. 129).

● **deindividuation** – being part of a large group of people can make us 'forget' ourselves. If we are less aware of ourselves we may behave impulsively and perhaps in a more anti-social way (see p. 109).

● **gender differences** – other people can encourage children to perform behaviours which are appropriate to their gender. They do this by rewards such as approval, or by providing gender-typed toys (see p. 191).

● **social identity** – we view other people's behaviour in terms of which group they belong to. If they belong to our own group (the in-group) we may treat them in a positive way, but if they belong to an out-group we are likely to discriminate against them (see p. 118).

- **labelling** – the labels which we give people can affect the way we treat them. If a teacher has labelled a child 'difficult', then when he asks a lot of questions in class it is because he is difficult, so he is reprimanded. If the child has been labelled 'bright' and asks a lot of questions, the teacher thinks this is because he is bright and may answer them.
- **bystander behaviour** – the presence of other people can affect the way individuals behave in an emergency. When alone an individual is usually quick to help, but when others are present they look to see what others are doing and if they appear unconcerned the individual is less likely to take action (see bystander behaviour p. 273).

Social norms

DEFINITION

Social norms are a society's unspoken rules about appropriate attitudes and behaviour – they define what is socially acceptable.

Social norms are learned from others in the group. The social group may be large, such as a religious or national group, or small, such as a football team. We refer to group norms when we are talking about a small group such as a football team or a group of friends. We need other people to provide us with acceptance and approval, but if this need is very strong we may change our behaviour and attitudes to conform to those of a group which we wish to join, or one which we belong to and want to support. If you want to explain someone else's behaviour, it is often helpful to look at which group they may wish to be identified with.

Examples of the ways in which social norms can influence and explain behaviour are:

- we **conform** to the norms of a group to which we want to belong, to the extent that we will say things we do not believe, as Asch found in his studies using a judgement of line lengths (see p. 107).
- we **help others** because of social norms relating to our obligations to others, so the norm of social responsibility says that we should help those who are less fortunate than ourselves (see p. 281). This means, for example, giving up your seat to an elderly person.
- social norms relating to **prejudice** and **discrimination** influence what people say and do in relationship to those they see as different from themselves. The norms in different groups may differ, so for instance racist jokes may be the norm in the workplace but not in another social setting (see p. 129).

Social roles

DEFINITION **Social roles** are the 'parts' we play in society.

There is a set of behaviour associated with most social roles – we expect someone performing a role to exhibit these behaviours, and we are expected to show certain behaviours towards them when they are performing that role (see pp. 212–16).

Here are some examples of the ways in which social roles can influence and explain behaviour:

- As social roles are associated with *expectations* about behaviour, this helps us to know how to behave, for example when you go to see your doctor you expect her to ask what your problem is. You also expect her to tell you what to do about it and, because your role is the patient, you listen and try to understand what she says. You are not expected to interrupt her. These behaviours are explained by the expectations associated with each role.
- We all perform several roles, each role requiring different behaviours. Imagine a mother who has just met her child from school and is chatting with another mother. She may take on her 'mother' role (bending down to admire a picture her child shows her) and then straighten up to continue in her 'friend' role, swapping ideas for holidays. Her behaviour will be different in each of these roles, and can be explained by the roles themselves.
- We perform a new role rather intensely and inflexibly at first perhaps because it does not feel comfortable, so we conform fairly rigidly to the behaviours and expectations of the role. We 'act' the role very consciously, and perhaps without much confidence. Once we **internalise** the role we have adapted it to suit our own needs and abilities, so we are able to perform it confidently and unconsciously. Our familiarity with a role explains how flexibly we perform it.
- People tend to behave in ways which are consistent with the role identified by their clothes, for instance a nurse's uniform can make people more caring or a prison guard's uniform can make them more aggressive (see deindividuation, p. 109). Clothes also announce to other people how you *want* to be treated. So if you are a job applicant you wear smart, formal clothes, but when socialising with friends you may wear jeans and trainers. Clothes enable us to perform a role more effectively, and uniforms in particular provide a 'mask' behind which we can hide, permitting us to do things which we would not normally do.
- Performing a social role gives us an opportunity to try out new behaviours, to discover what we feel comfortable with, to present a different 'face' to

the world, to experience being treated by others in a different way. An individual's self-concept develops partly from the social roles they perform.

Environment

DEFINITION **Environment** refers to our surroundings and experiences. In the nature/nurture debate the environment refers to the influence which our surroundings and experiences have on our behaviour.

Examples of environmental factors in human development include:

- parenting styles – how parents discipline their children (see aggression p. 142) and contribute to their self-esteem (p. 210)
- the amount of stimulation children receive during childhood (intelligence p. 179)
- the behaviour which children observe in their parents, peers or through the media (see aggression p. 139, gender p. 201)

THE IMPORTANCE OF THE ENVIRONMENT IN THE NATURE/NURTURE DEBATE

The **nature/nurture debate** is about which factors are the most important in making us the people we are. The nature side says that the majority of variation in human characteristics is due to innate factors, whereas the nurture side says that it is what happens *after* we are born that is the most important influence on how we develop. This latter view is the environmentalist view, that the majority of variation in human characteristics is due to environmental factors.

It is important to find out the extent to which we are influenced by these environmental factors. If these factors are shown to be important, we can do something to alleviate problems or enhance abilities. Research has shown that environment is influential, although some of the evidence is correlational so we cannot conclude that environmental factors alone cause improvements.

This is one of the reasons why the nature/nurture debate is likely to remain inconclusive. Other reasons include **ethical** and **methodological** difficulties of separating the influences of nature and nurture. For example, the changes in a child's development may be due to environment or to maturation. Research suggests that both play a crucial role, but one way of trying to identify inborn and environmental factors is to take a cross-cultural perspective.

Cross-cultural perspectives

DEFINITION A **cross-cultural perspective** compares people from different cultures in order to identify how much they show similarities and differences in particular behaviours or abilities.

THE IMPORTANCE OF CROSS-CULTURAL RESEARCH IN THE NATURE/NURTURE DEBATE

Cross-cultural research in psychology contributes to the nature/nurture debate because:

- it enables psychologists to investigate a behaviour or ability in people from different cultures, for example visual perception (see p. 244). If the ability appears in all the cultures, and is fairly similar, this suggests that it is innate, because, despite different environments, the behaviour is very similar.
- if the behaviour or ability appears in some cultures and not in others, or is very different in the cultures studied, then this suggests it is greatly influenced by the environment. These differences are due to the different experiences which each culture provides for its members.
- cross-cultural studies help psychologists to tease apart the influence of heredity and the influence of the environment. For example, research on **attachment** has shown that in Uganda, babies develop a single attachment, while in Israel they may develop several attachments. Because attachments are present in both cultures, this suggests that attachments have an innate basis, but the *number* of attachments depends on environmental factors because the number varies from culture to culture.
- cross-cultural studies highlight differences between cultures, and thus increase awareness of the cultural biases within which psychologists may operate. Awareness of such a bias enables psychologists to devise better studies and encourages co-operation between psychologists working in different cultures. Judging other cultures from one's own perspective is called **ethnocentrism** (see prejudice, p. 119).
- psychologists also use cross-cultural studies to compare behaviours across cultures rather than to gather evidence for the nature/nurture debate. They may be able to identify correlations between variables which differ between cultures and from comparison be able to suggest possible causes.

Summary

This chapter has identified reasons why we seek contact with others, and ways in which they may influence and explain our behaviour. It has noted some of the ways in which others help us to understand our world, to learn how to function in it and develop a sense of who we are. We have identified some of the factors in the environment which have an impact on human development and how they contribute to the nature/nurture debate. The value of cross-cultural research has been considered, both as a source of evidence for the nature/nurture debate and also as an opportunity for psychologists to compare different cultures in order to understand more about human behaviours and abilities.

Exercises

1 What is affiliation?
2 Why is affiliation important for humans?
3 Give one example of a way in which someone may influence a person's behaviour.
4 Give an example of how someone might explain another person's behaviour.
5 What are social norms?
6 Give an example of a social norm and explain how it might influence someone's behaviour.
7 What is a social role?
8 Give an example of the way in which a social role might explain someone's behaviour.
9 What do psychologists mean by environment?
10 Briefly explain how cross-cultural research contributes to the nature/nurture debate in psychology.
11 Why do psychologists study people from different cultures?

The Influences of Thinking and Perception

This chapter describes some of the ways in which psychologists explain how we perceive and make sense of our world and how we behave as a result of this understanding. This is an area of psychological study called cognition. As you can see from other chapters in this book, we use our cognitive abilities to make judgements about people and ourselves, to understand what it means to be male or female, to decide what is right and wrong. In other words, the way we think and perceive influences how we understand our social world.

Processing information

The information we receive from the world outside of our bodies has to go through changes before our brains can make sense of it, and even more changes before we can understand and act upon it. How do these changes occur? What factors influence our ability to deal with this information?

Cognitive psychologists try to answer these questions, and we will briefly review some of their explanations, starting with **transduction** – how we convert sensory information into a form that the brain can work with. Then we select information and organise it as we store it. Our minds are always trying to make sense of our experiences and we may use inference to do this. Let us look at these four processes in turn.

TRANSDUCTION

Transduction refers to the way sensory information is changed into electrical impulses so that the brain can use it. Examples of sensory information are light waves (which carry visual information to the eye) and sound waves (carrying auditory information to the ear). As the brain cannot process information when it is in this form, it changes this sensory information into a form it *can* use – electrical impulses.

The transformation to electrical impulses is carried out by receptor cells. These cells react to the sensory information they receive, for example receptor cells in the eye react to light waves, receptor cells in the inner ear react to sound waves. The receptor cells contain chemicals which react to the light or sound waves and this chemical reaction produces electrical impulses.

The impulses are then transmitted to particular parts of the brain for analysis. So light waves entering the eye are converted to electrical impulses which are then transmitted to the visual cortex, the part of the brain which specialises in analysing visual information.

SELECTION

The brain is constantly bombarded with information but we can only process a small part of it. Some information will be selected for further processing, the rest just fades away. We tend to select (or attend to) information which:

- is the first information we receive about someone or something, as in the **primacy effect** (see p. 284).
- is unusual or distinctive, so when two items of unusual information are presented together we assume they are associated – this is called an **illusory correlation** (see p. 297).
- we are primed for, perhaps because it is related to ourselves or because we are expecting it. An example is **labelling**, which may lead us to understand someone's behaviour in the light of the label they have been given, such as 'difficult' or 'mentally ill' (see p. 216).

By selecting information we also:

- 'hold on' to it while we process it further. In the 'halo effect' we select a positive (or negative) feature of another person and then process this information further as we generate a whole range of *other* positive (or negative) assumptions about them (see p. 287).
- tend to ignore *other* information, which then fades away. The child who can only attend to one aspect of a situation at a time fails to take account

of other relevant information. As a result the child will, for example, make faulty **moral judgements** based on their perception of events (see p. 255) or show errors in understanding of another's **gender** (see p. 193).

- tend to discount subsequent information which is contradictory, as happens when we stereotype on the basis of a selected feature such as skin colour or age.

ORGANISATION OF INFORMATION

The human brain has a very strong tendency to organise information, to put it into categories or to put associated information together. The way we organise this information affects our interpretation of people and of events. Some examples of this are:

- **Social categorisation** – we rapidly categorise people, and the basic categories are the in-group (those who belong to the same group as ourselves) and out-groups. We also put them into social groupings such as teenagers, women, Chinese, football fanatics, vegetarians, shop assistants, yuppies. If we belong to one of these groups then we will favour other members of this group simply because it is 'our' group. However we tend to have a lower opinion of groups to which we do not belong – out-groups (see prejudice p. 118). You can see that the way we categorise others (according to groups) in turn affects how we view them.
- **Personal constructs** – these are our personal ways of perceiving our world, they are highly individualised and we use them to interpret the behaviour of other people and as a guide for our own actions and responses to others (see p. 292).
- **Scripts** – these are sometimes called event schemas. They are knowledge structures based on previous experience of events. They contain information about the sequences of actions, the expected occurrences and behaviours and the roles people play (see p. 293). Examples of scripts are going to the doctor, attending a psychology class, visiting a friend in hospital, taking a child to school, going to a wedding.

INFERENCE

We are always trying to make sense of information, to the extent that sometimes we think we have seen or heard something which we have not, in other words we **infer** something. Making inferences involves adding more information, which may have come from our previous experiences. When someone smiles at me, I infer that they are friendly (from past experience I know that smiling and friendliness go together). From a particular behaviour (smiling) I infer a personality trait (friendliness). I could be wrong of course – they might have mistaken me for someone else.

Inference helps us to process information, make sense of ourselves and others, and form impressions of ourselves and others. You can see examples of each of these below:

- **Processing information** – when we meet someone who can be easily classified as a member of particular group, we may infer that they have the same characteristics as all other members of the group – we **stereotype**. When we stereotype we generate this set of inferences and this affects the way we process information about the individual. We look for (select) information which fits the stereotype and ignore information which does not fit. When information is ambiguous we tend to interpret it in a way which conforms to the stereotype.
- **Making sense of ourselves** – we use inference to understand more about ourselves, perhaps by observing the results of our own behaviour. When we perform a new **role** we have the opportunity to try out behaviours and so infer new information about ourselves, just as some of Zimbardo's 'prison guards' did (see p. 213).
- **Forming impressions of ourselves** – we make inferences about the kind of person we are by looking at the way other people treat us. If people laugh at your jokes you will infer that you are funny; if other people seem to like or approve of you, you infer that you are a worthwhile person. These inferences contribute to our **self-concept** (see p. 210).
- **Forming impressions of others** – if someone is described as 'warm' we infer that their other traits are positive. If they are described as 'cold' then our inference is that their other traits are negative ones. These are central traits because they bias our inferences about others (see impression formation p. 286).

Mental representation

Mental representation refers to the way we think about things. We have just considered some aspects of the way we process information, now we are going to look at three ways in which we represent this information to ourselves – schemas, mental images and mental concepts.

SCHEMAS

DEFINITION

A **schema** is a mental structure containing generalised knowledge and expectations about a person, object or event. Schemas (or schemata) develop as a result of our past experiences and provide a guide to future actions. A schema contributes to our processing of information because it influences what information we select, and how we organise and elaborate on it using inference. These points are discussed below.

Selection of information

A schema tells us what to look for, it directs our attention to related information. Your self-schema selects information relevant to yourself; people who are **gender-typed**, for instance, are more likely to attend to information related to gender. Once selected, this information is incorporated into the schema. Information which is not related, or does not fit easily into a schema, may be ignored and not processed any further. Because schemas 'filter out' information which is not relevant to the schema, we may have a distorted perception of the world.

Moreover, as the schema contains known information, it helps us to notice *new* information. For example, if I go to the bank one day and a different queuing system is in operation, this is new information which will contrast with my current 'bank' schema.

Organisation of information

Schemas provide ready-made structures for incorporating the information which has been selected. As the schema develops it becomes richer and more complex, incorporating for example behaviours, emotions and outcomes from past experiences. However, because information becomes generalised as it is absorbed into the schema, we may omit details and variations.

Inference

We use our schemas to make sense of situations and, where information is not actually provided, we 'fill in the gaps' from past experience. For example, your schema for a close friend enables you to make inferences. If a group of you are planning a night out and he says it does not appeal to him, the others might think he is being unsociable. You know he has been short of money, so you infer that his refusal is because he cannot afford a night out. Your inference is based on the information contained in your schema.

MENTAL IMAGES

These are patterns or pictures which we use to hold or represent information. We may use them for events and for people.

Mental images for events

According to Piaget, the child's ability to create mental images of events is a crucial aspect of its intellectual development. For example:

- A baby loses interest in an object when it is covered by a cloth and is no longer visible. However by 10 or 11 months of age it will continue to look for an object once it has been covered – this is called **object permanence** (see p. 228). Piaget claimed this was evidence that the child had a mental image of the object, because it retained the image when the object disappeared.
- Until about seven years of age, argued Piaget, children are unable to manipulate a sequence of ideas mentally because they are unable to create a mental image of the sequence. This effects their understanding of events (see reversibility p. 231).

Mental images for people

DEFINITION

- A **stereotype** is a rigid set of shared beliefs we have about other people because they belong to a particular group, for example women are nurturant, red-heads are hot-tempered or Germans are precise (see p. 114). **Stereotypes** provide us with a mental image of the person which does not correspond to that individual but to what we *infer* about that individual. Stereotypes influence our perceptions of others in several ways, for instance we discount information which does not fit the stereotype. If you meet a very easy going German you are likely to ignore this information because it does not fit your mental image of Germans.

- **Attachment** – as a result of its early experiences with the main carers, a baby develops a mental image of them. It can then differentiate between these people and strangers, which is evidence of attachment (see p. 75).

MENTAL CONCEPTS

The term **concept** refers to a group of related ideas. When we have a concept of something, we have an understanding of it, for example when we have a concept of gender we understand what it means to be male or female, what society's expectations are and so on. When we have a concept of self we know that we are separate from others, and we have an understanding of who and what we are. These concepts are abstract, which makes them difficult to define and measure.

The formation of mental concepts

Concepts take time to develop – while they are forming our understanding is still incomplete. In the younger child, limitations in its cognitive abilities affect how it forms concepts (see p. 230). As the child is only able to focus on one aspect of a situation at a time, and so can be deceived by appearances, its understanding is based on what it sees; it also has difficulties thinking about things in the abstract.

We use two strategies to form concepts; both reflect the characteristics of cognitive development:

- **Exemplars** – once we know the name for a particular thing (for example the child knows he is a 'boy', or someone is described as 'difficult'), we note the features associated with this thing or idea, and try to find more examples of it. As children tend to notice only one feature at a time, they make frequent errors in choosing what the relevant features are. It therefore takes them longer to form concepts than it does for an adult.
- **Hypothesis testing** – we do this when we have a clearer understanding of the features which define the concept. We form a **hypothesis** about which features define the concept and test it against new objects or ideas to see if our hypothesis is correct. If it is not, we change the hypothesis to fit the new information and test that one. Hypothesis testing is associated with the later stages in the development of concepts and is evident in children of about seven or eight years of age. Their thinking at this age tends to be governed by rules so it may be rather inflexible, as it is for example in the development of **gender concept** or **moral concepts**. In adults, hypothesis testing may occur quite early in the formation of concepts.

How do mental concepts influence our perceptions and behaviour?

Our concepts influence our perceptions and behaviours in a number of ways, for example they affect:

- our **perception of ourselves** – information in our self-concept may affect the way we see ourselves. For instance the **self-image** of someone who was taller than most other children may persist even if they are only average height as adults.
- our **perception of others** – a mental concept can influence our perception of others because when a concept has not fully developed we make mistakes in our perceptions. For example a child of three years old has an incomplete concept of **gender**, so she may think a woman has become a man when she puts on a moustache.
- our **behaviour** – because of disagreement over the concept of **intelligence**, it has been possible to discriminate against people on the basis of intelligence tests.
- our **reaction to others** – we tend to respond to people and judge them on the basis of concepts. For instance, we react to others on the basis of their gender, parents treat infant boys differently from infant girls, we punish aggression in girls more often than aggression in boys.

Summary

This chapter has brought together some of the cognitive explanations for our perceptions and behaviour. We have seen that the way we process information may have considerable influence on the interpretations we make, sometimes producing bias or inaccuracies. Nevertheless these techniques enable us to handle large amounts of information fairly efficiently.

Exercises

1 Briefly describe how sensory information is processed.
2 Give an example of how the selection of information plays a part in the processing of information.
3 Briefly describe one example of how our selection of information affects our behaviour.
4 How might the way we organise information influence our interpretation of an event?
5 How does inference play a part in the processing of information?
6 Give an example of the way in which inference affects our impressions of other people.
7 Outline an example of a schema.
8 What part does a schema play in the processing of information?
9 Give one example of way in which a mental image might influence our perception of events.
10 Give one example of a way in which a stereotype might influence our perception of another person.
11 Give an example of a mental concept and briefly explain how it might be formed.
12 How may a mental concept influence our behaviour towards others?

PSYCHOLOGICAL METHODOLOGY

SECTION

B

In Section B we will look at ways in which psychologists find out about people. You will see that there are a number of different research methods they can use, each one has some advantages and some disadvantages.

In Chapters 5 and 6 you will find out what each method involves, how psychologists decide which method is appropriate for what they want to find out, and how they actually design their research and report it so that other people can find out what they did and what they discovered. Chapter 6 is written to enable you to design your own research and report it clearly.

Chapter 7 covers the crucial topic of ethics, which refers to the way we protect the people we are studying when we do research. The ethical guidelines must be followed by anyone conducting research – whether a professional psychologist or a student studying GCSE psychology.

5

Ways of Discovering and Testing Psychological Knowledge

When writing about psychological research, Hugh Coolican says there are three major ways in which psychologists get information about people: 'You ask them, watch them or meddle.' In this chapter we are going to look at the ways in which psychologists ask, watch and meddle. In other words, we are going to look at research methods.

Methods of studying behaviour

There are a variety of research methods which psychologists use: some permit a high degree of control over participants, others are devised to study how people behave naturally.

OBSERVATION

When psychologists observe, they watch people's behaviour. Because of its complexity and the possibility of bias in the observer, it is usual to have more than one observer. If the behaviour is videoed, the observers will analyse the behaviour from the video. They need to be trained how to analyse and measure the behaviour they are interested in so that they all interpret it in the same way. This is called **inter-observer reliability**. They will have practised observing the behaviour and will note relevant behaviours on an **observation**

schedule. Figure 5.1 shows a simple schedule for noting the number of times behaviour is shown during an observation of pro-social play: you will see that each participant is identified by a number in order to preserve confidentiality (see ethics, p. 70). Alternatively, the participant's behaviour may be noted at regular intervals, say every 15 minutes.

Participant number	Number of times participant performed action				
	gave object	smiled at other	physically assisted other	agreed to help	encouraged other
P1					
P2					
P3					
P4					

FIGURE 5.1 Example of an observation schedule

DEFINITION   **Observation** is used to record and analyse behaviour when it occurs naturally (the observational study) or when it occurs in a specially controlled setting (the observational technique). The difference between them is detailed below.

The observational study
In an observational study the researchers have no control, they look at behaviour as it occurs naturally as in Patterson's study of aggression in children at play (p. 137) or Schaffer & Emerson's study of attachment behaviour (p. 83). Before starting the study, the observers try to become familiar with those they are observing in order to minimise the effect that their presence may have on them.

Advantages:
● the behaviour occurs in its natural setting
● observations provide very detailed information
● it can be used as a starting point for further, more controlled, research
● it can be used when other methods might be unethical.

Disadvantages:
● the presence of observers may affect the behaviour of those being observed
● it is difficult for observers to be completely objective
● it can be expensive and time-consuming to analyse the data
● there are so many variables which could affect behaviour that it is not possible to draw any firm conclusions.

The observational technique

When observation is used as a technique, the researcher has some control. It is frequently used with children or in social psychology research, and may be one of several methods which a psychologist uses in one investigation. In order that control can be exerted and the behaviour is easier to observe (such as through one way mirrors), the observations may take place in an artificial setting such as a research laboratory. Examples are Bandura's study of observational learning and aggression (p. 141) and Ainsworth's observations of children's responses when they experienced the 'strange situation' (p. 76).

Advantages:
- by controlling some variables (see p. 59) it is possible for the researchers to draw conclusions from their observations.

Disadvantages:
- the unfamiliar setting may affect participants' behaviour so it is less natural.

CASE STUDY

DEFINITION

The **case study** is an in-depth study of one person or a small group of people. It may include interviews, where the interviewer starts by asking specific questions, but the questions which follow will depend on how the person answers. Other people will be interviewed, to find out about the individual's past or present experiences and behaviours. Data provided by school or medical records may also be gathered. Case studies were used by Freud (p. 152) and by Bowlby (p. 80). They are often used for investigating people who show unusual abilities or difficulties, as in adults who have gained sight for the first time (p. 242).

Advantages:
- it gives a detailed picture of the individual
- it can be useful in treating individual problems
- it helps in discovering how a person's past may be related to the present
- it can form the basis for future research
- by studying those who are *unusual*, psychologists can discover more about what is usual.

Disadvantages:
- it relies on memory or records which may be poor or distorted
- it can only tell you about one person so you cannot **generalise** the information to others
- it relies on participants telling the truth
- the interviewer may be biased if they are looking for certain information.

SURVEY

DEFINITION

A **survey** asks people questions, either through a written questionnaire or face-to-face interviews. The questions must be carefully prepared so that they are clear, and do not persuade the participant to answer in a particular way. In order to ensure that people understand the questions and find them fairly straightforward to answer, the psychologist might first do a **pilot study**. This means giving the questions to a few people and asking for their comments, so there is an opportunity to make improvements before the proper study is run.

The questions may be closed or open-ended. Let us look at an example from Davey's research on prejudice (see p. 119) and consider the advantages and disadvantages of both types of question.

Open-ended questions

'What do you think of your child's school?'. The answer may provide a lot of information and is useful for more in-depth research. However, it would be difficult to compare with other people's answers, so the open-ended question is less useful when you are trying to *quantify* information.

Closed questions

'Is your child happy at school?' – yes/no. This produces one clear-cut answer which is easy to interpret and quantify, but most people would want to answer 'Well, it depends', yet because they are forced to choose yes or no, their answer will not reflect their real opinions. A compromise is the question which provides a range of answers, perhaps using a scale from 1 – 5 to reflect the strength or amount of agreement. This provides more detailed information which is still easy to quantify. An example is the social distance questionnaire relating to the study of **prejudice**, an extract of which appears in Figure 5.2

Advantages:
- surveys using questionnaires are quick and easy to operate
- a very large sample can be used
- people who are geographically distant can be studied
- questionnaires can open up new ideas for further research.

Disadvantages:
- the sample may be biased because the researcher has to rely on people returning the questionnaires (they may be returned by people who have plenty of time or strong feelings about the topic)
- face-to-face surveys are more expensive because interviewers have to be paid and trained

Please complete the questionnaire by following these instructions.
Using the scale of 1 to 5, write in each box in the table the number of the statement that agrees most closely with your feelings about being in each situation with a member of each group.

1 I'd actively encourage it.
2 It's alright with me.
3 I'm neutral.
4 I'd avoid it if I could.
5 I'm strongly opposed to it.

Social situation	White	Black	Catholic	Muslim	Jew
Be my friend					
Be my closest friend					
Work with me					
Work under me					
Be my boss					
Live next door					
Visit my home					
Date me or a member of my family					
Marry me					
Go to school with my child					
Totals					

Scoring: Add up the numbers in each column. The maximum possible is 50. The lower the score, for each group, the greater the participant's willingness to interact with a member of that group. The higher the score, the more the participant is reluctant to interact.

FIGURE 5.2 Extract from a Social Distance Questionnaire

- people may not give accurate answers because they are embarrassed, bored or do not understand the questions.

EXPERIMENT

This is where psychologists start meddling! The **experiment** has been widely used in psychology, because the psychologist has greater control over what happens and can therefore test cause and effect. In an experiment the researcher tries to keep all the variables the same except one – the **independent variable** (the IV). The IV is the variable which the experimenter manipulates in order to see what effect it has.

DEFINITION

In Darley & Latané's study of bystander intervention (p. 274) they wanted to investigate whether the number of people who knew of an emergency would affect the participant's behaviour. Each participant was given the same instructions and heard the same seizure over the intercom – these variables were kept constant. The variable which was being *manipulated* (the IV) was the number of other people who were thought to hear the seizure.

The effect that the IV has on the participants is called the **dependent variable** (the DV). The DV in this experiment was the participant's behaviour after hearing the seizure.

Experiments differ in the extent to which the psychologist has control of the variables. There are four types of experiment, as shown below.

Laboratory experiment

In the **laboratory** experiment there is a high level of experimental control. The psychologist manipulates the IV, assigns participants to the control or experimental condition and has control over the environment in which it takes place. The Darley & Latané experiment is an example because they had a control condition (participants alone) and experimental conditions (participants and others listening).

Field experiment

In the **field** experiment the psychologist manipulates the IV but the experiment takes place in a 'real life' setting, so there is less control over variables such as the people who take part or when the study happens. The experiment on helping behaviour by Piliavin and his colleagues (p. 274) is an example. The participants were people travelling on the New York subway who did not know they were participants in an experiment.

Quasi experiment

The **quasi** experiment is one in which the IV already exists so the researcher cannot 'create' a difference for the purpose of the experiment. Naturally occurring independent variables include age and gender, for example Burgner & Hewstone's study (p. 200) investigating reasons for failure and success given by boys and girls. There is debate as to whether naturally occurring IVs can be included as experiments, because, for example it is not gender itself which creates any difference, but something which is *associated* with gender.

Natural experiment

The **natural** experiment occurs in real life. The researchers are studying an independent variable which they have not been able to manipulate in an environment which they have little control over, for example research on the outcomes of the Headstart programmes comparing children who had taken part with those who had not (p. 182).

You will see below that what is a disadvantage in one type of experiment becomes an advantage in another.

Advantages:
- in a **laboratory** experiment it is possible to test cause and effect; this is less true with quasi experiments and much less true in **field** or **natural** experiments
- in the **field** and **natural** experiments we are able to see how people behave *naturally* as a result of the manipulation.

Disadvantages:
- As **laboratory** experiments are artificial this may effect participants' behaviour and may also produce results which do not apply to real life. Participants know they are taking part in an experiment and they may use clues within the experiment to guess what it is about – the clues are called the **demand characteristics.**
- In **natural** and **field** experiments the researcher cannot be sure that the results *are* due to the manipulation because there are so many other variables which cannort be controlled. Psychologists therefore have to be very cautious when they interpret the results in these two types of experiments.

PSYCHOMETRIC TESTS

DEFINITION   **Psychometric tests** are tests which have been devised to measure characteristics such as intelligence or personality. They are usually pencil and paper tests which are carefully designed to enable psychologists to compare an individual's results with those of people in general.

Psychometric tests are used only after considerable research to ensure they are:

- **standardised** – psychometric tests are given to a large number of people to work out the norm for a particular characteristic or ability. For example, an IQ of 100 is the norm, it is the most common score. The process by which the norm is established is called **standardisation.**
- **valid** – this means they test what they are *supposed* to test, but this is problematic because intelligence and personality are abstract. They are not things you can measure objectively, as we can measure a person's height or weight. In addition, psychologists do not agree on what intelligence or personality *are*, so there is disagreement about what should be measured. Critics argue that intelligence tests only test the ability to *do* intelligence tests.

- **reliable** – this means that each time someone does the test their results are very similar.

Psychometric tests are used in employment, education and business to identify needs in management training or eligibility for a particular school or suitability for a career (see intelligence p. 171).

Advantages:
- psychometric tests are cheap to run
- they are quick
- they can give useful information about an individual.

Disadvantages:
- they are expensive to buy
- they may be used by people who do not understand the information they provide
- they require sophisticated marking and interpretation
- they may not measure what they are supposed to
- they may be biased
- they make people think abstract abilities such as personality or intelligence *are* easily measured.

CORRELATIONAL STUDY

Sometimes psychologists want to find out what behaviours go together, for example to see whether the amount of television watched is related to the amount of aggression shown. Both the variables may be *already* occurring but the psychologist wants to see if they are related. This can be done by calculating a **correlation**.

DEFINITION This is not a research method. A **correlational study** is a way of analysing data to see if two variables are related. The data may have come from questionnaires or observations, for example. There are two patterns of correlation:

- a **positive correlation** occurs when one variable increases as the other increases, for example Murstein found a positive correlation between the levels of physical attractiveness in male and female partners (p. 101)
- a **negative correlation** occurs when one variable increases as the other decreases, for example the lower the security of a child's attachment, the greater the child's disobedience.

The relationship can be plotted on a **scattergram** (see pages 63–4 for examples). If there is no upward or downward pattern in the scores, this indicates that the two variables are not related, so we say there is zero correlation. It is important to remember that a **correlational** study can only show a *relationship* between two variables; we cannot assume that one variable causes the other.

Advantages:
- a correlational study provides information about variables which we cannot control
- it may form the basis for a follow-up study to test cause and effect
- it allows us to predict the value of one variable if we know the other one.

Disadvantages:
- we cannot conclude that one thing causes another, only that the two variables are related, as in Eron's study of the amount of violent television watched by eight year old boys and their aggression levels at 18 years old (p. 140).

Types of research study

Psychologists who are interested in how something changes can study people in one of two ways – using a longitudinal or a cross-sectional study. We will consider both of these and then look at the cross-cultural study, which is one way of discovering the effects of heredity and the environment on behaviour, and so provide evidence for the nature/nurture debate. When conducting any one of these three types of study, researchers will use some of the **research methods** we have just looked at.

LONGITUDINAL STUDY

DEFINITION   In a **longitudinal** study, the researcher studies the same individuals over a period of time so they can monitor changes in the variables. Schaffer & Emerson (p. 83) observed the development of attachment behaviours over 12 months; Eron's correlational study of televised aggression and aggressive behaviour lasted more than 10 years (p. 140).

Advantages:
- we can identify changes which are common to most people
- we can compare the long term effects of an experience (for example children who experienced 'Headstart' compared with those who did not)
- we can identify characteristics which persist and those which tend to disappear
- there are no participant variables
- we can study people in considerable depth.

Disadvantages:
- some participants will drop out over the years so their data will be of limited use
- long term funding is required which may be hard to find
- it is difficult to change the study once it is under way
- findings may be out of date by the conclusion of the study
- social change at any stage in the study may affect the variables being measured (for example the rapid increase in unemployed fathers and working mothers which occurred towards the end of the 1980s).

CROSS-SECTIONAL STUDY

DEFINITION   A **cross-sectional** study enables us to investigate changes by comparing people who are at at different ages or stages (as in the study of divorce) and studying them all at the same time. Rather than following children from 4 to 16 years of age in a longitudinal study, for example, we can study 4, 8, 12 and 16 year olds. This is a **quasi** experiment and is the kind of study Piaget used to investigate children's cognitive development.

Advantages:
- it provides immediate results
- it is cheaper than the longitudinal study
- there is less likelihood of participants dropping out.

Disadvantages:
- there are individual differences between groups which can bias results although a large sample will reduce this
- social changes may create differences between groups (the 10 year olds may have experienced major educational change which the 14 year olds have not)
- it tends to exaggerate differences between ages.

CROSS-CULTURAL STUDY

A **cross-cultural** study enables psychologists to compare people from different cultures. This is one way of discovering the influence of heredity and environment on topics such as the roles of women or levels of aggression. Early cross-cultural studies tended to be **ethnocentric**: researchers viewed other cultures through their *own* cultural lens. Thus there was a tendency to find that others lacked abilities (such as 3-D depth perception – see p. 245) which were evident in the researcher's culture. Imagine researchers coming from a culture in which violent men had large beards. What assumptions would they make about the man in Figure 5.3?

FIGURE 5.3 How might someone with different cultural assumptions view this man?

Although ethnocentrism is still a difficulty, researchers are more aware of such a **bias**, and now researchers from different cultures frequently co-operate on joint cross-cultural studies. This helps to reduce another problem, which is that to gain a full understanding of someone's behaviour requires an understanding of the culture in which they live.

Advantages:

- results can provide evidence for the nature/nurture debate by identifying characteristics which seem to be universal, and those which differ from culture to culture
- they can highlight the differences between cultures and make us ask if we are right in our own assumptions about what is good or bad, changeable or unchangeable, normal or abnormal.
- they help psychologists compare behaviour between cultures, to identify correlations and possible causes.

Disadvantages:

- they can be expensive and time-consuming
- it can be difficult to be sure that you are looking at, or doing, exactly the same thing in each culture
- even if you are, you may be *understood* differently in each culture
- they can be used to suggest that one's own culture is superior.

Summary

As you can see from the studies described in this book, psychologists often use more than one method in their research. For example, in the Schaffer & Emerson study (p. 83), interviews with parents may have produced some biased information. This was balanced with observation of the adult-child interactions which gives a more objective view. By using two or more methods, researchers can counteract the disadvantages of one method and thus gain more complete and reliable data. The remaining chapters in this section of the book provide more information on the subject of research methodology. The next chapter describes how to carry out research, including the use of methods we have reviewed here, and the final chapter discusses ethical concerns in psychological research.

Exercises

1 From this book, find one example of each of the following. In each case, say why you think the psychologist chose this particular way of studying people:
   a) observational study
   b) case study
   c) survey
   d) experiment
   e) psychometric test
   f) correlational study
   g) longitudinal study
   h) cross-sectional study
   i) cross-cultural study

2 Fill in the blanks below, using the words from the list above.
   a) A _____ is a way of assessing a particular ability.
   b) A _____ is a way of discovering whether two variables are related.
   c) One way of comparing the influence of heredity with that of the environment is to do a _____
   d) An _____ enables the researcher to test cause and effect.
   e) A disadvantage of a _____ is that you cannot generalise from your findings.
   f) A _____ enables us to study development over a short period of time.
   g) The _____ can provide a lot of information fairly cheaply.
   h) An advantage of the _____ is that there are no subject variables.
   i) An _____ allows the researcher to find out how people behave in everyday life.

Planning and Reporting Research

When psychologists want to find out more about a topic they will read what other psychologists have done. They may find that nobody has looked at exactly what interests them, or that someone has but there were flaws in the study which affected the results. They would then plan their own research, recording what they do and what they find, then write it up as a report, which may be published in a psychology journal so that other psychologists can read it and benefit from it. This is one of the ways in which psychological knowledge develops. In this chapter you will find out how psychologists plan and report their research. As you need to know this for the examination, and in order to plan and report your own practical exercise, the chapter is written as though you are the psychologist.

Using this chapter for your practical exercise

This chapter tells you how psychologists plan their research. A description of research methods is provided in Chapter 5, so you will find it useful to turn back to check these methods with their advantages and disadvantages.

Having decided on an appropriate research method, this chapter tells you how the researcher selects participants and controls variables which could affect the results. Use this information in order to plan your own practical exercise. The chapter also tells you how to collect and present your data and draw conclusions from it.

There are a number of ways of writing a research report, but the usual order of information is:
- INTRODUCTION – including context, aim, hypothesis, IV and DV if appropriate
- METHOD – including design, sample, materials, procedure

- RESULTS – including where appropriate, in written and visual form, tables, mean and range
- DISCUSSION – relating results to aim or hypothesis, interpretation of results, evaluation of study.

CHECK
This chapter is divided into the four sections described above and at various stages you will see a 'CHECK' marker in the margin, to remind you of information which you should include in each of these sections of your report.

Introduction

As a researcher you must first decide what you want to study: you need to look at the work and theories of other psychologists so that you can understand the topic that interests you. Your Introduction must include information which is relevant to your aim and method, so the reason for your aim and choice of research method will be clear.

Say you want to conduct a study similar to Patterson's observational study (see p. 137) on the outcomes of aggression in young children: you include a description of Patterson's research (with results and conclusions) along with a brief explanation of reinforcement. You explain why the observational method is appropriate for this type of study and then formulate your aim, which could be:

> *The aim of this study is to observe outcomes of aggression in 3 year old children.*

Alternatively, you might want to investigate ways of reducing prejudice. From the material on the causes of prejudice and its reduction (see p. 131) you decide that encouraging empathy might be useful in creating more positive attitudes towards members of an 'out group' and thus reducing prejudice. You decide to test this idea in your research, so you write:

> *The aim of this study is to see if encouraging empathy makes people's attitudes more positive towards members of an 'out group'.*

You must now decide which research method is the most appropriate for conducting your study, and say why. As you want to see whether encouraging empathy improves people's attitudes, you will be testing cause and effect. An **experiment** is the most appropriate research method (see p. 41). This is because it enables you to isolate one variable (the **independent variable** – empathy) and see what effect it has on another variable (the **dependent variable** – attitudes to others). For more on variables, see p. 42.

The next task is to decide how to encourage empathy, measure attitudes and define an 'out group'. You may decide the out group will be refugees and that you will encourage empathy by asking people to read an emotional article which details the plight of refugees. Because it is written to encourage emotions (such as empathy), we will describe it as an 'emotive article' through the rest of this chapter. One group of people will read the emotive article and a comparison group will read a non-emotive article. A questionnaire will be used to measure participants' attitudes towards refugees, which will be given before and after they read the article.

CHECK

The Introduction to your report must state your aim and research method, and provide relevant background material so the reader can understand the reasons for your aim and choice of research method.

HYPOTHESIS

DEFINITION

If you conduct the **observational** study you have no expectations of what will happen, but in the experiment you do, because you want to see whether empathy improves attitudes – whether the IV affects the DV. In other words the purpose of your study is to test an **experimental hypothesis**. You must state your hypothesis and it must be a prediction of what you expect to find, for example:

> *The experimental hypothesis is that reading an emotive article about refugees will make attitudes towards them more positive.*

If you are using the **correlational** method (p. 44) to investigate whether there is a relationship between two variables, your hypothesis is called a **research hypothesis**. Imagine that your aim was to replicate Murstein's study (p. 101) to verify that there is a positive correlation between the physical attractiveness of partners when rated by others. Again, your hypothesis predicts what you expect to find, for example:

> *The research hypothesis is that there will be a positive correlation between the physical attractiveness of partners when rated by others.*

INDEPENDENT AND DEPENDENT VARIABLES

An experiment allows you to manipulate the IV in order to see what effect it has on the DV (see p. 41–42). If your chosen research method is an experiment, you must state what your IV and DV are. For the empathy experiment you would write:

> *The IV in this experiment is the emotive article.*
> *The DV in this experiment is the attitude to refugees.*

If you look at the middle of p. 51 you will see that the experimental hypothesis for this research incorporates the IV and the DV.

CHECK   Your Introduction should also include your hypothesis (if you are conducting a correlational study or an experiment) and an IV and DV (if you are conducting an experiment).

Method

This is where you describe how you put your study into effect, detailing your design, sample, materials and procedure. The imaginary examples of an observational study and an experiment are used to illustrate some points. However, the next section on **experimental design** relates only to experiments.

EXPERIMENTAL DESIGN

In an **experiment** you compare data from two (or sometimes more) groups of participants:

- In **laboratory** or **field** experiments you have an experimental group (which experiences the IV) and a control group (which do not). The control group experience exactly the same treatment as the experimental group *except* for the IV, so that any difference between them must be due to the IV you have manipulated. In these types of experiments *you* choose how participants are allocated to groups (or conditions).
- In the **natural** and **quasi** experiments participants automatically fall into one of the two conditions, for example males compared with females; adopted children compared with children in a residential nursery; younger people compared with older people. You are not able to assign participants to groups – they automatically fall into one group or the other. The difference between the *participants* is the IV.

Experimental design refers to the way that you divide your participants into two groups so that you can compare them. Below we look at the three ways of doing this – independent measures, repeated measures and matched pairs designs. Some of these designs can only be used in certain circumstances (which are noted below), but where you have a choice you must weigh up the advantages and disadvantages of each design, decide how they relate to *your* research and then decide on the most appropriate. You must give the reasons for your choice of design in your report.

Independent measures design

DEFINITION

An experiment using **independent measures** has different participants in each condition:

- In **natural** and **quasi** experiments participants *have* to go into one of the two groups – the groups form themselves as you saw above.
- In **laboratory** and some **field** experiments *you* are manipulating the IV and are able to choose which participants are assigned to the experimental group and which to the control group, as you would do in the empathy experiment. You do this by **random allocation**, which ensures that each participant has an equal chance of being assigned to one group or the other (for details of randomising, see sampling on p. 55)

The major disadvantage with this design is that individual differences can affect the results, for example in the empathy experiment there may be a greater number of poor readers in one group. There are several ways of reducing the effect of these participant variables: you can have a large sample, you can pre-test all participants on a variable which might affect the results, such as a reading test, and use the test to ensure that reading ability is equally distributed between the two conditions; alternatively you can use a repeated measures design (see below).

Advantages:
- this is the quickest and easiest way of allocating participants to groups
- there are no **order effects** (which occur with repeated measures, see below).

Disadvantages:
- participant variables may bias results
- a large sample is needed to reduce the effects of participant variables
- pre-tests are expensive and time-consuming.

Repeated measures design

DEFINITION

In a **repeated measures** design every participant goes through the experimental *and* the control conditions. This is an advantage because as the same people are in both conditions there are no **participant variables**. However there is a drawback because participants may behave differently after they have been through one condition and thus affect your results – this is called **order effects** or **practice effects**.

To take the empathy experiment, participants in the experimental condition read the emotive article, but empathy which is created may carry over when they are tested in the control condition. This would affect the second set of attitude scores and therefore your results.

To get around these problems you **counterbalance** the order in which participants experience the conditions. You split your sample in half, one half does the experimental condition (A) then the control condition (B); the other half does the control condition (B) then the experimental condition (A). This is called the ABBA design: it cancels out any effects which are due to the order of conditions that the participants experience.

Advantages:
● it eliminates participant variables because individual differences such as reading ability, concentration and intelligence are the same in both the experimental and control conditions
● it is therefore possible to have a fairly small sample.

Disadvantages:
● due to order effects, **counterbalancing** must be employed
● participants may decide not to return for the second part of the experiment
● this design cannot be used in **quasi** or **natural** experiments because participants automatically fall into one of two groups.

Matched pairs design

DEFINITION   With **matched pairs** there are different participants in each group but they are matched in pairs on the basis of variables relevant to the study, such as age, gender, intelligence, reading ability or socio-economic background. This may require pre-tests in order to ensure good matching, then one of each pair is assigned to the experimental condition and the other to the control condition. The perfect matched pairs design is one which uses identical twins!

Advantages:
● you can have a fairly small sample, though you may need more before you start in order to select good matches
● the effects of individual differences are reduced
● there are no **order effects**
● it can be used in quasi experiments by matching participants in the important variables *except* for the IV, for example a male and a female would be matched on the basis of age, intelligence, socio-economic background.

Disadvantages:
● it can be expensive and time-consuming
● accurate matching is quite difficult – either you spend time and money trying to achieve this or you have reasonably well-matched pairs but a larger sample
● participant variables may still affect results.

SAMPLE

DEFINITION   Your sample is the participants you use in your research, and you choose them because they *represent*, to some extent, a certain **population**. If you wish to study one year olds these are your **target population**, but because you cannot study all one year olds you take a sample. You must decide if there are any characteristics which might affect a person's eligibility for your research. For example if you are studying visual perception your participants should all be sighted; if you are studying attitudes to refugees your sample should exclude refugees.

You decide how large the sample will be, based on factors such as your design (**independent measures** requires more participants than **repeated measures**), time available (a small sample is usual in an **observational** study because it is time-consuming and you are not testing a hypothesis). Although a larger sample is more representative of a population, most researchers use perhaps 20 to 30 participants. You only need a small sample for your practical exercise.

Once you have decided on the numbers and characteristics of your participants you must select them. If your sample is representative of the target population, then you can generalise your results from the sample to the target population. Four sampling methods are described below (random, quota, opportunity and self-selected). Note that some are more representative than others. When choosing your sampling method you must weigh up the advantages and disadvantages of each, decide how they relate to *your* research and then decide on the most appropriate. Weaknesses, such as a biased sample, may affect your **results** and **conclusions** and you may want to mention this in your discussion of the results.

Random sampling

DEFINITION   Be warned, this is not what you think it is – random sampling is highly controlled! It means that every member of the target population has an equal chance of being selected. This is an ideal, and in practice to obtain a random sample you ensure that you select people from a range of backgrounds. If your target population is seven year olds, you could select children from different types of primary schools. To select, say, 30 participants you could first collect the names of all seven year olds attending two inner city, two suburban and two rural primary schools, perhaps 170 names in all.

To ensure each child has an equal chance of being selected you give each name a number, and then using a 'lottery' type of number selection, take the first 30 numbers selected to give you the names of the children who will form the sample. Examples of the 'lottery' style of selection are taking bingo balls out of a box, computer generated numbers or random number tables. Raffle tickets can be used, as long as they are well mixed and the selector can not differentiate between tickets before they are pulled out of the drum or box.

Advantages:
● participants are representative of the target population
● as they are representative you do not need a large sample.

Disadvantages:
● this method can be time-consuming
● people may not agree to take part once they have been selected
● you can not use random sampling in some types of research, such as field experiments.

Quota sampling

DEFINITION

If you have ever been stopped by someone on the street doing market research, they are probably using quota sampling. This means selecting a sample which is in proportion, in the relevant characterics, to the population as a whole. What on earth does this mean? Imagine you are conducting a survey of men to find out what qualities they value in their friends. You need to find out what proportion of men in the population fall into categories such as: self-employed, working class, professional, unemployed, married, divorced, single, 20 – 30 years old, 30 – 40 years old and so on.

You can get this information from census data, which might show for example that 10% of males are self-employed and 20% are working class. You select people on the basis that they fit in to these categories until you have filled your quota, so that 10% of your sample are self-employed, 20% are working class, and so on.

Advantages:

● it produces a representative sample
● for this reason a large sample is not necessary.

Disadvantages:

● it is time-consuming and expensive to fill the quota
● it is not always possible to use quota sampling, for example in a field experiment.

Opportunity sampling

DEFINITION

Here you ask anyone who fits your requirements or rely on people becoming participants by chance. If you wanted to study gender differences in teenagers, you might use the first males and females you could find, as long as they were within the age range and agreed to take part. An example of opportunity sampling is selecting names from a telephone directory, but this is not a very representative sample because many people are not listed in a directory. Opportunity sampling occurs in field experiments such as Piliavin's subway experiment (p. 274) because participants were the people who happened to be in the carriage where the 'emergency' took place.

Advantages:
- it is easy and fast
- it is used in natural and field experiments.

Disadvantages:
- the sample may be biased because you may only ask people to take part who look approachable and co-operative, which will affect your results
- samples will not be very representative in field or natural experiments
- in order to increase representativeness, a large sample is necessary.

Self-selected sampling

DEFINITION A self-selected sample is one where *participants* choose to take part, for example people who return questionnaires or surveys, or who have volunteered to take part in a study (by responding to advertisements in newspapers or on the radio). Research has shown that these people are unlikely to be representative of the population, for instance they may be more outspoken, have more time or have strong feelings about the topic you are researching.

Advantages:
- people offering to take part are less likely to drop out
- surveys enable you to have a large sample
- they are easier and cheaper to conduct because you do not have to go through a selection process.

Disadvantages:
- a self-selected sample is likely to be biased because it is not representative of the population.

Not all experiments study people, for example researchers have investigated racism, stereotyping and bias in the media, possibly comparing two newspapers or two television channels. These could be classsed as quasi experiments because the IV (for example the two television channels) is naturally occurring. This type of research is called **content analysis** because researchers analyse the content of programs or articles, as did Manstead & McCulloch in their study of sex-role stereotyping in television advertisements. They analysed several hundred advertisements in terms of the central figures in the ad, their roles, the type of product and so on (see p. 202 for more details).

VARIABLES

Your Method will include information such as where and how the study was conducted, what materials you used and what you said or did with participants. When planning these aspects of your practical exercise you need to consider **variables**. These are discussed in more detail below.

Measuring the variables

You must decide how to measure the variables in your research – in the imaginary **observational** study the variables you measure are the outcomes of aggression. You will therefore need to define aggression (pushing – how hard? grabbing – a toy? an arm? facial expressions – which ones? verbal behaviour – what kind?) and how to measure it (how often it occurs or how long it lasts or both?). How do you define and measure 'outcomes' (the response of the other child? whether ownership of an object is gained?) Will you measure aggression towards things as well as people?

How will you conduct these **observations**? Will you watch six children for a 15 minute period or two for a full play-group session or any child who comes to the sand box? How will you observe the participants – will you be hidden from them or sit in a corner of the room or join in their activities? Will you video the children and analyse the behaviours afterwards?

You explain how the measures are devised. In an observational study it is useful to run a **pilot study** because it enables you to watch the kind of behaviour you will be analysing, and thus devise the most useful measures.

In the empathy **experiment** you measure the **dependent variable**. You explain how the questions were devised (perhaps based on the social distance questionnaire used to measure prejudice (see Figure 5.2 p. 41). Say why and how questions are scored, for example on a 1–5 scale (see p. 41), and say what a high score indicates, for example, a positive attitude. You might include 'decoy' questions which are designed to mask the purpose of the questionnaire. If you do, say which they are and do not include the scores in your calculations. Once again a **pilot study** is a useful way of testing that people can understand your questions and that they are worded so that you get a range of answers.

You must say why the measures you are using are suitable. For example, in the empathy experiment, attitudes could be assessed by **interviewing** participants before and after they read the article, but they may not give you an honest answer. The anonymity of a written **questionnaire** is preferable because it is likely to give more accurate information in this particular study.

Confounding variables

DEFINITION A **confounding variable** is anything which systematically affects your results. It is usually due to a fault in the design, such as **order effects** or **sampling**.

In the empathy experiment, the emotive article will be chosen because it encourages an emotional response, probably by personalising the plight of the refugees by describing what two or three of them have experienced. If the article read by the control group was a long account of numbers of refugees and the names of countries to which they had dispersed, then you may find there is no increase in empathy in this condition.

However this could be due to the 'dry' style of the article, which would be a **confounding variable**. To eliminate this you ensure that the articles are as similar as possible in terms of length, complexity of language, size and style of print, number of illustrations and so on. You explain that this is how you control variables to ensure if there is an increase in positive attitudes it is due solely to the emotive nature of the article – the IV.

Situational variables

You must ensure that the environment in which the research takes place is the same for all participants. If some do a task when the room is very noisy they may perform very badly in comparison with others, which will affect your results. You therefore control all **situational variables** and say how you do this, for example briefly describe the environment in which the research will take place, at what time and so on.

Standardised procedure

You must also ensure that each participant is treated in exactly the same way. In an **experiment** the only thing which changes is the IV. Every participant must do exactly the same tasks, with the same materials, in exactly the same order – this is called a **standardised procedure**. Each should be given exactly the same instructions (**standardised instructions**) ideally by the same person in the same way. One way of ensuring that instructions are the same is to provide written instructions, which should be simple and clear.

MATERIALS

Describe any equipment (for instance the empathy articles), toys or other materials which you used. If sketches or diagrams provide more detail include them in an Appendix. Copies of questionnaires or observational schedules should be attached, along with the marking or scoring system, in an Appendix.

PROCEDURE

In this section you describe exactly what you did in the order in which it was done. Say how you controlled variables, how you measured them and your standardised instructions. If you ran a pilot study to check your design, observations or questions, state this along with any amendments you made. Describe how you conformed to **ethical guidelines** and what you said when **debriefing** your participants.

CHECK

There are no rules about the order in which information is presented in your Method, but it must include the following information (if appropriate): research method, experimental design, sample and sampling method, how the variables were measured and variables controlled. Say why these choices were appropriate and describe how you put them into effect.

Results

This is the section of your report where you present the data from your study and analyse it. Very basic data (such as scores from each participant on each question of a questionnaire) may be attached as an Appendix, but the summary of this data should appear in the Results section.

Continuing the empathy research, imagine you have used the independent measures design and the total scores for each participant are presented in a table such as Table 6.1 below. What you are really interested in is any *change* in scores, so the table also includes the calculated difference between each participant's 'before' and 'after' scores. Note that participants are identified by number (remember **ethics!**).

	Empathy score		
Participant number	Before reading	After reading	Difference
Control group			
P1	44	48	+4
P2	31	34	+3
P3	50	53	+3
P4	49	55	+6
Experimental group			
P5	28	41	+13
P6	32	38	+6
P7	41	45	+4
P8	47	52	+5

TABLE 6.1 Table showing attitude scores by participant

Depending on the type of data you have, you may be able to present it in a visual form which will show its characteristics more clearly. Different types of data require different visual representation:

- **bar charts** show amounts or the number of times something occurs
- **graphs** show data which changes over time
- **pie charts** show data as a proportion of the whole
- **scattergrams** show the pattern of relationships in a correlational study.

BAR CHARTS

The bar chart is used to show amounts or the number of times something occurs. A bar chart of the difference in attitude scores in Table 6.1 would look like Figure 6.1 below.

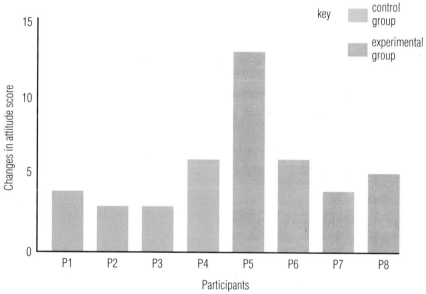

FIGURE 6.1 Bar chart showing differences in attitude scores by participant

GRAPHS

The graph is used to show how something changes over time. Imagine you collected data on the number of friends children had at various ages, then calculated the average (or mean) number of friends at each age, results might look like those in Table 6.2

Age of child	2	4	6	8	10	12	14
Mean number of friends	1	4	5	7	6	7	8

TABLE 6.2 Table showing mean number of friends at various ages

To put this data in a graph, you put the regular information (ages) along the bottom axis and the data which varies along the upright axis. A graph of the data in Table 6.2 would look like Figure 6.2 below.

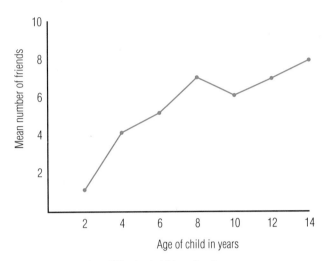

FIGURE 6.2 Graph showing mean number of friends of children at various ages

PIE CHARTS

The pie chart is used when you want to show proportions of a whole. For example in the Thomas, Chess and Birch study on temperament (see p. 165), they classified children in one of four categories. The 'pie' in Figure 6.3 represents all the children, and it is divided into segments which correspond to the proportion (or percentage) of children in each category.

FIGURE 6.3 Pie chart showing proportion of children in each category of temperament

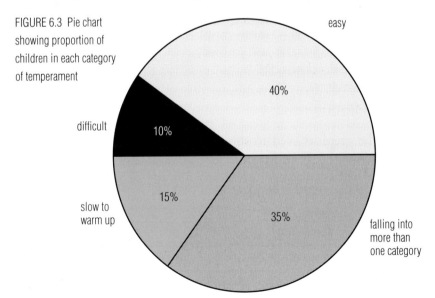

SCATTERGRAM

The scattergram is only used in a correlational study: it enables you to see whether there is a pattern of relationships between two variables (see p. 44). Let us imagine you replicate Murstein's study (see p. 101) of the similarity in attractiveness of couples, and ask participants to rate each male and female from 1–10, 10 being very attractive. From this you calculate the mean rating for each partner – imaginary data is presented in Table 6.3.

Couple number	Mean of male score	Mean of female score
1	7	4
2	3	4
3	8	7
4	5	6
5	4	3
6	4	5
7	5	4
8	6	8

TABLE 6.3 Table showing mean attractiveness rating for each partner in a couple

When you draw a scattergram each axis represents a variable. A scattergram of the information in Table 6.3 is shown in Figure 6.4, each cross represents the ratings for the partners in the couple.

The scattergram in Figure 6.4 shows a **positive correlation** between variables. If you drew an imaginary line through the crosses it would go upwards from

FIGURE 6.4 Scattergram showing mean attractiveness rating for each couple

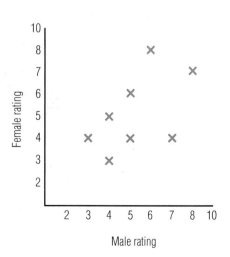

the junction of the two axis. If this imaginary line ran *down* this would indicate a **negative correlation**, which occurs when one variable decreases as the other increases. If there is no upward or downward trend in the crosses this indicates there is zero correlation between the variables – in other words there is no relationship between them (see Figure 6.5).

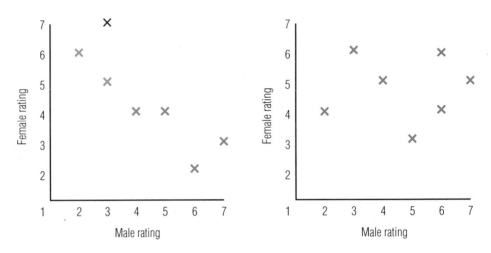

FIGURE 6.5 Scattergram showing negative correlation   Scattergram showing zero correlation

ANALYSING RESULTS

So far you have only presented data, but in order to draw conclusions from it you must analyse it. As you read through this section it should become apparent that analysing your data helps you to draw more accurate conclusions – it may not show you what you think it does! The empathy scores in Table 6.1 (p. 60) will be analysed as an example.

The mean

You can see by looking at Table 6.1 that the increase in empathy score is greater in the experimental group. What you need to know is how big the difference is, and whether it is likely to be due to the IV. You can check this by working out the mean (or average) score for each group. Add up the scores for each group and divide it by the number of scores:

Total score for control group = 16, divide by 4 = mean of 4

Total score for experimental group = 28, divide by 4 = mean of 7

Because the experimental group have a higher mean score, you might conclude that the IV has made a difference, but look at the data in another way and you might not be so sure.

The range

By calculating the range of scores you can see how much they vary. You do this by taking the lowest score away from the highest score in each group:

> Control group – highest score minus lowest is 6 – 3 = range of 3

> Experimental group – highest score minus lowest is 13 – 4 = range of 9

Because the range of scores is much larger in the experimental group this shows they varied much more than the scores from the control group. When there is a large difference between the two ranges it could be that a participant in one group has a very high or low score.

This happens here because P5's score is much higher than the others in the group. If P5's score was taken out of the calculations, the mean score for the experimental group would be 5 (much closer to the mean score of 4 in the control group) and the range would be 2 (similar to the control group's range of 3).

By calculating the range you have discovered that one participant's score is distorting the data. If this extreme score is discounted the difference between the two groups is small, not enough for you to be confident that the IV has had an effect.

CHECK

The Results section presents the data which you have obtained in your research (unless it is very detailed, when it goes in an Appendix). Use a visual representation if this helps the reader understand the data (see pp. 61–4). Where appropriate calculate means and ranges. All data must be presented neatly, accurately and fully labelled.

Discussion

Once you have analysed the data you should be able to relate it to the aim or to the hypothesis in your study and draw some **conclusions**. If your study does not have a hypothesis, for example if the aim of your study had been to observe the outcomes of aggression in three year old children, then your conclusions would provide comments about any patterns or trends which you can identify.

If your study *is* testing a hypothesis then you must say what your results are and whether they support, or do not support, your hypothesis. As we have just seen when analysing the empathy data, this can be difficult to decide. Psychologists would do a statistical calculation on the data, which would tell them how likely it is that their results do support the **experimental hypothesis**. You do not have to do this, so your decision must be based on your analysis of results and the size of your **sample** (the fewer the participants, the larger the difference must be before you can conclude that your hypothesis is supported). Although empathy results show that reading the article did create more positive attitudes, the one extreme score has exaggerated this difference – without it the differences between the two groups is small. Having explained this you would conclude that:

> *Reading the emotive article did not affect attitudes towards refugees, so the results do not support the experimental hypothesis.*

To draw **conclusions** from the results of a correlational study you must judge the extent to which the scores fall along a fairly straight upward or downward line. Once again, the fewer scores you have, the closer they should be to the line for you to conclude that:

> *The results show that there is a positive correlation between the attractiveness of male and female partners in a couple, which supports the research hypothesis.*

Once you have drawn conclusions from your data and related them to your **aim** or **hypothesis**, you must also say how they relate to what other psychologists have found on the same topic. Are they similar, are they what you would expect? If not, what other explanations could there be for your findings?

Finally you must evaluate your own study, regardless of whether or not your hypothesis was supported. For example in the empathy study, *all* participants showed an increase in empathy – why? Perhaps completing the questionnaire raised their awareness of the suffering of refugees, and it was this which increased empathy, not the emotive article.

To evaluate your research, ask yourself: How did participants respond to your instructions? How accurately did your observations reflect what happened? Did participants understand the questions in the questionnaire? Did the children answer thoughtfully or guess? Would a larger sample have made a difference to your results, and therefore your conclusions? What were the weaknesses in your sampling? Did participants make any useful comments when you debriefed them? Think about the answers to these questions and what impact they may have made on your results and conclusions. Critical evaluation and suggestions for improving the study help psychologists to draw more accurate conclusions and to design better studies.

CHECK   Make sure your Discussion draws conclusions from your data and relate it to your aim (or hypothesis if appropriate), saying whether or not they are what you expected (and whether the hypothesis is supported or not) and give your reasons. Interpret your findings by linking them to relevant psychological material. Evaluate your study – say what went wrong, what could be improved, whether any of the faults explain unexpected findings.

CHECK   Your report should also include a title, contents, numbered pages and numbered appendices if appropriate. The details provided in your report should enable someone else to copy your study, so you must provide all relevant information clearly and in the right order. Where relevant, use the correct terms as they have been explained in this chapter, such as variables, standardised instructions, opportunity sampling, mean, bar chart and so on.

Exercises

1 What is the aim of Schaffer & Emerson's study on p. 83?
2 Write a hypothesis for Byrne's experiment on p. 99.
3 What is the IV and the DV in Ruble, Balaban & Cooper's experiment on p. 194?
4 What is the difference between a population and a sample?
5 A psychologist selects a sample by choosing every 100th name in the electoral register. What kind of sampling is this? Say how representative it is likely to be and explain your answer.
6 Give one advantage and one disadvantage of any two experimental designs.
7 What are standardised instructions?
8 What information do the mean and the range give us?
9 Would it be appropriate to draw a pie chart of the friendship data? Explain your answer.
10 If a positive correlation is found between two variables, what conclusion can we draw?

Ethical Concerns in Research

7

Ethics are the desirable standards of behaviour we use towards others. If we behave ethically, then we treat others with respect and concern for their well-being. We do not take advantage of their trust or their lack of knowledge. Ethics apply to human beings and to animals.

Ethical concerns in research

Psychologists must conduct their research within the guidelines of the British Psychological Society. This is because:

- psychologists have legal and moral responsibilities to those who help them in their research – every individual has rights, and these must be respected and protected.
- psychology will continue to need human participants in research, and must therefore ensure that trust which participants show is justified and protected.
- in order to retain public confidence in psychology we must demonstrate our concern for the rights and well-being of other human beings. In the last 30 years there has been increasing concern that psychologists behave ethically and treat the people who help them in their research as equals. This is one reason why they are now called participants, when they used to be called subjects.
- everyone working within psychology has a responsibility to others in the discipline – any action which discredits our own work also discredits the work of psychology as a whole.

The British Psychological Society has therefore published guidelines specifying ethical concerns and how they must be addressed. These guidelines apply to anyone working within psychology, so this includes students of psychology. When devising and carrying out your own practical investigation for the GCSE course you must remember to adhere to the guidelines detailed below.

AVOID DISTRESS

You must ensure that those taking part in research will not be caused any distress. This means, for example, that you must not embarrass, upset, frighten, offend or harm participants. For example if your study involved showing them gruesome pictures, this could upset them. This is also an issue in cross cultural research, for example a question asked may offend the cultural norms of one culture but not another. Participants in research put their trust in the psychologists. If we distress them in any way we betray that trust and discredit the profession, as well as making it less likely that *others* will agree to participate in research in the future.

INFORMED CONSENT

Participants (or those responsible for them if they are children) must consent to take part in studies. Before the study begins the researcher must outline what the participant will be asked to do so that when consent is given the participant has made a conscious decision to take part in the research knowing what it will entail.

An exception to this is in a **field** experiment or some kinds of **observational** study when it is not possible to gain consent. This is acceptable as long as what happens to the participants is something which could just as easily happen to them in everyday life. For example, if research involves observing people in a bus queue, those people may be observed by *anyone* when they are in the queue.

AVOID DECEPTION

Participants must be deceived as little as possible, and any deception must not cause distress. Before gaining their consent you tell your participants what your study involves and what to expect. If you deceive them, then they will have agreed to take part without knowing fully what to expect. Sometimes deception is unavoidable, but the true nature of the research should be revealed at the earliest possible opportunity, or at least during debriefing. When the participant is likely to object or be distressed once they discover the true nature of the research at debriefing, then the study is unacceptable.

WITHDRAWAL

Participants have the right to withdraw from a study whenever they wish. They must be told this at the start of the research and reminded of their right to withdraw if it is a long study or if they appear to be distressed. By reminding them of the right to withdraw you are stressing that they are under no obligation and can act to protect themselves at any time if they feel uncomfortable.

CONFIDENTIALITY

Information about the identity of participants and any information gained from them is confidential. For example, you must never give the names of participants, or any information which would make them identifiable unless the participants agree.

PROTECT FROM RISK

Participants should be protected from risk. For example frightening them could cause a heart attack. Any risk they experience should be no greater than what they would encounter in their everyday lives.

DEBRIEFING

Participants must be thoroughly debriefed at the end of the study. This means that you must give participants a general idea of what you were doing and why you were doing it. This is one way of showing your concern about their well-being and ensuring that they would be prepared to take part in future research. If serious deception has been involved the researcher must ensure that the participant feels comfortable about their part in the research, and if necessary they should be followed up to ensure there are no ill-effects later on.

ANIMALS

Where animals are to be confined, constrained, harmed or stressed in any way, the researcher must think whether the knowledge they would gain makes the way the animals are treated justifiable. Researchers should find other ways of researching if possible, must use as few animals as they can, must meet their needs for food and space. Any procedures which may cause pain and distress can only be done by those holding a Home Office licence.

CONDUCT

You must always behave honestly – you do not use other people's wording and claim it is yours, you do not invent data, you do not copy other people's work. You must not pretend that you know more than you do as people might think you are competent to help them with their problems because you are studying psychology. You must be very cautious if they ask your advice.

The guidelines in practice

It is sometimes difficult to plan research within these guidelines. Most research requires some degree of deception, for example. Nevertheless, psychologists have devised clever ways of running studies which do not break these guidelines: others have not. You can see that some of the research reported in this book breaks these **ethical guidelines**, possibly because the research took place before the guidelines became so strict.

When devising research studies, psychologists are strongly recommended to seek the advice of their colleagues to ensure that these guidelines are being met, particularly when they are uncertain about a particular aspect of the study. A colleague may, for example, be able to suggest an alternative design which would minimise the amount of deception. Wherever psychological research takes place there are Ethics Committees to monitor and advise on ethical issues in research.

CHECK

As a student carrying out research for your practical exercise, you must check with your teacher that you are competent to carry out the research. You must ensure that your practical exercise is designed and conducted within these guidelines, and that the way you answer your examination questions shows that you understand and respect these guidelines.

Exercises

Find three studies in this book which break these ethical guidelines. Explain why they do.

SOCIAL AND ANTI-SOCIAL RELATIONSHIPS

SECTION

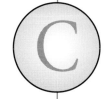

In the first two chapters of Section C we look at the individual's relationships with other people. We examine the development of the infant's first relationships and why they are important, and then move on to children's friendships. We consider why other people are important to us, what effect they have on our behaviour and why we prefer some people more than others. This is covered in Chapters 8 and 9.

In Chapters 10 and 11 we consider relationships with others which are unpleasant or unfair – anti-social relationships. We look in particular at how prejudice and aggression originate, their affect on our behaviour towards others, and finally we review ways in which such anti-social behaviour can be reduced.

As you are reading, note the tabs alongside the text. These indicate definitions, core topics (which are explained in chapters 1–4) and methodology (which is explained in chapters 5–7).

Making Attachments to Others

8

The newborn infant is utterly dependent on others if it is to survive – others provide food, warmth and protection. But if the infant is to thrive, it needs more than physical care. This chapter considers the child's emotional relationships with other human beings. These relationships are important for the development of the child's social skills and cognition, and in this chapter we will find out how children develop an emotional bond with others. We are interested in the different kinds of bonds, why they are important and what happens if they are broken, or do not even form in the first place.

The development of attachments

DEFINITION

An attachment is defined as a close emotional bond to another person. Infant behaviours such as crying, making eye contact and grasping form the basis of its interaction with others. These are all types of **attachment behaviour**. Other attachment behaviours develop during the first two or three months – smiling, reaching and arm waving for example. These behaviours invite carers to respond to the baby, they learn how to attract its attention, make it smile or to understand its needs. This is how attachments form, from the interaction between the two people.

For the first three months, most babies respond equally to any caregiver, but then they start to respond more to the people who are familiar to them. So a baby may wave its arms or smile when it sees its father's face, but there will be little reaction from the baby when it sees a stranger. The baby continues to respond most to those it interacts with frequently until about six or seven months of age. It then begins to show a special preference – an attachment – to certain people. We consider that the baby has formed an attachment to someone when it shows two particular behaviours:

FIGURE 8.1 This baby gains security from its mother

- **separation distress** – if the baby cries when its mother leaves the room, we conclude that the baby feels insecure when the mother is out of sight
- **stranger fear** – if a stranger comes close to the baby and it turns away from the stranger and towards another person, we conclude that it is fearful of strangers and gains security from this person.

Some babies show these behaviours much more frequently and intensely than others, but nevertheless they are seen as evidence that the baby has formed an attachment when it looks to that person for security, comfort and protection. Such an attachment has usually developed by 12 months old.

The quality of attachments

Psychologists have identified two ways in which attachments can vary:

- the **strength** of the attachment, which means how strong the attachment behaviours are – for example, how often the child goes to its attached person or how tightly it clings
- the **security** of the attachment, which means how confident the child is that its special person will provide what it needs.

The security of a one-year old's attachment to its mother was tested by Mary Ainsworth (1978) in her 'strange situation' studies. She **observed** children's behaviour when mothers and strangers came into and left the room. She **concluded** that there were three types of attachment, as shown in Table 8.1.

Type of attachment	% of children	Attachment behaviours
Securely attached	70	Happy when mother present, distressed by her absence, went to her quickly when she returned, a stranger provided little comfort
Insecurely attached – anxious avoidant	15	Avoided the mother, indifferent to her presence or absence, greatest distress when child alone, a stranger could comfort just as well as the mother
Insecurely attached – anxious resistant	15	Seemed unsure of mother, more anxious about mother's presence, distress in her absence, would go to her quickly when she returned then struggle to get away, also resisted strangers

TABLE 8.1 Three types of attachment identified by Ainsworth

A third type of insecure attachment was identified by other researchers, which they called '**insecure – disorganised**'. These children appeared to be dazed or confused as they showed avoidance and clinging at the same time.

Factors affecting the quality of attachments

Psychologists have proposed a number of reasons why attachments vary like this. Factors which seem to be important for the development of attachment are described below.

SENSITIVE RESPONSIVENESS

SOCIAL

The sensitivity which the carer shows towards the baby's needs has an important influence on the development of attachment. This was shown in Rudolph Schaffer and Peggy Emerson's study, which is detailed later in this chapter. They called it **sensitive responsiveness** and it means responding appropriately to the baby's needs and signals, for example being able to differentiate between the baby's cry of hunger and the cry of pain.

CHARACTERISTICS OF CARERS

SOCIAL

The carer's characteristics appear to be important for the development of a secure attachment. Alan Sroufe (1977) describes mothers as 'psychologically unavailable' when they avoid or reject their babies. Their lack of interaction with their infants may lead to Ainsworth's 'anxious avoidant' attachment. In contrast, some research shows that when mothers are rejecting, their babies may become more clingy.

CONSISTENCY OF CARE

This means that the carer should be seen often by the baby, and they should behave in a similar way all the time. So if a carer is moody and withdrawn sometimes and then very responsive and entertaining, the type of care is not consistent. This may make it more difficult for the baby to develop a secure attachment. One study found that some one-year olds who were securely attached became anxiously attached by 18 months old when their mothers were very highly stressed.

AMOUNT OF STIMULATION

Schaffer & Emerson also found that stronger attachments were related to greater amounts of stimulation from the carer. Stimulation includes using different tones of voice, changing facial expressions often, touching and playing with the baby.

FIGURE 8.2 This baby's attention is captured by his mother's facial expression, she is providing stimulation and is sensitive to her baby's need to be close to her face in order to see it clearly.

TEMPERAMENT

INBORN

Some babies dislike new experiences – they may cry a lot and be very hard to comfort. These are characteristics of the 'difficult' temperament (see p. 167) and this behaviour is similar to that of Ainsworth's 'anxious resistant' attachment. Children with a 'difficult' temperament may have problems developing their attachments. Their carers may find it hard to be loving and caring because they cannot understand these children's needs and carers may feel they are not caring very well. In this case the attachment may be weak or insecure because *neither* partner is able to build the attachment easily.

Why are attachments important?

Psychologists have studied topics such as how well children play with others, how they solve problems, how aggressive they are. They found that children with secure attachments have fewer difficulties as they go through childhood. Children who fail to develop a good early attachment, or those with insecure attachments appear to experience more problems as they grow up. Attachments seem to be very important for three main reasons, all of which are covered in other chapters of this book and which are referred to briefly below:

SOCIAL

- **social development** – learning how to get along with others, acting responsibly and morally. Research on children up to five years of age indicates that securely attached children show more social behaviours, more empathy and are more popular with their peers, whereas insecurely attached children show more attention seeking behaviour and are more likely to show pleasure at the distress of others.
- **emotional development** – being confident, trusting others and developing self-esteem. Research shows securely attached children have higher self-esteem at five years of age, whereas insecurely attached children show more tantrums and aggression.

COGNITION

- **cognitive development** – talking, thinking and understanding the world. Research on children up to four years old shows securely attached children are more flexible and resourceful, show longer attention spans and are more confident in attempting problems and use their mothers more effectively for assistance.

Research therefore suggests that the security of the attachment is correlated with successful development. One of the psychologists who felt that a secure attachment was crucial for long term development was John Bowlby, whose work we now turn to.

Evidence for Bowlby's theories of attachment

John Bowlby was working from the 1940s until the 1980s. He was a psycho-analyst, believing that early experiences have a profound effect on later life and his ideas on attachment have been very influential and controversial. We will first review some of the evidence on which his ideas were based then summarise his key points. In the section after that we will examine evidence which undermines his ideas.

BOWLBY

METHODS

Bowlby was working with emotionally disturbed juveniles (young people) during the 1940s and as part of this work he investigated their early years using the **case study** method. This involved interviews, and looking at past school and medical records. Bowlby divided the young people into two groups, with 44 participants in each. One group comprised juvenile thieves, the other consisted of juveniles who were emotionally disturbed but had no known criminal involvement.

His **results** showed that more than half of the juvenile thieves had been separated from their mothers for longer than six months during their first five years. In the other group only two had such a separation. He also found several of the young thieves showed 'affectionless psychopathy' (they were not able to care about or feel affection for others). Bowlby **concluded** that the reason for the anti-social behaviour in the first group was due to separation from their mothers.

Criticisms of Bowlby's research include:

METHODS

- weaknesses in the **case study** method, for example retrospective research is not always reliable because records may be incomplete and people's memory of the past is often biased and partial (see p. 39).

METHODS

- there was a basic error in the design of his research which makes his conclusions invalid. It *appeared* that a large proportion of maternally deprived children became juvenile thieves simply because one of his groups consisted of participants who were already juvenile thieves. To test the effect of maternal deprivation he should have compared a group who had experienced separation from their mothers with a matched group who had no separation. If there was a difference in the outcomes between the two groups, he could *then* have concluded that it was due to maternal deprivation. This is an example of a **confounding variable** (see p. 59).

SPITZ & WOLF

Rene Spitz and Katherine Wolf (1946) conducted an **observational** study of babies being brought up by their mothers in a prison. As a result of a prison re-building programme, these babies were separated from their mothers at the age of six to eight months old (when first attachments first occur). The separation lasted for three months during which the babies were cared for by other mothers. Spitz & Wolf noted that the babies cried more and failed to gain weight during this time. However, when they were re-united with their mothers they returned to normal. They **concluded** that the negative effects were due to separation from their mothers.

Spitz & Wolf have been criticised for concluding that separation from the mothers caused these effects, which could have been due to other factors, for instance:

- the *other* changes which they experienced, such as disruption in familiar patterns of care and comfort or being in a different physical environment.
- the substitute care was provided by young mothers who did not know these babies, and some of the factors which are important for the development of attachment (p. 77) are relevant here. The care was probably performed with little emotional commitment, and some of the new carers may have been 'psychologically unavailable' to the babies. The new carers would be unable to show sensitive responsiveness to the baby's efforts to communicate and may have provided low levels of stimulation.

GOLDFARB

W. Goldfarb (1943) studied the development of children who spent their early months in an orphanage. He compared one group who were fostered in the first year with a second group who remained there for another two years. **Results** showed that at 12 years of age both groups showed emotional problems, but those who stayed longer in the orphanage scored lower than those who left early on a range of measures, such as **IQ tests** and sociability, and showed higher levels of aggressive behaviour. Goldfarb **concluded** that this poorer development was due to their longer time in the institution, where no attachment figures were available to them.

COGNITION

This research has been criticised because it did not fully consider the reasons *why* some children were fostered at an early age and others were not. It could have been that the more responsive children were fostered, which is why they showed higher levels of sociability and intelligence at 12 years of age.

ROBERTSON & ROBERTSON

James and Joyce Robertson (1968), in their studies of children separated from their mothers, noted that the child's behaviour changed through three stages. This was vividly demonstrated in their film of John, who stayed in a residential nursery when he was 17 months old while his mother had a second baby. During the nine days he was there, they observed the following stages, which comprise the **distress syndrome**:

1 **protest** – the child cries, protests and shows physical agitation
2 **despair** – the child is miserable and listless
3 **detachment** – the child seems to have accepted the situation and shows little interest when reunited with the attached figure. He may be active in separating himself from the attached figure, struggling to be put down if cuddled for example.

The Robertsons **concluded** that the child experiencing separation from its mother would show this pattern of distress because the bond had been disrupted.

Bowlby's maternal deprivation hypothesis

Bowlby also noted evidence for attachments in the young of animals and proposed that attachment in the human infant is an **instinct**, and it is directed only towards one person. He argued that the mother also has an instinct to care for her child, so both the infant and the mother have a biological need to form an emotional bond. If the mother is not available to the baby, then a 'permanent mother substitute' would do. This instinct is at its strongest during the first year or so of the baby's life. Bowlby proposed that if the child did not form an attachment within its first three years then it was too late for one to form. These three years are the **sensitive period**, the period when the child is most able to form this attachment.

INBORN

As a result of the evidence we have already examined, Bowlby (1951) proposed his **maternal deprivation hypothesis**. The hypothesis is that if a child does not develop a strong unbroken attachment with its mother (or permanent mother substitute) during the sensitive period, or if the attachment is broken, then the child would develop long-term social and emotional problems, possibly even affectionless psycopathy. He argued that the attachment to the mother is unique in its quality and its importance – it is as vital as food and forms the basis for all future relationships

As we will see shortly, research has confirmed the importance of attachment and the evidence of problems when attachments are broken. The major criticism is aimed at Bowlby's explanation for these problems – that they are due to maternal deprivation – and it is this claim which generated the research we will examine now.

Evidence undermining Bowlby's ideas

To begin with we will review some evidence which contradicts Bowlby's claims, and will then reassess his **maternal deprivation hypothesis** in the light of this evidence.

SCHAFFER & EMERSON

Rudi Schaffer and Peggy Emerson (1964) conducted a **longitudinal** study over 12 months which investigated the way infants formed attachments, details of which are given below.

Schaffer & Emerson (1964)

The **method** used was naturalistic observation and interview.

The **sample** comprised 60 infants living in Glasgow.

The **procedure** was that the babies were visited monthly and observed when they were with others. Schaffer & Emerson decided that the baby had developed an attachment to a carer when it showed 'separation upset' after the carer left.

The **results** of the observations showed that:

- the first attachment appeared at about seven months old
- many of the babies had more than one attachment by ten months old, they showed attachment to mother, father, grandparents, brothers, sisters and neighbours
- the mother was the main attachment figure for about half of the children at 18 months old: the main attachment figure for most of the others was the father
- attachments were most likely to form with those who responded accurately to the baby's signals: if the main carer ignored the baby's signals then there was often greater attachment to someone the baby saw less, but who responded to it more.

Schaffer & Emerson **concluded** that babies could develop several attachments at the same time, and that where there was a main attachment, it was not always to its mother. They also concluded that the strength of the attachment was due to the amount of 'sensitive responsiveness' the carer showed, not to how much time the carer spent with the baby.

You can see from this description that the Schaffer & Emerson study contradicts Bowlby's claim that there will be one main attachment and that this special attachment is to the mother. It also shows the importance of the father, yet Bowlby said the father had no direct emotional importance to the child. **Results** indicate that **sensitive responsiveness** makes a major contribution towards the development of attachment, and this is something that *any* carer can show.

SOCIAL

HODGES & TIZARD

This **longitudinal study** by Jill Hodges and Barbara Tizard (1989) followed the development of children who had been in residential nurseries from only a few months old. The care provided was of good quality, but carers were discouraged from forming attachments with the children. At about three years of age some were adopted, some returned to their mothers, the rest remained in the nursery. They were also compared with a **control** group, who had spent all their lives in their own families. The children were assessed at two, four, and eight years old and again at 16 years of age, when they were interviewed, as well as their parents and care-workers. However, the researchers noted that results from the control group may have been biased because some parents who had experienced problems in rearing their children decided not to take part in the final assessment.

METHODS

Results indicated that at two years of age none of the institutionalised children had formed an attachment, but by eight years of age those who were adopted had formed good attachments. Also their social and intellectual development was better than that of children returned to their own families. Those returned to their families showed more behavioural problems and the attachments were weaker. Nevertheless all those children who had spent their early years in institutions showed some difficulties in their social relationships, particularly with their peers. Figure 8.3 shows the number of children who were, according to their mothers, attached at eight and 16 years of age.

We can **conclude** from this evidence that Bowlby was correct to emphasise the importance of the early years because all the institutionalised children showed some difficulties in their social relationships later on. However these results show that children *can* form attachments after 3 years of age, which Bowlby claimed was too late because it was after the **sensitive period**. It also contradicts Bowlby's claim that the best place for children is with their own

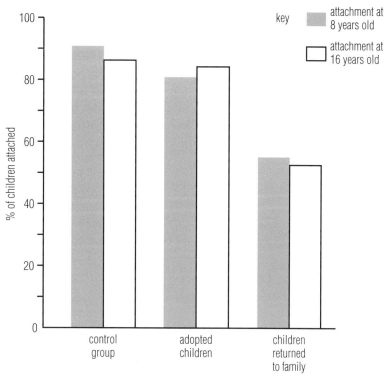

FIGURE 8.3 Bar chart showing attachment to the mother at 8 and 16 years of age

families because this research shows children did better with adoptive parents than in their birth families.

ROBERTSON & ROBERTSON

After observing and filming 17 month old John when separated from his mother (see p. 82), James and Joyce Robertson (1968) noted that his distress could have been due to one or more of the following variables:

- being in a strange and stressful environment
- being deprived of maternal care
- being separated from his mother.

The Robertsons subsequently cared for two girls during a temporary separation from their mothers. The Robertsons were able to isolate the last variable – physical separation from the mother – by providing the other two. Each girl visited them with her mother before the mother went in to hospital. They made sure that the care they gave was similar to the mother's – similar routine and plenty of individual attention. One of the Robertsons was always present to look after and comfort the child. Each child brought momentos from home and was encouraged to talk about her mother.

Results showed they experienced mild distress but otherwise adapted well to the change. The Robertsons concluded that this was because the new situation was familiar and that both children formed an attachment to their new carers. In addition, keeping the child's memory of the mother alive prevented disruption to the bond. However these conclusions can be criticised because the children were girls and the original study was of a boy – **gender differences** could have accounted for the lower level of distress shown. In addition, these are all **case studies** so we cannot generalise the results to the population as a whole.

HAROLD SKEELS

In 1949 Harold Skeels and his colleagues tested the IQ of 25 children in an orphanage who were between one and two years old. (A person's IQ is their score on an intelligence test, and an IQ of 100 indicates a normal score for that age.) Half of the children, those with a mean IQ of 64, were then sent to a school for mentally retarded girls. Here they were looked after by individual girls in an environment with many more toys and attention. The mean IQ of the children remaining in the orphanage was 86.

Results of IQ tests administered two years later showed the mean IQ of children moved to the school had increased to 92 whereas for those in the orphanage it had dropped to 60. The researchers followed these children through to adulthood and in 1966 reported that most of the latter group had stayed in institutions, whereas all of the other group had normal self-supporting lives, marrying and having children.

We can **conclude** that it is the lack of *stimulation* which leads to poorer

FIGURE 8.4 How important do you think this father is for his children's social, emotional and cognitive development?

cognitive development, not necessarily **maternal deprivation** as Bowlby claimed. This study also shows that early problems can be overcome, whereas Bowlby claimed that this was very unlikely.

MICHAEL RUTTER

Michael Rutter (1970) has provided a comprehensive reappraisal of children's attachments which we will look at shortly. First we will examine the evidence from his own research on the long term effects of early separation from mothers. His **sample** comprised 9–12 year old boys from London and from the Isle of Wight. He looked particularly at anti-social behaviour. **Results** indicated that:

- there was more anti-social behaviour in boys from families where the parents' marriage was rated as 'very poor' or where parent-child relationships were cold or neglectful
- there was no difference in anti-social behaviour between boys who had separated from *one* parent and those who had separated from *both* parents
- when a parent died, a child was only slightly more likely to become delinquent than a child from an 'intact' home
- boys who were separated because of illness or housing problems did not become maladjusted.

Rutter **concluded** that there was no correlation between separation experiences and delinquency. He argued that delinquency is not caused by disruption of the bond (as Bowlby claimed) because when disruption was final with the death of a parent, there was only a slight increase in delinquency.

He concluded that there *was* a correlation between family discord and delinquency, suggesting that family discord (such as arguing, lack of affection, stress) distorted relationships. Rutter argued this was not particularly related to early childhood as Bowlby claimed. The distorted relationships may be linked to insecure attachments, perhaps even preventing the formation of attachments.

Deprivation and privation – what are they and how do they affect children?

Rutter (1982) evaluated Bowlby's ideas using a wide range of evidence, some of which we have just examined. This evidence led him to the view that Bowlby's emphasis on the importance of attachment and bonding was correct, but he was wrong in some of his claims. In particular Rutter asserts that:

- the quality of the child's main attachments are actually very similar, although one may be stronger than the rest
- the damaging influences Bowlby cited were due to a variety of circumstances which have different effects, not simply to 'maternal deprivation'
- the term 'maternal deprivation' masks two very different circumstances: privation and deprivation.

We will look in particular at privation and deprivation and how they affect children.

PRIVATION

DEFINITION

Privation occurs when there is a failure to form an attachment to *any* individual. This may be because the child is brought up in a residential nursery with many different carers, or because family discord prevents the development of attachment to any figure. Privated children do not show distress when separated from a familiar figure, which indicates a lack of attachment.

SOCIAL

COGNITION

Research indicates that privation may be related to long-term problems such as anti-social behaviour, affectionless psychopathy, and disorders of language, intellectual development and physical growth. However these problems are not due specifically to the lack of attachment to a mother figure, as Bowlby

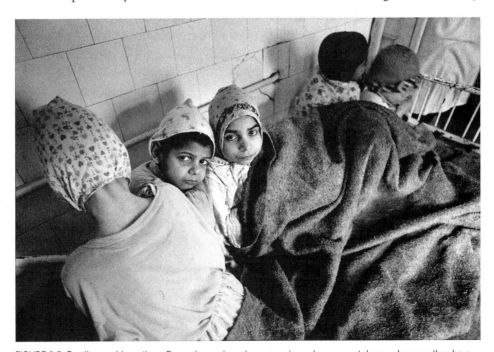

FIGURE 8.5 Bowlby would say these Romanian orphans have experienced permanent damage because they have experienced maternal deprivation. As you read Rutter's criticism of this view you can see there are alternative explanations.

claimed, but to factors such as the lack of intellectual stimulation and social experiences that are usually associated with an attachment. In contrast to Bowlby's claim, it seems that such problems can be overcome later in the child's development, with the right kind of care, as we have seen in the Skeels study and research by Hodges & Tizard.

DEPRIVATION

Deprivation refers to the loss of the maternal attachment, due to separation from the attachment figure. There are short and long-term effects of deprivation, which we will now review.

Short-term effects

The short term effects of separation have been described in the Robertson study – the **distress syndrome** – although children under six months of age do not show this effect because attachments have not developed. Distress is reduced when:

- the attachment is protected, as shown in the Robertsons' later study. As a direct result of their work, and that of Bowlby, hospitals changed their practices so that now children have frequent and extensive contact with attachment figures – parents are sometimes able to stay with their children overnight.

- there is no change in the child's environment other than the loss of the attachment figure, so for example it is better for a child to be cared for in its own home when separated from a main attachment figure
- the child has other attachments which it is able to maintain, such as to another parent, grandparent or siblings
- the child continues to receive warm, consistent, responsive care.

Long-term effects

The long term effects of deprivation may include:

- a change in the nature of the child's attachment – it may become more insecure. The child may show **separation anxiety** for a year or longer. However, a child with a secure attachment seem to be able to withstand the effects of deprivation more than a child whose attachment is insecure.
- an increase in anti-social behaviour where the separation has been related to family discord or a history of disturbance in the life of the young person. Children in these circumstances may be more likely to have insecure attachments.

There appear to be few ill-effects when separations are due to holidays, hospitalisation or when the child has experienced successful separations previously. In this latter case the child may have established a secure attachment which enables it to withstand separations.

Other factors

Another area of research has investigated how children differ in their ability to cope with the effects of separation from an attached figure. Factors such as the age of the child, their temperament and gender affect their ability to cope with disruption of their attachments. We will look at these factors in more detail now, as we consider the effect of divorce on children.

The effect of divorce on children

One example of the disruption of attachments is when parents separate or divorce. As the incidence of divorce increases, so has research on its effects on children. However, this topic raises difficulties for psychologists, some of which are described in Box 8.1 below.

8.1

CHILDREN AND DIVORCE – SOME RESEARCH CONCERNS

METHODS

In order to study children and divorce you would need to make decisions on the following topics.

The **type of study**:

- A **longitudinal** study provides information on particular children at each stage of divorce. You gather information about them before the divorce process starts – are they outgoing, moody, quiet, slow to learn, happy at school, naughty and so on. This provides a baseline for your measurements, so you can monitor how these characteristics change, and which new ones appear. However, a longitudinal study would take several years to complete and children may drop out as the divorce proceeds.
- A **cross-sectional** study takes children whose parents are at various *stages* of divorce. Because the children at each stage must be comparable, they need to be matched on variables such as age, gender, family background, intelligence and emotional profile. A cross-sectional study therefore requires a large sample. As you cannot discover what your participants were like before the divorce, you cannot be sure how much of their behaviour during your research is typical of them or due to the divorce. Nevertheless this gives more rapid results than a longitudinal study.

The **sample** – whatever type of study you chose, you would need to find parents who were going to divorce, or who were already in the process of it. How would you do this? One method could be to advertise, but this would give you a biased sample. Parents who responded might be mostly those going through a relatively painless divorce; a representative sample should include those whose divorce is very difficult. A valuable source of information on parents who are about to divorce would be marriage guidance clinics, lawyers or social workers. The work of these people is confidential so contacting people through these sources would require great care.

Ethical concerns in such a study include:

- **distress** – a study might involve observing parents and children, interviewing them as well as their friends, family, teachers. This may cause additional distress in what is going to be a distressing experience. One solution could be to use researchers who are also trained as counsellors. This means they may be able to reduce the distress and even help the participants.
- **withdrawal from a study** – you must remind participants that they can withdraw from a study at any time and, as divorce is a distressing experience for all involved, it is quite likely that some participants will withdraw. You will need to make allowances for this when deciding on your sample size.

Despite methodological difficulties, psychologists have been able to study divorce. We will examine some of the research, which shows that children differ in their responses. We will then summarise the main consequences of divorce for children. In doing so we will look at how some of these effects can be reduced.

WALLERSTEIN & KELLY

In a **longitudinal** study of the families of 60 divorcing parents carried out by J. Wallerstein and J. Kelly (1987), the **results** showed that:

- divorce is usually disruptive whatever the child's age and the divorce itself does not automatically mean the end of disruption – a third of the children showed significant disturbance more than five years later
- children aged between three and five years old showed the most severe immediate symptoms but fewer long term effects
- the effects of divorce last longer in older children, because those who were two to six years old when separation occurred appeared to show fewer signs of distress after ten years than children who were nine or ten years of age when separation occurred. The latter group showed more signs of distress ten years later.
- older children showed more sadness or anger and these symptoms persisted for up to ten years.

HETHERINGTON, COX & COX

Mavis Hetherington and her colleagues (1982) compared children whose parents had divorced (and who were living with their mother) with children in non-divorced families. **Results** indicated that in the divorced families:

- boys appeared to show conduct disorders and suffer more than girls in the short term; there was more tension between mothers and sons than mothers and daughters
- mothers became less affectionate and more inconsistent in their discipline
- a strong attachment to the custody parent seemed to make conduct disorders less likely
- a stable and happy home environment reduced the upset for the child
- parents found it easier to keep a stable and happy home life for their children when they had help and emotional support from family and friends, rather than coping with problems alone
- children with the 'difficult' temperament show more problem behaviour if the mother was depressed and had poor social support
- after six years the children were more independent.

They **concluded** that there were two phases in the child's response to divorce:

- the **crisis phase**, when the emotional and behavioural responses may be quite marked and when children typically feel angry, guilty, afraid or depressed; this phase occurs during the reorganisation and change in family balance after divorce
- the **adjustment phase**, when children show they are adapting to the new situation, they show less disturbance than children remaining in intact homes where there is still discord.

HOW CAN THE EFFECTS OF DIVORCE BE REDUCED?

Helen Bee (1992) has summarised some of the ways in which the effects of divorce can be reduced. You will see that this brief list links directly with some of the psychological material we have come across in this chapter.

Maintaining attachments

When separation takes place, the effects will be reduced if the child has frequent contact with the non-custodial parent. Both parents will experience stress – they may be withdrawn, angry, depressed, having financial or housing problems. Nevertheless they should both try to maintain a good quality of interaction with the child and be consistent in their behaviour

Maintaining continuity and stability

If there are few other changes in the child's life – the same school, home, contact with grandparents and so on – then separation will be less disruptive. Every effort should be made to ensure that, as much as possible, all other

FIGURE 8.6 If there is a major change in this baby's life, these grandparents will provide some stability

aspects of the child's life remain stable. Economic security reduces problems and stress and makes continuity in the child's life more likely.

Avoiding conflict

The more stressful the home environment, the greater the likelihood of problems for the child. As this discord may be more damaging than the divorce itself, every effort should be made to reduce the child's experience of conflict. This includes both parents agreeing on child rearing and discipline *after* the divorce.

Individual differences

Parents and others involved in the child's life should be aware that they need to be sensitive to the individual differences between children, such as:

- **gender** – boys may be treated more harshly than girls in times of conflict in the home. Boys may have more tense relationships with the mother. Girls may have better 'coping mechanisms' in times of stress but their problems may emerge several years later in adolescence.
- **age** – because it is difficult for young children to understand what is happening they will need extra reassurance. Teenagers are likely to experience a conflict of loyalty which is very difficult to negotiate – support from friends and family along with tolerance and patience will help.
- **temperament** – where there is marked discord in the home, the child with an 'easy' temperament seems to experience less conflict. Children with a

'difficult' temperament are twice as likely to be the target for potential criticism. These children will need extra effort to cope with their experience of divorce.

Social support

SOCIAL

Support from friends and family can ease the difficulties associated with divorce. They can provide practical support, continuity in the children's life and reduce the stress experienced by the adults in the divorce.

Summary

There is little doubt that attachments play a crucial role in the child's development, yet at the same time children vary considerably in their ability to develop attachments and to withstand disruption to their attachments. Bowlby's arguments for the crucial role of the mother have been disputed as psychologists investigated a variety of circumstances and outcomes related to privation and deprivation. Developmental problems related to the difficulties experienced in the early years of life may be overcome with the right kind of care. Nevertheless, the research we have examined in this chapter has led to greater knowledge about how we can care for children to minimise the ill-effects of early experiences and help them withstand loss and disruption to their attachments.

Exercises

1 What do psychologists mean by an attachment?
2 Describe how parents or care-givers can influence the development of attachment.
3 Why are attachments important?
4 What is maternal deprivation?
5 What is the difference between deprivation and privation?
6 Explain how privation may affect children.
7 Describe one study which supports Bowlby's ideas about the effect of maternal deprivation and one which contradicts him.
8 Compare and contrast the results and conclusions of two studies which provide contradictory evidence relating to attachment.
9 Psychologists have studied the effects of divorce on children. Describe the results and conclusions of one of these studies.
10 From what you have learned in psychology, how can parents reduce the effect of divorce on children.

Widening Social Relationships

We take for granted the fact that much of our time is spent with other people: they are the context in which we live our lives. Other chapters in this book examine our earliest relationships, our attitudes to others and how they influence our development. But why do we choose certain people as friends or partners, and why do they choose us? This chapter starts by providing some answers to these questions. It then moves on to look at how other people affect our own behaviour. Here we see that we are influenced by other people to a much greater extent than we think. The chapter offers some explanations of why this influence is so powerful.

How do children develop relationships with their peers?

As a child matures, its relationships with peers develop. Early relationships are based on play with whoever is available. By four years of age children will be co-operating and playing complex games together, where there will be several 'players' and the success of the game depends on each one's contribution. During these early years the child is learning a multitude of social skills: how to get along with others, how to resolve problems, to give and take, to see things from someone's else's viewpoint, what they like or dislike about others. By adolescence qualities such as trust and mutual support are key features of friendship.

Research suggests that the following are some of the factors related to a child's ability to make good relationships with its peers:

SOCIAL

- **opportunities for interaction** – parents who encourage other children to come to play, provide games involving co-operation and give their children experience of pre-school groups also have more popular children.

- **a secure attachment** – securely attached children tend to have better relationships with their peers in the early years. The child who is supportive and friendly is more popular than the child who is aggressive or punitive.
- **conformity to group norms** – more popular children tend to be able to fit in with the **group norms**. They wait before trying to join in, whereas the child who is aggressive or unco-operative may well be rejected by the group.

When people consistently prefer to spend time with each other rather than with others, then that is evidence of friendship. Robert Selman (1980) investigated children's friendships by giving them a problem relating to a friend and asking them what they would do. From their answers he proposed that there are *levels* of friendship, namely:

- level 0 – friendship is based on whoever is closest, so it is unlikely to last
- level 1 – one-way assistance: if there is a disagreement you make it up by giving something to the other child
- level 2 – two-way co-operation: the child can understand different levels of intimacy (which is typical of pre-adolescents)
- level 3 – the relationship becomes more intimate and there is mutual sharing; if there are differences between you this can deepen the friendship; solutions to problems may need to be sensitively handled
- level 4 – the child realises that sometimes friendships cannot be changed to accommodate every individual: sometimes a friendship has to end because an individual can only be expected to change to a certain degree.

Selman did not give ages – he said the level of friendship depends on the child's experiences and how well the child is able to reflect on them. These in turn depend on the child's cognitive development and social skills (see p. 98).

Changes in friendship patterns

We have noted that by about four years of age a child starts to show the beginnings of friendships. What will be the changes in friendship patterns as this child grows up? The three major elements appear to be the number of friends, their gender and the nature of the relationship with them. Research suggests that friendship patterns change according to the child's age, which can be loosely divided as – up to six years old, 6–13 years old and 14 or older. Let's look at how friendships differ in each of these phases.

FRIENDSHIPS UP TO SIX YEARS OLD

Children in this first phase show friendship towards those they spend more time with. This may be because the children live next door to each other or see each other frequently at playgroup. Perhaps they both share the same play interests – dressing up games, for example – and so spend more time together than with others. Even at three years old, the majority of children spend more time with others of the same sex.

They treat their friends differently, they show more positive and less negative behaviour towards friends than non-friends, and try to respond to friends' needs. They may share sweets or toys, which relates to Selman's level 1.

FRIENDSHIPS BETWEEN SIX AND 13 YEARS OLD

SOCIAL

By about seven years old, children's friendship patterns start to change. Their friends are now mostly of the same sex and there is a difference between the size of the friendship group, namely:

- boys tend to form larger groups, and relationships with others in the group are fairly loose. It is relatively easy for another boy to join the group or to leave it.
- girls tend to form smaller groups of perhaps two or three and their relationships are more intimate – there is more sharing of secrets and worries. It may be harder for a girl to join or leave the group.

When asked about friendship, children at this age say friends should help each other out. This usually means material help such as taking computer

FIGURE 9.1 This child doesn't seem to be part of a group. Can you think of any reasons why?

games to play at a friend's house or helping a friend to tidy her room so they can both go swimming. They say this is the kind of thing friends do and it relates to Selman's level 2.

FRIENDSHIPS FROM 14 YEARS OLD ONWARDS

SOCIAL

By about 14 years of age a youngster's peer group is one of the most important influences on his or her behaviour and development. Research suggests that small group friendships move gradually to become part of a larger mixed-sex group, and from this evolve boy-girl (heterosexual) relationships.

Nevertheless earlier same-sex friendship groupings may survive through this change, and emerge intact and more intimate. According to research evidence, this may be because people understand friends can not provide *all* needs, and friendships need to be flexible in order to survive. Friends now tend to give psychological as well as material support, for example giving advice or not laughing at a friend's embarrassment. This relates to Selman's levels 3 and 4.

COGNITION

The changing pattern of children's friendships is related to cognitive development. As the child becomes able to understand more abstract and complex features of relationships and to see things from someone else's point of view, it can understand the needs of others. Some of the reasons why we form friendships will now be examined in more detail as we look at interpersonal attraction in adults.

What attracts one person to another?

In Chapter 3 there is a discussion of the reasons for affiliation – why people need each other. We need others for reassurance or a sense of identity, but the study of attraction is an attempt to explain why we like *particular* people. Psychologists have suggested several reasons for attraction: we will examine four of these in turn – similarity, familiarity, physical attractiveness and social exchange theory.

SIMILARITY

Similarity between two people is one reason why they become friends. Research has shown that people prefer others who are from similar backgrounds, similar ages, similar attitudes, similar beliefs, similar interests and so on. Steven Duck (1988) suggested that this attraction is because we have similar **personal constructs** (see p. 292) – we see the world in the same way.

COGNITION

This makes it easier and more pleasurable to interact. But similarity seems to be important in the continuation of relationships: being with people who share our attitudes and values gives support for our own beliefs. Research shows that partners who stayed together tended to be more similar in age, intelligence and physical attractiveness than partners who separated.

Evidence for the importance of similarity is provided by Donn Byrne's experiments using the 'bogus stranger' technique, described below.

D. Byrne (1961)

The procedure was that participants first completed an attitude scale, thus providing information about their attitudes to a range of topics, using a seven-point scale. Later they were given an attitude scale which they thought had been completed by someone else – the 'stranger'. This was in fact a fake scale which showed the 'bogus stranger' to have attitudes which were either very similar or very dissimilar attitudes to those of the participant. Each participant was then asked a series of questions about their feelings towards the 'stranger'.

Byrne's **results** showed that participants liked the similar 'stranger' more than the dissimilar one, they would prefer to work with them, and they evaluated the similar person more favourably in terms of intelligence, morality and adjustment. He concluded that similarity leads to attraction and to higher evaluation.

METHODS

Critics have argued that Byrne's method is limited because the only basis for making judgements is the information provided by the seven-point attitude scale. In real life we have much more information, such as the person's appearance, what they say, their non-verbal behaviour, in addition to the context in which a meeting takes place.

In contrast to Byrne's research, Theodore Newcomb (1961) followed the actual development of friendships between male students who were given free housing in exchange for their participation in his investigation. Newcomb assessed their attitudes towards a range of issues, before and during their stay in the house, as well as recording their attitudes to the others in the house during their residence. His **results** showed that participants who were attracted to each other also agreed on values, issues and on their attitudes to others in the house. From this he **concluded** that attitude similarity is a key determinant of attraction.

FAMILIARITY

Research has shown that we prefer people who are familiar to us. For example, studies of housing projects confirm that the more likely it is that two people will casually pass each other, the more likely they are to form a relationship. One reason for this is that they have more opportunity to interact and so get to know one another.

However, it seems that even without interaction we prefer something familiar, whether it is a real person, a nonsense word or the photograph of a stranger. Robert Zajonc (1968) investigated this effect, which he called **mere exposure**, by showing his participants a large number of photographs of unknown people although some of the photographs reappeared several times. Participants were then asked how much they liked each of the faces shown in the photographs.

Results showed that there was a **positive correlation** between the number of times the photograph had been seen and how much the face was liked. Zajonc **concluded** that people were liked more when they were familiar.

A similar result was noted in a study which brought participants together several times as they were tasting various drinks. Afterwards the participants had to rate how much they liked each of the other participants. The more contact there was, the more they liked the other person. Why should this be so? It could be that we feel more secure with something familiar, but too much familiarity can lead to boredom, which lessens attraction. However these last two studies only show a **correlation**, so we cannot conclude that familiarity causes liking.

METHODS

PHYSICAL ATTRACTIVENESS

Physical attractiveness appears to be a crucial factor in the first stages of a relationship. This is supported by evidence from a 'computer dance' for students, which is described below.

E. Walster et al (1966)

The **procedure** required students to complete a personality assessment, thinking they would be matched with a partner by computer. In fact the researchers randomly selected the partners except that the man was always taller than the woman. Each student was also rated by independent judges on their physical attractiveness. Half way through the evening the participants were asked questions such as how attractive they found their partner and how keen they were to see them again.

Results showed a strong correlation between physical attractiveness and liking, so students who found their partners very attractive also liked them a great deal. There was no correlation between liking and other factors, such as intelligence or similarity of attitudes.

It was **concluded** that because physical attractiveness was the only factor correlated with liking, this is the main factor in attraction to another person. However this does not mean that it *causes* liking because participants may have liked their partners and *therefore* thought them physically attractive.

There are a number of reasons why we may be attracted to someone who is physically attractive. Two of the reasons are:

COGNITION
- the **halo effect** – which means we infer that people who have a particular quality have other, similar qualities (see p. 287). We think someone who is physically attractive is likely to have other attractive features – they will be pleasant, warm, intelligent and so on.

COGNITION
- the **primacy effect** – this is when the *first* thing we notice has the strongest impact on our impression of the other person (see p. 284). We are likely to notice physical appearance before we notice personality aspects.

This work on physical attractiveness could make many of us rather depressed about making friends and finding a partner, but there is hope! For example research suggests that people who are very attractive are not the most popular. This may be because they create envy in others, or because they fail to live up to the expectations created by the **primacy effect** or the **halo effect**.

When seeking a partner, it appears that we look for someone we consider to be about the same level of attractiveness as ourselves. Rather than risk rejection by someone who is stunning, we seek an equal. This was tested by Bernard Murstein (1972) and is known as the **matching hypothesis**. Using individual photographs of couples who were in long-term relationships, Murstein asked judges to rate each photograph for attractiveness on a five-point scale.

Results showed that there was a positive correlation between the ratings for each partner and Murstein **concluded** that individuals of similar physical attractiveness were more likely to form an intimate relationship than individuals of different levels of attractiveness. If you want to check the matching hypothesis, look at the photographs in the 'Marriages' section of your local newspaper.

SOCIAL EXCHANGE THEORY

Some psychologists have suggested that we look at our relationships in terms of rewards and costs. We enter a relationship when the rewards ('he is really good-looking'; 'she makes me laugh') are greater than the costs ('I'll have to go out of my way to see her'; 'he talks about himself a lot'). This is called **social exchange theory** and was developed by J. Thibaut and H. Kelley (1959).

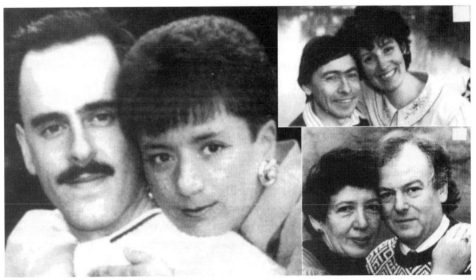

FIGURE 9.2 Why do you think Dateline chose these photographs?

You can see how the ideas in social exchange theory can be related to the three reasons for attraction which we have already considered. For example, the *rewards* of a friendship with someone who is similar means you can do the things you like with someone else. If you were not similar, then you could spend a lot of time doing things you don't like – the costs would be too high for this relationship to get going!

Social exchange theory explains the **matching hypothesis** which predicts that we will not waste our time searching for a dream partner. If we did, the costs (time, disappointment, rejection) would be greater than the rewards (the chance of finding a dream). Similarly we are not drawn to someone much less attractive than ourselves, because according to social exchange theory, although the costs may be fewer, the rewards are small too.

Research also suggests that we prefer people who are competent but also sometimes those who are *incompetent*. How can we explain this contradiction? According to social exchange ideas, we are attracted to those who are competent because they may be able to help us, or we can bask in their glory. However, if people are *very* competent this makes us feel inferior, so the costs outweigh the rewards of getting to know this person. Equally, when someone who is normally competent *fails*, this increases our liking for them because it makes us feel superior, which increases the rewards.

So **similarity**, **familiarity** and **physical attractiveness** influence who we are attracted to. **Social exchange** theory suggests how we evaluate these factors, and also explains why we are attracted to certain people and whether or not relationships will develop and endure.

The presence of other people and their effect on our behaviour

SOCIAL

You may be surprised at how much other people can affect your behaviour. Do you feel different when you are part of a large group of people? If you have to do some work in class, does it matter whether you work alone or in groups of six? Although you may not be aware of it, many of the things we do, or don't do, are influenced by other people. We are going to look at four ways in which the presence of other people affect our behaviour – social loafing, social facilitation, social conformity and deindividuation.

SOCIAL LOAFING

DEFINITION

When people are working together in a group, each individual tends to reduce their own effort – this is called **social loafing**. It happens whether people are clapping or pulling in a tug-of-war. So our behaviour is affected, even though no-one tries purposely to change it. Bibb Latané has demonstrated social loafing in a number of studies, an example of which is given below.

Latané et al (1979)

Participants were asked to shout and clap and make as much noise as they could, sometimes alone, or with one other or in a group of four or six. They wore headsets so they did not know how much noise the others were making. The researchers recorded the amount of noise the participant made.

Results showed that the larger the group, the less effort the individual made. The individual's output of sound, when working with five others, was reduced to about one-third.

Latané and his colleagues **concluded** that people were making less effort because others were contributing to the task.

Research has identified a number of explanations for social loafing, such as:

● each individual thinks their own effort will make little impact on the outcome: the larger the group, the lower the impact so the lower the effort
● the individual thinks others in the group are not fully committed and does not want to be the 'sucker'
● the individual's own effort cannot be identified from amongst the rest of the group
● the task has little importance to the individual.

If these factors are eliminated, is there less social loafing? A later study by Latané and his colleagues (1980) provides the answer. They organised a swimming gala, with spectators, trophies and of course competitors, all of whom swam in relay as well as individual events. Some lap times were announced and some were not.

Results showed that when lap times were not going to be announced, competitors swam slower in the relay than they did as individuals – this is evidence of social loafing. However, when swimmers knew their lap times were to be announced, they swam faster in the relay than in the individual events. **Conclusions** were that identification of an individual's effort in a group task eliminates the effects of social loafing.

SOCIAL FACILITATION

Do you hate being watched when you are doing something difficult? If so, you are not alone. Most of us perform worse when we are watched, unless we are doing something easy, in which case we perform better. This is known as the social facilitation effect – the presence of other people improves ability to perform a well-learned task and interferes with performance of a complex task. Their effect depends on the actual situation, as we shall now see.

DEFINITION

Coaction effect

This occurs when two or more people are doing something side by side, such as the typists shown in Figure 9.3, or candidates in an examination room. Although they are not competing against each other, the presence of another person tends to improve, or speed up, our performance in a task.

SOCIAL

Audience effect

Being *watched* by others also affects an individual's performance – this is known as the audience effect. Research shows that an audience has one of two effects:

● participants doing an easy task perform *better* when there is an audience
● participants doing a difficult task perform *worse* when there is an audience.

This difference has been been explained by the arousal hypothesis and by evaluation apprehension.

● **the arousal hypothesis** – Robert Zajonc (1966) proposed that it is the mere presence of others which affects our performance because we have an innate response to the presence of others – we become aroused. This arousal stimulates us, so that if we are doing something we are good at, we do it better. However, we are *already* aroused when we are doing a difficult task (such as one which is complicated or new), so the presence of others

INBORN

FIGURE 9.3 According to the coaction effect, these typists working in 1929 were typing faster than if they had been working alone

creates an overload of arousal and interferes with our ability to do the task. For example, researchers assessed the ability of some pool players over several games and rated them as either above or below average. The researchers then stood by the pool table as play was going on, to see if their presence had any effect. **Results** showed that better players became more accurate and the performance of the below average players deteriorated. We could **conclude** that this difference was due to the presence of others.

● **evaluation apprehension** – Nickolas Cottrell (1972) found that when an audience was blindfolded there was no social facilitation effect. He **concluded** that it was not the presence of others which created this effect but their ability to evaluate us. He proposed that arousal is learned, because we come to associate other people with being evaluated. If we are confident about our ability, then the arousal caused by being watched makes us do the task well. If we are not confident, then whilst trying to do the task we are constantly worrying about what those others will think if, or when, we make mistakes – he called this evaluation apprehension.

The experiment as evaluation

One criticism of many of these studies of social facilitation was that because participants were taking part in an experiment they already knew they were being evaluated. In order to remove this effect, Bernard Schmitt and his col-

LEARNING

METHODS

leagues had people take part in an experiment without realising it. The details are shown below.

It can be seen from Table 9.1 that the participants completed the easy task faster in the mere presence condition and fastest when being evaluated by another. However they took longer to complete the difficult task when others were present, although the number of errors are not shown here. Schmitt **concluded** that performance on a well-learned task *is* improved by the mere presence of others, and this improvement increases when others can evaluate performance. In contrast, performance of a difficult task deteriorates in the presence of others.

Schmitt et al (1985)

Participants thought they were about to take part in a 'sensory deprivation' study (which means they cannot see, hear and so on). Before taking part, they were asked to enter information on a computer. This included entering their name and later on entering it again *backwards* with numbers in between each letter. The computer automatically recorded how long each of these tasks took. Have you guessed that this part is actually the experiment, and one of these was the easy task and the other the difficult one? Participants were divided into 3 conditions:

- **alone** – participants were left alone to enter the information and were told to ring a bell when they had finished.
- **mere presence** – participants entered the information whilst there was another person (a confederate) in the room wearing a blindfold and earphones who was facing away from them: they were told that this other person was already part way through the sensory deprivation experiment.
- **evaluation apprehension** – participants entered the information with someone watching just behind them.

Results The number of seconds taken by each participant to complete the easy and the difficult task is shown in the table below.

Nature of task	Participant alone	Mere presence	Evaluation apprehension
Easy	15	10	7
Difficult	53	73	63

TABLE 9.1 Completion time in seconds (from B. Schmitt et al 1985)

SOCIAL CONFORMITY

DEFINITION Although most of us like to feel we make our own decisions, in reality we often adjust our actions or opinions so that they fit in with those of other people. This is known as **social conformity** and we will discover more about it as we look at the work of three psychologists.

Muzafer Sherif

SOCIAL Sherif (1935), who was newly arrived in the U.S.A., was interested in how people conformed to the **social norms** he saw in this unfamiliar culture. His study used the autokinetic effect, which occurs if you shine a dot of light in a darkened room. The light *appears* to move, although it remains still.

One by one the participants sat in the room and told Sherif how far they estimated the light moved. After several trials each participant's estimate began to narrow down to a fairly consistent figure. After this Sherif put the participants together in the room, and asked them to call out their estimates each time they saw the dot of light.

SOCIAL The **results** showed that the fairly consistent estimates which participants had given in private began to change when participants were in a group. Participants' estimates started to converge so that eventually a common figure emerged. Sherif **concluded** that through social interaction people change their own views so that they merge into a common standard – a **norm**. Critics of this conclusion argued that participants changed their views simply because they were uncertain about the distance the light moved.

Solomon Asch

One of these critics was Solomon Asch (1958) who asked whether an individual would go against the **group norm** when there was *no* uncertainty. He devised a series of experiments which were supposed to be tests of 'visual perception'. In each there was a group of confederates (who were being instructed by Asch but pretended to be participants) and one naive participant. Asch presented the group with lines of different lengths, and they had to judge which one was the same length as the test line.

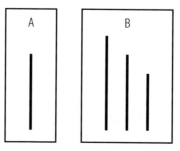

FIGURE 9.4 An example of the test line and the comparison lines in the Asch experiment

On some occasions the confederates would all give a wrong answer, and Asch was interested to hear what the participant would say. Would he conform to the rest of the group, and give an answer which was clearly wrong, or would he say what he really thought?

Results showed that when participants were tested alone there were virtually no mistakes in judging the correct line. But when in a group, Asch found that 25% of participants conformed to the rest of the group on *most* of the occasions when the group was wrong and 75% conformed to the 'wrong' answer at least *once*. There were 25% of participants who did not conform at all. Asch **concluded** that the majority of people succumb to group norms and conform even when they know the group is wrong.

When questioned afterwards, most participants showed they were fully aware that they had lied. They gave reasons such as 'I didn't want to spoil the experiment', 'I didn't want to let the others down'. Asch argued that it is just such pressures which the individual feels in a group and they conform for exactly those kind of reasons. Asch varied the format of this study, finding that:

SOCIAL

- conformity increased when lines were similar in length so that the correct answer was less clear
- conformity increased if group members were thought to be high status
- conformity decreased if one other in the group gave a right answer before the participant had answered, and also when the participant could give a private (written) answer
- when only one other (a confederate) gave a wrong answer there was no conformity.

Asch **concluded** that the crucial influences on conformity are when information is ambiguous (which is related to Sherif's conclusions), when others are high status, when others are unanimous and when dissent is public.

Critics of Asch pointed out that some participants were very conforming, and others very independent. These individual differences are not apparent from the way Asch presented the 'average' scores. Another point is that his participants may have been affected by the **demand characteristics** of the experiment. For example, the lack of response of the others in the group was unreal (see Figure 9.5). When a subsequent study reversed the roles (with a confederate giving a wrong answer amongst a group of participants who gave the right answers) the participants started laughing at the wrong answer, as did the experimenter himself!

METHODS

These studies suggest that others may influence our behaviour when:

- we conform to group norms to gain approval or maintain the coherence of the group: this is called **normative** influence – our behaviour changes but not our views.

FIGURE 9.5 The only person who doesn't know what is going on is the naive participant – No.6. In this photograph he is giving his estimate after each of the five men before him have given an obviously wrong answer. (from S. Asch 1958)

● we are uncertain and look to others for information: this is called **informational** influence – our behaviour *and* our views change.

DEINDIVIDUATION

DEFINITION

Have you ever been at a rock concert or football match and felt yourself swept along by the mood of the crowd? If so, you have experienced **deindividuation**, a state in which you are more likely to behave impulsively and in accordance with the mood of the crowd. This state is created by the close proximity of large numbers of people and psychologists have used the idea of deindividuation to explain why people, when in a crowd, are more likely to behave anti-socially. The state of deindividuation is created by a number of factors, we will review three of them – anonymity, arousal and group unity.

Anonymity

One factor seems to be anonymity: being part of a crowd makes it more difficult to be identified, so we feel free to do things which would normally bring unpleasant consequences. The effect of anonymity was tested by Philip Zimbardo (1969). He had female participants, in groups of four, give 'electric shocks' to his confederates. In one condition the women wore identical coats and hoods so they were anonymous. In the other condition, the women were

FIGURE 9.6 The proximity of large numbers of people may lead to deindividuation and an increase in anti-social behaviour

individuated – they wore their own clothes, had name tags identifying them and spoke to each other using their own names.

Results showed that the anonymous women gave twice as many shocks as the individuated ones. Zimbardo **concluded** that anonymity permits uninhibited behaviour. However, the experiment was criticised because the 'anonymous' women looked like members of the Ku Klux Klan (a group associated with aggression and violence towards black people). When the experiment was repeated with a group who wore nurses uniforms, the 'nurses' gave fewer shocks than the individuated participants. This suggests that anonymity is not a major factor in deindividuation. Because the participants dressed as nurses gave fewer shocks, this suggests that **roles** have a powerful effect on behaviour (see p. 214 for another study on roles by Zimbardo – the Prison Simulation experiment).

Arousal

We saw earlier under **social facilitation** that the presence of other people increases arousal, so being part of a large crowd can be very stimulating. This excitement can be one of the main reasons for joining a crowd.

Group unity

Being part of a group increases our sense of identity, it meets our need to belong. For some people, one of the attractions of large crowds is to feel carried along, or even submerged by others. We saw earlier that some people conform to **group norms** and are therefore more likely to do what others do. Our attention is drawn to what is happening around us, and the behaviour of others reinforces our own actions.

LEARNING

According to this view, group behaviour reinforces whatever the group norms are – if they are aggressive then aggression will increase; if they are peaceful, then peaceful behaviour will be maintained. Research of riots in Britain in the last 20 years supports the idea that 'mob violence' is not random, but that anti-social behaviour may be restricted to particular targets and only certain *kinds* of anti-social behaviour occurs.

DEINDIVIDUATION AND ANTI-SOCIAL BEHAVIOUR

So, when we are in a crowd we become less aware of ourselves and literally 'lost' in the crowd. This reduced self-awareness leads to the state of deindividuation, in which there are fewer restraints on our own behaviour, and in which we are more easily influenced by the behaviour of others in the crowd. As a result we may be aggressive or destructive, doing things we would not normally do if we were alone.

These factors were identified by Leon Mann (1981) who examined newspaper reports of the behaviour of crowds watching people who had been threatening to commit suicide, such as jumping from high buildings. He found that on some occasions the crowds actually tried to encourage these individuals to jump! This happened when the crowd was large, was in darkness, and was not too close to the person contemplating suicide. These three factors all increase the anonymity of the individual in the crowd, and, with the other components of deindividuation, show how being part of a crowd can lead to anti-social behaviour.

Summary

This chapter has provided psychological evidence for the importance of others. As we change, so do our relationships with others. From childhood to adulthood our relationships become more complex as our understanding of ourselves and others becomes richer. We like people who are physically attractive, as well as those who are familiar or similar, although this last quality seems to be the most important for the maintenance of a friendship. But we do not need to have established a relationship with someone for them to influence us. The mere presence of other people is sufficient to affect our behaviour in a variety of ways.

Exercises

1 How do friendship patterns change as children grow older?
2 How do relationships with peers change as children grow older?
3 Describe one study of interpersonal attraction.
4 Describe and explain one reason why one person may be attracted to another.
5 Explain one way in which someone's behaviour might be affected by the presence of other people.
6 According to psychologists, how might the presence of other people affect an individual's behaviour?
7 Describe the results and conclusions of one study which shows that the presence of other people may affect an individual's behaviour.
8 What are social norms? Give one example of how they may affect behaviour.
9 Describe one reason why affiliation is important for humans.
10 How might inference affect our attraction to other people?

Prejudice

Read the national newspapers or listen to conversations and you will come across examples of prejudice. People express negative attitudes towards others because they are of a different religion, a different culture, a different race. We make assumptions about others based on their sexual orientation, their age, their physical appearance, their life-style. Why do we do this? In particular, how is it that we can hold negative attitudes about people we have never met? If we meet them, how do these attitudes affect our behaviour and theirs? This chapter presents some of the answers to these questions which are provided within psychology, and looks at ways in which prejudice and discrimination can be reduced.

Prejudice, stereotypes and discrimination

As we will be looking at each of these topics in some depth, let us start with a definition and brief description of each of them.

PREJUDICE

DEFINITION   Prejudice can be defined as a rigid attitude, which is usually negative, towards a particular group of people, based on characteristics which are assumed to be common to all members of the group. Although prejudice can be positive or negative, psychologists have been much more concerned with its negative aspects because of the damaging effects.

Our attitudes to people can be seen as having three related parts, sometimes called the A B C of attitudes. In terms of prejudice, these are:

- **Affective** – what we feel towards a group, which is unfavourable or **negative** emotions
- **Behaviour** – how we treat members of that group, which is to **discriminate** against them
- **Cognitive** – what we think we know about the group – the **stereotype**

Prejudice is commonly used to refer to the affective *and* the cognitive parts because they are closely related, whereas discrimination tends to be seen as more separate. We will come back to discrimination later in the chapter.

If we are prejudiced we prejudge people, inferring their characteristics and behaviours and treating them unfairly and perhaps cruelly. Early research on prejudice focussed on racism, but people may be prejudiced on the basis of sex, age, religion, nationality, sexual orientation, body size and so on.

STEREOTYPES

DEFINITION

A stereotype is the cognitive part of prejudice, the set of shared beliefs we have about those who belong to a particular social or physical category, for example fat people are jolly, people wearing glasses are intelligent, black people are good at sports, English people are cold. Beliefs such as these are acquired from other people. Stereotypes provide us with a simple, generalised version of what people who belong to this category or group are like. Stereotypes can be positive or negative, but if these traits are negative they form the basis for prejudice. Even if we have never met anyone belonging to this group, if the stereotype contains negative information we may feel dislike towards any member of the group – we are prejudiced towards them. This is not always the case, for example, children can provide stereotypical information about a particular group but there is no evidence of dislike or fear when the stereotype contains negative information. So they are showing the cognitive but not the affective aspect of prejudice

Evidence of how stereotypes can affect our perception of others is provided by a study in which participants watched a video of two people having a discussion in which one of them pushed the other. The psychologists manipulated the race of the actors – either two white, two black, or a black and a white actor. Participants who saw the black actor doing the shoving rated his behaviour as more violent compared with those who saw the white actor doing the shoving. These **results** provide evidence of racism, because they show that participants interpreted the behaviour they saw on the basis of the actor's *race*. This single feature was enough to affect their judgement.

Now that we have clarified some of the terms we will be examining, we are

'That's the end   'Rather'.
of the season
for him, eh, what?'

'I say old chap,   'Let's not get worked up.
was that you   It's only a game
stamping on my face,   and all that sort of thing'.
eh what?'

FIGURE 10.1 These extracts are taken from a book written for French children. At this point in the story, the English characters are playing rugby and you can see how the writer stereotypes the English.

able to consider three explanations for the affective aspect (the feelings) and the cognitive aspect (the stereotype) of prejudice: these are psychodynamic, cognitive informational and social learning explanations.

Psychodynamic explanations for prejudice

Psychodynamic ideas focus on the emotional and motivational reasons for stereotyping and prejudice. According to this view, prejudice has its roots in the unconscious, in particular the need to express emotions such as frustration, anger and fear in ways which are acceptable.

THE AUTHORITARIAN PERSONALITY

The notion that **prejudice** can be due to a personality type was proposed by Theodore Adorno (1950) in America. In his research to find an explanation for the behaviour of Nazi soldiers in World War II he interviewed and tested hundreds of people. He and his colleagues found a particular pattern of personality characteristics which they called the **authoritarian personality**. Those with an authoritarian personality are:

- hostile to those who are of inferior status
- obedient and servile to those of higher status
- intolerant of uncertainty or ambiguity
- conventional, upholding traditional values.
- fairly rigid in their opinions and beliefs, seeing most things in terms of black or white

These characteristics were more likely to be found in people who had a very strict upbringing by critical and harsh parents. Adorno argued that they experienced unconscious hostility towards their parents which they were unable to express towards them.

Using Freud's proposal that when we have unacceptable feelings we use **ego defence mechanisms** (see personality p. 154) to cope with them, Adorno proposed that those with the authoritarian personality would be hostile to those who were weaker than themselves – this is called **displacement**, and it explains the affective part of prejudice.

The stereotype (the cognitive part of prejudice) is explained by the rigid attitude of the authoritarian personality – the tendency to categorise and simplify things in absolute terms of black/white, good/bad, weak/strong and so on.

This notion of the authoritarian personality explains why some people may be predisposed to become prejudiced, however:

- Adorno found a **correlation**: we can only conclude that parenting style, personality and prejudice are related in some way; we cannot conclude that one of these factors *causes* another. For example, the cause could be that children learn these behaviours through observation and imitation of their parents – through social learning.
- research also shows that not all prejudiced people had harsh parents, and some prejudiced people showed few features of the authoritarian personality
- the authoritarian personality does not explain why many people are prejudiced, nor does it explain why we are prejudiced against certain groups. The next explanation, scapegoating, explains these points.

SCAPEGOATING

According to this explanation of prejudice there are *always* frustrations in living, and these can build up to unacceptable levels in some people, particularly if they are in difficult circumstances such as unemployment or poor housing. The **frustration-aggression hypothesis** proposes that this frustration leads to hostile feelings which have to be released (see p. 136).

Often this hostility and aggression cannot be directed at the causes – because they are many and complicated, we may not even know what they are. Instead it is **displaced** on to groups which society considers to be acceptable targets for hostility and aggression. These groups are used as **scapegoats**, we blame them for our frustration and release our aggression against them. Politicians may create scapegoats in order to re-direct public frustration away from themselves. In the 1930s, for example, Adolf Hitler blamed Germany's economic problems on Jews – they became the scapegoats.

There is evidence that those who feel most threatened during an economic recession show an increase in prejudice against particular groups. C. Hovland and R. Sears (1940) amassed statistics relating to lynchings of black Americans in the U.S. and failures in the cotton crop from 1880 to 1930. They found a **negative correlation** between these two variables – the number of lynchings increased as economic conditions deteriorated. This is how scapegoating explains the affective (emotional) aspect of prejudice.

COGNITION   The cognitive aspect is the shared belief (the **stereotype**) that society holds about a particular group – we believe they are to blame for our problems and that it is acceptable to be hostile towards them. So scapegoating explains why many people may be prejudiced, and why they are prejudiced only towards certain groups, although as we see later, groups which are the targets of scapegoating may change (see p. 122).

Cognitive-informational explanations of prejudice

These explanations propose that prejudices originate in the way people process information. As we shall see, people tend to *distort* information in order to process it.

SOCIAL CATEGORISATION

COGNITION   One of the basic cognitive processes is categorisation, the tendency to group things together. Henri Tajfel (1971) pointed out that when we categorise people we divide them into two basic groups – the in-group ('us') and the out-group ('them'). Research has shown that when we categorise things we:

● exaggerate the differences between the categories, in this case between the in-group and the out-group
● we see the members of the out-group as more alike than they really are, which is reflected in everyday comments such as 'they're all the same, these youngsters' or 'those Japanese all look alike to me'. We assume they have similar characteristics – we stereotype.

Tajfel called this **social categorisation** and it explains the cognitive basis for prejudice but not the reason why we have negative feelings towards the out group. This is explained by social identity theory.

SOCIAL IDENTITY THEORY

Tajfel showed that not only do we categorise people but we favour the in-group over the out-group. In a series of **experiments**, Tajfel and his colleagues assigned participants to groups by the toss of a coin, so it was clear that their membership of a particular group was *only* due to the toss of a coin. **Results** showed that when asked to allocate points, participants largely favoured members of their own group – they **discriminated** against the out-group.

FIGURE 10.2 Are members of the same group as alike as we tend to think?

SOCIAL

This preference for in-group members has been produced in many other experiments, and **results** show that we think members of the out-group are less attractive, less intelligent, less able and so on. When our group fails it is due to bad luck; when the other group fails it is because they are not very good.

Why do we do this? In their **social identity theory**, Henri Tajfel and John Turner (1979) argue that membership of our group – our psychology class, football team, neighbourhood and so on – is an important source of pride and self-esteem which we enhance by:

● increasing the status of the group to which we belong – the in-group
● denigrating or belittling groups to which we do not belong – the out-group.

The more we need to raise our self-esteem, the more we are likely to denigrate the out-group, which is why some people are more prejudiced than others. Social identity theory explains the affective part of prejudice, although, critics argue that the evidence is based largely on experimental work, and that in real life we enhance our own group, but we are much less likely to denigrate others.

Social learning explanations of prejudice

LEARNING

The social learning view is that prejudice is learned through observational learning and reinforcement. According to this explanation, children learn the content of stereotypes (the cognitive part) and how to feel about others (the affective part) by observing people and imitating them (see p. 16).

Those who act as models for children's behaviour are likely to be **powerful** and **similar** to the child, so parents will be important models. They also provide **reinforcement**, which makes it more likely that the child will continue with behaviour which it has imitated. Alfred Davey and his colleagues examined the attitudes of children and their parents towards various ethnic groups, as described on p. 120.

Participants who strongly favoured their own group and were hostile to others were classified as **ethnocentric** (which means seeing one's own ethnic group as superior and using it as the standard for judging others). The **results** showed that overall there was no correlation between the attitudes expressed by children and those expressed by their parents. However there *was* a **positive correlation** between strongly held attitudes in parents and children –

Albert Davey et al (1983)

The **sample** comprised 256 children of white parentage, 128 of West Indian and 128 of Asian parentage, between 7 and 11 years old. The children were given various tests and their parents were surveyed using face-to-face interviews.

Materials were a series of open-ended questions initially about the child's school and friends and later about attitudes to other ethnic groups. A sample of the questions is shown below:

- What do you think of your child's school?
- Are there any children you don't like your child to play with? Why is that?
- Some people think it's a good thing that children of different races should be in the same school. What do you think?

The **procedure** used interviewers from the same ethnic group as those being interviewed, and for the Asian parents they spoke the same language. Questions were linked by informal comments, so that the interview was more like a natural conversation.

All parents received **standardised instructions** – "I'm ...(researcher's name). I'm connected with the study that ...(child's name) took part in at school, about children growing up and their ideas. Do you mind if I take notes? You do understand that this is completely confidential. We're not using anyone's names. We just want to compare the ideas of parents in London and Yorkshire about children growing up."

ethnocentric parents had children who were ethnocentric and parents who were low in ethnocentrism tended to have children who were low also.

Davey and his colleagues noted that many parents commented that the school had an important role in educating children about *other* religions and cultures. In addition, half of the West Indian and Asian children wanted to be white, regardless of where they lived or what the ethnic mix of their school was. Davey **concluded** that this showed the children felt that white children got better treatment.

Although we cannot explain the correlation in ethnocentrism by saying the child has learned it by observing the parent's behaviour, this could be one reason. So how might prejudice originate according to social learning theory?

STEREOTYPING AND SOCIAL LEARNING

The social learning view is that the cognitive aspect of prejudice (stereotyping) is learned by observing models who say, for example, 'Look at that parking – women drivers!' or 'He's a typical Scot, never spends a penny if he can help it'. These models:

- encourage children to categorise people according to group labels
- provide information about the characteristics of a group
- show the child that stereotyping is acceptable.

COGNITION

We learn stereotypes as children, but because they filter out inconsistent information (see p. 31), it is likely that information from later models may have little impact on the stereotype. This has implications for reducing prejudice.

PREJUDICE AND SOCIAL LEARNING

Not only do children learn the cognitive aspect of prejudice from **models**, but models provide information about how they *feel* towards others. Adults who express suspicion, resentment or superiority over a group provide information about the feelings they have, which children may imitate without understanding. An investigation into the preferences of 5–10 year

FIGURE 10.3 Does this information fit your stereotype of an older person?

old English children was carried out by M. Barett & J. Short (1992). **Results** showed that French and Spanish people were liked most and Germans least, although the children knew very little about these nationalities.

LEARNING

Social learning theorists propose that children, through being selective about *where* they imitate behaviour, and *how* they are reinforced, come to internalise what they see and hear. They learn the **social norms** of their society, which groups are used as **scapegoats**, and how adults feel about members of these groups.

SOCIAL

An example of how such norms can be changed comes from the U.S.A. During World War II, American government propaganda shaped American attitudes to Japanese and Germans as negative, and towards Russians (who were allies) as positive – hardworking and so on. After the war, as the Americans and the Russians became enemies, the propaganda changed and the Russians were portrayed in a negative way – as cruel, for example.

Research showed that American attitudes towards Russians became much more negative – the **social norm** towards Russians changed. It became acceptable, even proof of being a good American, to denigrate the Russians. This shows how the targets of prejudice – the scapegoats – can be changed by the media and politicians (see social filters pp. 297–8).

To summarise then, each one of these three explanations provides us with some answers about the origins of stereotyping and prejudice, but none is complete in itself. The authoritarian personality explains why an individual may become prejudiced, whereas scapegoating theory says why large numbers of people may be prejudiced. In these cases, prejudice is necessary to maintain well-being, as it is for our self-esteem in social identity theory. In contrast, social learning theory proposes that we learn to be prejudiced, and who to be prejudiced against. Box 10.1 on p. 123 shows a brief summary of the explanations.

The relationship between prejudice and discrimination

You will see from the definitions below that prejudice is an attitude and that discrimination may be the behaviour associated with it:

DEFINITION

Prejudice is a negative attitude towards a particular group of people, based on characteristics which are assumed to be common to all members of the group.

DEFINITION

Discrimination is treating people unfavourably on the basis of their membership of a particular group. Discrimination is usually, but not always, the behaviour resulting from prejudice. Discrimination includes ignoring

10.1

SIMILARITIES AND DIFFERENCES IN EXPLANATIONS OF PREJUDICE

	PSYCHODYNAMIC EXPLANATION	COGNITIVE INFORMATIONAL EXPLANATION	SOCIAL LEARNING EXPLANATION
How does the theory explain stereotyping (the cognitive part of prejudice)?	the authoritarian personality has rigid views scapegoating involves a socially shared belief that a particular group is responsible for society's problems	we classify others into in-group and out-group, members of the out-group are seen as very similar to each other	stereotyping is learned from others – both the content of stereotypes and how to stereotype – through observational learning and reinforcement
How does the theory explain negative feelings (the affective part of prejudice)?	the authoritarian personality displaces hostility on to others who are less powerful people displace frustration and anger on to a socially targeted group – the scapegoats	people denigrate and have negative feelings towards members of an out group in order to raise their own self esteem	negative attitudes towards others are learned through observational learning and reinforcement

someone, keeping a distance, using an unfriendly tone of voice, showing preference to others over them, harassing or even attacking them.

C. Word and colleagues (1974) devised a study which showed the effects of discrimination very vividly. The study investigated the self-fulfilling prophecy (see p. 220), the way that someone's attitude to another person can affect that person's behaviour.

Researchers observed the behaviour of white college students interviewing either black or white 'applicants' (confederates of the researchers). They noted that the students held shorter interviews and sat further away from black 'applicants'. In a second stage, white confederates were trained to do interviews using the *same* behaviour (such as sitting further away). Once trained, they 'interviewed' only white applicants.

Judges watched videos of the white applicants' behaviour to rate them on ability and performance. The **results** showed that the applicants with the lowest ratings were those who received the discriminatory treatment. The researchers **concluded** that poor performance was due to discriminatory treatment, not to any genuine lack of ability.

These results demonstrate that:

- although it is illegal to discriminate, we can still show discrimination by non-verbal behaviour
- we may not be aware of discriminating in this way
- the behaviour of those who experience discrimination is affected by the way others treat them.

It is often assumed that those who are prejudiced show discrimination, and that someone who discriminates against another person is prejudiced towards them, but the link may not be quite as direct as it seems. An example comes from research in the U.S.A. by Richard La Piere (1934). He toured the U.S.A. with a Chinese couple, visiting 250 hotels, restaurants and similar places. Despite prejudice against the Chinese at this time, they were only turned away from one establishment. At the end of the trip each of the establishments were sent a **questionnaire** asking, amongst other things, whether they would accept Chinese customers. Over 90% of the returned questionnaires said they would not.

You should be able to think of several reasons why so many establishments said they would discriminate but did not do so. Research has shown that prejudice is more likely to lead to discrimination if:

- we are very prejudiced
- our prejudice relates directly to us, for example if it is necessary for our self-esteem

COGNITION

- our prejudice is easily accessible – it will be if we rely on stereotypes to judge others
- the law permits it – Thomas Pettigrew (1971) found that after the introduction of a new anti-discrimination law 60% of people became more positive and people's attitudes became less prejudiced.

SOCIAL

- situational pressures allow or encourage us to express it – for example if the **social norms** or the **roles** we are playing allow us to express prejudice by discriminating.

So the link between prejudice and discrimination is not direct. R. Minard (1952) studied black and white coal miners in West Virginia and **results** showed that there was complete integration below the ground (at work) but almost complete segregation above ground (at play). He **concluded** that one set of **social norms** operated below ground whilst the social norms operating *above* ground were those of the wider society in which these men lived. Some miners may have been prejudiced but felt unable to show it below ground but above ground they were able to show it, just as those who were *not* prejudiced may have felt compelled to discriminate in their social lives above the ground in order to conform to the behaviour or expectations of others (see conformity, p. 108).

How can prejudice and discrimination be reduced?

Psychologists have studied many ways of reducing prejudice (a negative attitude) and discrimination (the related action). Success is related to the *cause* of prejudice and discrimination in the first place. For example, it has been argued that those with the authoritarian personality are unlikely to change their attitudes because these are necessary for the release of their hostility.

Several strategies for reducing prejudice and discrimination have been proposed and tested. We will review six of them now – social contact, co-operation, promoting positive images, challenging social norms, challenging stereotypes and creating empathy.

SOCIAL CONTACT

COGNITION

If prejudice and discrimination are based on lack of knowledge about members of other groups, increasing the contact between members of these groups should give people more information about others, and thus break down stereotypes. However, research has shown that it is not simply enough to bring people together. These were the **conclusions** from an American study which arranged for very prejudiced white and black people to work together

FIGURE 10.4 Increasing contact may not be sufficient to reduce prejudice and discrimination

on a series of joint tasks. **Results** showed that six months later 40% of the participants were much less prejudiced, 40% had not changed their attitudes and 20% had become *more* prejudiced.

In the 1970s, Elliot Aronson noted there had always been contact between black and white Americans, yet prejudice and discrimination had not reduced. He argued that because whites saw black workers only doing menial jobs, contact merely *reinforced* their prejudice. Research shows that the more effective ways of reducing prejudice and discrimination through social contact are:

COGNITION

- if those experiencing prejudice and discrimination are of *higher* status than the discriminator (for example having better jobs or a higher level of education). When members of two groups are in contact, it is invariably the higher status members who dominate – they tend to initiate things, their views are more likely to be followed. If the members of both groups are of equal status it is not enough to 'tip the balance' in favour of those experiencing discrimination.
- if the individuals who are in contact are seen as representative of a group, and not as individuals. When seen as individuals, prejudice towards the individual may be reduced, but is less likely to generalise to *all* members of that group.

CO-OPERATION

A well-known study of intergroup behaviour was devised by Muzafer Sherif and his associates (see p. 127). This **Robbers' Cave** study provides evidence that contact between the members of two groups is insufficient to reduce prejudice and discrimination and that co-operation can be effective.

The **results** of observations showed that in the first stage both groups quickly established their own culture – naming themselves the 'Rattlers' and the 'Eagles' and developing **group norms**. There was a little in-group favouritism at the expense of the out-group. But hostility quickly arose in the second stage, with competition. Groups derided and attacked each other. Each group became more united, and the more aggressive boys became leaders. During the third stage, when the boys shared social situations, there was still considerable prejudice and discrimination towards each other. It was not until the fourth stage that this changed – when the boys *had* to **co-operate** the intergroup hostility disappeared.

Sherif and his colleagues **concluded** that:

- Newly created groups quickly develop group norms.

Sherif et al (1961) The Robber's Cave experiment

The **research method** was a **field experiment** using a **matched pairs** design. The type of study was a longitudinal study taking place over 3 weeks using the **observational technique**.

The **sample** was 22 middle-class white boys, aged 12 years, who were attending a summer camp called Robber's Cave. They were not known to each other and all were psychologically well-adjusted from stable homes. The participants were matched in pairs as closely as possible for physical and psychological characteristics. One of each pair was assigned to one of two groups.

The **procedure** comprised four stages during which camp counsellors (who were in fact trained researchers) observed the boys' behaviour. For a few days normal summer camp activities took place. The second stage started when a series of intergroup contests was announced by the counsellors. The group winning the series would get a silver cup, and each boy would get a penknife. The third stage began after the contests ended, when the two groups had contact with each other, for example they all went to see a film. In the fourth stage *all* the boys had to to co-operate on tasks such as pulling a truck back to camp in order to get there in time for lunch.

- Conflict between groups leads to prejudice and discrimination towards the out-group and increases unity of the in-group.
- Co-operation between groups reduces prejudice and discrimination.

In another study of co-operation, Elliot Aronson and his colleagues (1978) were called in by a Texas school to devise some ways of reducing prejudice between the white and black students, they devised the **jigsaw technique** to increase co-operation. This involves small groups of racially mixed students, each of whom has to work on a *part* of a lesson. In order for the whole class to cover *all* the material, the individuals in the groups have to work together first, and then they have to communicate their group work to the rest of the class.

When Aronson evaluated the strategy he found increased co-operation, self-esteem and academic performance. He also noted more positive perceptions of those of the other racial group, but these new perceptions were not generalised to *every* member of the racial group. It appeared that these students saw each other as *exceptions* to the **stereotypes,** but the stereotypes themselves

SOCIAL

did not change very much. So although co-operation strategies *can* reduce prejudice, the individual may not **generalise** these new attitudes to others when they are in a different setting.

Research on joint tasks in other real life settings, such as industry, have produced similar results. The following factors appear to improve the success of co-operative strategies:

- the joint tasks have to be of value to *all* participants, as with the Robber's Cave experiment
- the competitive element should be eliminated as much as possible – many of our social environments are competitive, the classroom, the sports field, the workplace
- participants should succeed in the joint task, because research shows that if a mixed group fail in their task, then the blame may fall on the members of the minority group (they become the scapegoats). The task must be fairly easy to accomplish, or at least be difficult to label as a 'failure', so that the group experience success.

One explanation for the success of the co-operation strategy in the Robbers' Cave study was because the *differences* between the boys was artificially created. They were all basically very similar. Real life is different – there are *physical* differences between people which make them easy to categorise, there may be **social norms** *supporting* prejudice in one setting but not in another, there may be differences in social status between groups. These factors also need to be tackled.

SOCIAL

PROMOTING POSITIVE IMAGES

COGNITION
In order for prejudice and discrimination to be reduced, perceptions of the minority group must be changed. In this chapter we have noted a number of ways in which this may occur, and several stress the important of positive images. For example, prejudice is reduced when the members of the minority group:

- have **higher status** than the prejudiced individual
- are **portrayed positively** by the media, so if minority group members are presented in positions of achievement, responsibility or expertise, this should contribute to the reduction of prejudice
- see **positive, high-status models** from their own group, which encourages them to fight negative attitudes and resist the expectations of others which may lead to the self-fulfilling prophecy (see p. 220). This has been one of the aims of social movements such as the Black Power, Feminist and Gay Liberation movements in recent decades, who have worked to increase the assertiveness and self-confidence of their members.

CHALLENGING SOCIAL NORMS

SOCIAL

Social norms can be affected officially (by making laws) and unofficially (when the individual challenges what is considered acceptable or appropriate behaviour). We saw from Thomas Pettigrew's study that people's **attitudes** became more positive as a result of anti-discrimination laws. If the law makes it illegal to discriminate, then people's behaviour will change. However, we have seen that people may remain prejudiced even though they do not discriminate. Indeed, Pettigrew's research also showed that forcing people to change will actually *strengthen* some people's prejudice and discrimination.

A **cross-cultural** study carried out in Holland and America looked at how racism is communicated between white people (racism is being prejudiced and discriminating against someone because of their race). **Results** showed that in the wider society there may be a social norm not to *show* racism, but within various subgroups (such as the family, in the workplace, amongst neighbours) racist talk and behaviour was acceptable. This suggests that challenging racism at the *official* level is only part of the solution. Racism, or indeed any form of prejudice and discrimination, needs to be tackled at the

FIGURE 10.5 When members of minority groups increase their self-esteem they are more able to challenge stereotypical expectations

unofficial level as well, which means the *individual* refusing to conform to social norms if they permit prejudice or discrimination and challenging others when they conform to these norms.

CHALLENGING STEREOTYPES

COGNITION

If we can show that stereotypes do not 'fit' reality, they may weaken and so prejudice and discrimination may be reduced. For example the media can challenge stereotypes by:

- increasing the exposure of people who do not fit the stereotype – several of the photographs in this book have been chosen because they challenge stereotypes
- presenting characters in plays or films in non-stereotypical ways – a black headteacher, a female judge, a male nurse, an active pensioner
- providing information which frequently *conflicts* with a stereotype.

Sandra Bem has shown how strong a stereotype can be in her work on gender, and points out that parents have an important role in *counteracting* stereotypes and in identifying to children when stereotypes are being portrayed in the media. Adults can also draw attention to information which shows the stereotype does not fit, for example challenging the male stereotype by saying 'look how that man is crying, he must be very unhappy'.

CREATING EMPATHY

If we experience the effects of prejudice and discrimination, we might try to change. Jane Elliott (1980) used the brown-eyes/blue-eyes technique to help her class of nine year-olds understand the effects of stereotyping, prejudice and discrimination. She told them that brown-eyed people were better and more intelligent than those with blue eyes, and should therefore be given extra privileges. The children started to behave according to these artificial stereotypes: the brown-eyed became more dominant and produced better work; the blue-eyed became angry or depressed and their work deteriorated. The next day she told them she was wrong and that blue-eyed people were superior: the patterns of behaviour quickly reversed.

On the third day she told them the truth, that there were no such differences but that she wanted them to feel what it was like to be judged on the basis of one, irrelevant, physical feature which they could not change, in other words to experience prejudice and discrimination. Helping people to empathise like this can be an effective strategy for the reduction of prejudice and discrimination in children and adults.

Summary

The explanations for stereotyping, prejudice and discrimination share some common elements. The role that social factors play appear to be very important, as evidence shows that attitudes can be changed by propaganda, by laws, by the media and by individuals. Efforts to reduce prejudice and discrimination need to take account of possible causes. If they support the individual's sense of self-esteem or sense of belonging to a group, then to change the attitude means to threaten the individual. Discouraging children from adopting stereotypical attitudes or modelling discriminatory behaviour should reduce prejudice and discrimination in young people. The responsibility of those in positions of influence to behave in non-discriminatory ways is also of crucial importance both for changing attitudes and as models for others.

Exercises

1 What is a stereotype?
2 Describe one explanation of stereotyping.
3 Give one example of a stereotype and explain how it might affect someone's behaviour.
4 Describe how a stereotype might affect our perception of someone.
5 Explain the difference between prejudice and discrimination.
6 Briefly explain how prejudice can affect an individual's view of other people.
7 Describe one psychological explanation of prejudice.
8 Describe two different explanations of stereotyping, explaining one way in which they are similar and one way in which they differ.
9 From what you have learned in psychology, describe one way of reducing prejudice.
10 Describe two ways of reducing discrimination, using evidence from psychological research.

Aggression

Aggression is a major source of concern in many societies and most of us recognise it when we see it. We say people are aggressive when we refer to their manner of speaking, the way they play a sport or a musical instrument, the way they treat others or solve problems. So 'aggression' is used to describe someone's energetic approach to something as well as to describe a film which consists mostly of fighting, destruction and killing: our concern here is the kind of aggression which is intentional and destructive. What causes this behaviour? We start by looking at answers to this question which, as you will see, reflect different ways of explaining human behaviour. Then we consider the way that parents might influence their child's aggression and finally we review the work of psychologists who have looked at ways of reducing aggression.

What is aggression?

DEFINITION

Although there is no agreed definition, **aggression** is generally considered to be behaviour which harms, or intends to harm, someone or something. Aggression can be verbal as well as physical and is regarded as anti-social behaviour. Violence generally refers to the use of deliberate physical force. If we take into account the *reason* behind the aggression we can distinguish between:

- **hostile** aggression – harming someone with the purpose of hurting them
- **instrumental** aggression – harming someone in order to achieve a goal, perhaps because they are attacking you.

Although this distinction is still not clear, our focus will be on hostile aggression. The explanations for the causes of aggression come from ethology, psychodynamic and learning theory, and you will see that some explanations stress the role of **innate** factors, while others stress the role of the **environment**. In other words aggression is a topic in the **nature/nurture debate**.

Ethological explanations for aggression

Ethology is the study of animals in their natural environment and ethologists are interested in how animal behaviours increase their chances of survival and the reproduction of their species. The ethologist Konrad Lorenz (1966) argued that aggression is **innate** – he called it the 'fighting instinct' which is present in all species. It is used for survival, enabling members of a species to gain a mate, to protect their territory or their young.

INBORN

All **instincts** generate a drive or energy which is constantly renewed. If aggressive energy is not discharged, the excess may be used destructively on other members of the species. Lorenz proposed that animals had evolved ways of releasing excess energy which are not destructive, for example they use **appeasement rituals**. This means that when one of the pair behaves in a particular way, the other stops fighting. For example, if you watch two cats fighting, one may stop and turn his head to the side, exposing his neck. Lorenz said this particular behaviour is ritualised in cats and inhibits the aggression of the other cat.

What has this got to do with human aggression? Lorenz claimed that aggression fulfilled similar purposes for humans – by nature we are warriors. We also have appeasement rituals to stop the other aggressing, for example smiling, kneeling or bowing the head. However, with the development of weapons of destruction (cannons, machine guns, bombs) which *separate* human aggressors, these appeasement rituals cannot come into effect.

Humans have also devised ways of releasing aggression without destruction. For example, aggressive behaviour in a competitive sports setting is controlled by rules, referees and acceptable forms of aggression, which Lorenz proposed were a way of releasing pent-up aggression safely.

This ethological explanation for aggression has been criticised because:

- more recent ethological research has shown that animals such as chimpanzees *do* kill members of their own species, sometimes even the infants
- most evidence of early societies suggests that man has not been a warrior but a hunter-gatherer
- COGNITION   we cannot **generalise** directly from non-human to human behaviour because humans are much more complex, so for example humans have language and this can affect how an **instinct** is expressed
- research on reducing aggression through watching or taking part in competitive sports shows that this actually increases aggression

FIGURE 11.1 Weapons such as these prevent our instinctive appeasementment rituals from overriding our aggression, according to Lorenz

SOCIAL

- **cross-cultural** research shows wide variations in the levels of aggression in different societies, suggesting social norms are more influential than innate factors.

Psychodynamic explanations for aggression

INBORN

Sigmund Freud, who represents the psychodynamic approach, tried to find an explanation for all the killing in World War I. Like Lorenz, Freud proposed that aggression is **innate** – he claimed that each of us have an instinct for self-destruction. He called this the **death instinct** (or thanatos) and aggression is the drive which enables us to satisfy this death instinct.

However the death instinct conflicts with the **life instinct** (eros), yet both these instincts are constantly in need of satisfaction. They are both part of the **id** – the part of personality comprising our innate desires which demand immediate satisfaction (see p. 153 for details of the id, ego and superego). The **ego** (the part of personality which tries to satisfy our desires in a realistic way) manages these conflicting instincts and avoids self-destruction by directing our self-destructive energy outwards. In Freud's view, then, we aggress against others in order to preserve ourselves, otherwise we might become depressed or even suicidal.

However, the **superego** is mindful that we must not hurt others. It is the superego which channels this aggressive energy into socially (and morally) acceptable activities. Freud proposed that these might be competitive sports, exploration, or even observing someone else being aggressive. These experiences would be **cathartic** – they would release the build up of aggression.

There are several criticisms of this explanation:

- Research shows that participating in or observing competitive sports does not reduce aggression, in fact this tends to *increase* aggression
- Other psychodynamic views say that aggression *can* be controlled if the ego and superego are strong enough
- There are many people who do not show aggression, do not get involved in competitive sports and yet do not become self-destructive
- Freud's theory is difficult to test because it uses concepts which are not directly observable.

Learning theory explanations for aggression

LEARNING

From the **learning theory** viewpoint, aggression is not an innate drive, it is learned in the social setting. Each of the explanations which follow use various aspects of the social setting to explain how learning occurs.

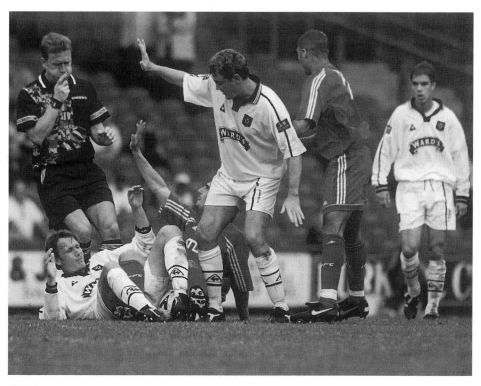

FIGURE 11.2 Humans have devised ways of controlling the level and type of aggression which is permissable

THE FRUSTRATION-AGGRESSION HYPOTHESIS

INBORN

LEARNING

J. Dollard and his associates (1939) combined Freud's belief (that aggression is innate) with learning theory to propose that aggression is caused by frustration. This became known as the **frustration-aggression hypothesis**, which proposes that people are motivated to reach goals, but if they are blocked, then frustration occurs. For example, if a task is too difficult or someone stops us from doing something, we will become frustrated. When we are frustrated, we aggress. Equally, if someone is aggressive it is because they are frustrated.

The notion of frustration is useful because we can see that although frustration may *cause* aggression, this may not be directed at the cause of frustration. This happens in **displacement** (which is a **defence mechanism**, see p. 154), when aggression cannot be aimed at the real target, so another target is substituted. An example of displacement is **scapegoating**, when aggression is turned on to an individual or group who is not the cause of frustration but who is 'safe' because they are less powerful (see p. 116).

However, some studies showed that aggression is only raised slightly when participants are frustrated, and later Dollard and his colleagues changed the hypothesis to say that frustration causes aggression but the individual might not *show* aggressive behaviour. There are several reasons for this, such as:

● they might think it wrong to behave aggressively
● they may have learned not to show aggression
● they might be frightened that the other person would be aggressive towards them
● they might think that although the other person made them frustrated, it was not done on purpose.

So frustration does not always lead to aggression; it depends on the individual's past experiences, the other people involved in the situation and its meaning for the individual.

AGGRESSIVE-CUE THEORY

The notion of frustration was taken up by Leonard Berkowitz (1966) who argued that frustration does not cause aggression directly but *does* arouse anger. The anger in turn creates a *readiness* to act aggressively. What happens next is due to the individual's learning. In other words, if there are aggressive cues in the environment – a gun for example – this makes the individual more likely to be aggressive.

LEARNING

This is an example of **classical conditioning**, in which two stimuli are paired together several times until the conditional stimulus alone creates a response (for details see p. 11). Berkowitz proposed that people learn to associate particular stimuli such as a gun, or a boxing match, or a person with *anger* or ways of *releasing* anger (the conditional stimulus). When the individual is frustrated this creates anger and a gun, for example, is a 'cue' for aggression. Berkowitz found that participants who were made angry showed higher levels of aggression when there was an 'aggressive' cue around, such as a weapon, rather than a badminton racket.

Several studies have confirmed this 'weapons effect' but others have not. One explanation could be that the presence of weapons intensifies the anger, but this will *only* be expressed in a way which the individual feels is appropriate at that time. The Berkowitz study gave participants the opportunity to be aggressive while they were taking part in an experiment, and their behaviour could have been affected by the **demand characteristics**. Similar studies carried out in a natural environment (**field** experiment) show that the less worried the individual is about being judged, the more they tend to show the weapons effect.

OPERANT CONDITIONING

LEARNING

According to **operant conditioning** principles, behaviour is shaped and maintained by its consequences. Behaviour which is **reinforced** is likely to be strengthened, if it is **punished** it is likely to weaken (for details see p. 12). We will consider reinforcement and punishment in turn, but first look at the picture on the following page.

Reinforcement

If the little girl in Figure 11.3 manages to get the toy off the little boy, then she is rewarded – she has got what she wanted. Next time she wants something off another child she will grab it. She is receiving **positive reinforcement** for her aggression and so is likely to repeat it. This is just what Gerald Patterson and his colleagues (1967) found in an **observational** study of young children – those who got what they wanted through aggression were more likely to be aggressive again.

On the other hand, what if this little boy fights back and is able to hang on to his toy? Patterson found that if this happened, the boy would be more likely to fight back *next* time. This is an example of **negative reinforcement** – if a behaviour (fighting back) stops an unpleasant experience (being attacked) then the behaviour is rewarding, so it is more likely to be repeated.

Aggression may be rewarded because it gains approval from others. Robert Sears and his colleagues (1977) found that boys were sometimes rewarded for

FIGURE 11.3 What will happen if this little girl's aggression is successful?

aggressive behaviour by their parents, who saw it as appropriate behaviour for boys and therefore approved of it. There are many other reinforcements for aggressive behaviour, in children and adults, such as increased status, increased self-esteem or more attention from teachers or peers.

Punishment

Punishment is aimed at *weakening* behaviour, making it less likely to happen. Results from the Sears study showed that girls were punished more often than boys for aggressive behaviour, whether it was directed at other children or at their parents. Some psychologists argue that this is why girls show *less* aggression than boys, because they are punished for it and boys are reinforced for it.

However, research on the effects of punishment show that it is not very effective in reducing aggression. This may be because:

- punishment increases the individual's frustration, and this has to find an outlet which is often in the form of aggression (as we noted in the frustration-aggression hypothesis p. 136).
- those doing the punishing are **modelling** aggression (see next section), so the child can also find new ways to be aggressive by imitating that behaviour – small children can be seen 'punishing' their teddies or dolls in exactly the same way as their parents have punished *them*! Research suggests that to be effective in weakening behaviour, punishment must given in the context of a good relationship between child and punisher. We will look at why this might be so when we examine the role of parents later on page 142.

- we are punishing a child to get what we want, so we show the child 'this is how you get what you want'.

SOCIAL LEARNING THEORY

This explanation proposes that aggression comes from observing the aggression of others and imitating it. This is known as **observational learning**. Reinforcement and punishment also play a part in social learning theory. The main principles were devised by Albert Bandura and his colleagues, who conducted many experiments early in the 1960s. We will look at at their work shortly, but let us first see how social learning theory explains aggression.

LEARNING

Bandura proposed that children learn by observing the behaviour of other people (known as models) and may subsequently imitate it. He found children are more likely to imitate certain kinds of models, those who are:

- **similar** to the child, such as a sibling or someone of the same sex or same age
- **powerful,** such as a parent, teacher, sports person, pop star, cartoon character
- **caring** towards the child, such as a parent, relative, teacher
- **rewarded** for their behaviour, such as another child who successfully grabs a toy; or a character in a film who receives approval from others for being aggressive. This is called **vicarious reinforcement** because the observer receives reinforcement *indirectly*.

Research showed that children only perform behaviours in particular situations, so they had learned the behaviour but only *performed* it at certain times. Why? Bandura used **operant conditioning** principles to explain this – behaviour is shaped by its consequences. So, if a situation provides rewards for a child, then the behaviour will be performed: if it is not rewarded, or is punished, then it is less likely to be repeated. For example, a child might learn that his teacher disapproves when he acts out violent scenes from a film he has seen, so he no longer performs it in front of the teacher. But this behaviour wins admiration from his peers, so he only does it in the playground, out of the teacher's sight. You will notice these points as we examine some of Bandura's work on aggression.

In Bandura's early **experiments**, an adult modelled aggressive behaviour towards a large inflatable doll – called a Bobo doll. The children then had the opportunity to play with the doll while the model was nearby. This provided a 'reminder' for the child of the model's behaviour. The photographs in Figure 11.4 were taken during these experiments.

However, Bandura and his colleagues also wanted to see what would happen if the model was *not* present during the play stage and whether a same-sex

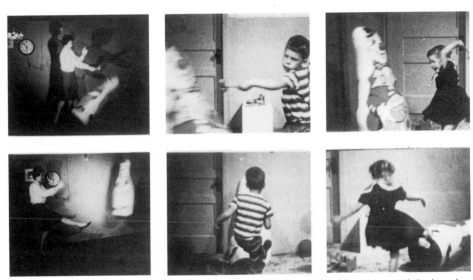

FIGURE 11.4 Here you can see the aggressive behaviour of the female model, and the subsequent behaviour of a boy and girl who watched the model (from A. Bandura et al 1961)

model was imitated more than an opposite sex model. This research is described on page 141.

Bandura and his colleagues **concluded** that children exposed to aggressive models may imitate the aggressive behaviour and are more likely to do so if the model is the same sex. This research also provided evidence that children knew what behaviour was appropriate for those models, because some of them commented that 'ladies shouldn't do things like that'.

In a variation of this study, Bandura asked each of the children to reproduce as much of the model's behaviour as they could remember; they were rewarded for doing this. **Results** showed that *all* the children were able to reproduce most of the aggressive acts. We can **conclude** that all the children had *learned* the behaviour, but the likelihood of them **imitating** it depended on factors such as the sex of the model they had observed and whether their performance of the behaviour was rewarded.

The media has frequently been blamed for providing models for aggressive behaviour, but does research support this? There is considerable evidence for a positive correlation between the amount of time an individual spends watching aggressive or violent television programmes and their level of aggression. A **longitudinal** study conducted by Leonard Eron (1983) found such a correlation for boys when they were 8 and 18 years old. One possible explanation is that people who are aggressive prefer to watch these types of programmes, not that violent programmes encourage aggression. However, such programmes *do* offer models of aggressive behaviour which show the

LEARNING

Bandura, Ross & Ross (1961)

The **design** of the study was an independent measures design of three groups of participants – one experimental group saw an aggressive model, another saw a non-aggressive model and a third was the control group. The **participants** were 36 boys and 36 girls from 3–5½ years old who were attending a University nursery school.

The **method** involved assessing each participant's level of aggression before assigning them to a group. In the two experimental conditions, participants were divided into sub-groups of boys and girls. Each participant was taken individually to play in a room in which there was an adult and a number of toys (a Bobo-doll, mallet, dart guns, crayons, tea set and plastic farm animals). In the aggressive condition, the adult started to punch the Bobo doll and hit it with the mallet (physical aggression) and spoke aggressively ('Hit him', 'Kick him'). In the non-aggressive condition the adult assembled toys and ignored the Bobo doll. The control group did not go through this stage. The children in each of the conditions were taken individually to another room containing a similar range of toys and left to play whilst their behaviour was observed.

The **results** showed that children exposed to aggressive models did show significantly more aggressive behaviour than those in the control group. There was no significant difference in aggression between those seeing non-aggressive models and the control group. The children also showed more imitation of the same sex model and boys performed more acts of aggression than girls, as Table 11.1 shows.

Sex of participant	Aggressive female model	Aggressive male model
Female	19	9
Male	17	38

TABLE 11.1 Mean scores of imitative aggression (from A. Bandura et al 1961)

viewer new ways to be aggressive, and also make people more immune to the effects of aggression so they are more tolerant of it in society.

Overall, critics of learning theory explanations argue that:

INBORN

- they overemphasise the influence of the environment and experience and underestimate the importance of inherited factors

- because **classical** and **operant conditioning** are based on research with animals, they fail to take account of the human ability to think, reason and remember alternative strategies for behaviour; however this criticism is not so relevant to social learning explanations.

To summarise then, the ethological and psychodynamic explanations for aggression propose that it is innate. In contrast, learning explanations stress the role of the environment, which means that our experiences with family, friends and school, as well as the media have an impact on aggression. Box 11.1 provides a comparison of these explanations.

11.1

SIMILARITIES AND DIFFERENCES IN EXPLANATIONS OF AGGRESSION

	PSYCHODYNAMIC EXPLANATION	LEARNING EXPLANATION	ETHOLOGICAL EXPLANATION
Are there innate factors?	yes	no	yes
What causes aggression?	thanatos – the death instinct	frustration, cues, reinforcement, punishment, imitating models	instinct for survival
How important are parents?	very important	very important	not important
What social factors are important?	opportunities to release aggression	aggressive cues, models, others who provide reinforcement/ punishment	appeasement rituals, opportunities to release aggression
How difficult is it to reduce aggression?	fairly difficult	it is possible	difficult

The effect of child-rearing styles on aggression

As you might expect from the material we have already covered in this chapter, there is considerable evidence that the way parents bring up their children is related to the levels of aggression the children show. Let us look first at two studies which produced very similar results.

Diana Baumrind (1971) observed families of pre-school children, noting several aspects of the parents' behaviour towards their children, namely:

- the amount of **warmth** the parents showed
- how **clear** and **consistent** the parents' rules were
- how **independent** children were expected to be
- how much the parents **talked** to and **listened** to their children

A study by Robert Sears (1977) and his colleagues looked at how 379 parents in Boston disciplined their five year old children. Six years later they followed the children up to assess their levels of aggression and moral development. From the **results** of both of these studies, the researchers **concluded** that there were three distinctive child-rearing (or parenting) styles:

- **permissive** parents were warm but were inconsistent with rules, they did not discuss or explain things to their children and used little discipline. Their children tended to be aggressive and remain aggressive.
- **authoritarian** parents were cold and did not discuss or explain things, they expected their children to be independent, do as they were told and disciplined them often and quite harshly. Their children were aggressive when young, though they were less aggressive but more anxious six years later.
- **authoritative** parents were warm, explained to their children what was expected of them and why, and made rules clear and consistent, their discipline was restrained and fair. Their children were less aggressive and remained that way.

Eleanor Maccoby and John Martin (1983) have added a fourth child-rearing style:

- **neglecting** or **rejecting** parents rejected or were indifferent to their children and therefore did not get involved in child-rearing. These children tended to show higher levels of aggression, and difficulties in relationships with others, which persisted as they grew up.

These four parenting styles are illustrated in Table 11.2

	WARM	COLD
DISCIPLINE	authoritative	authoritarian
LACK OF DISCIPLINE	permissive	neglecting

TABLE 11.2 Table showing the relationship between warmth, discipline and parenting styles

LEARNING

So how might parenting style be related to a child's aggression? There are a number of possible explanations, which relate to the theories we have looked at earlier in this chapter. For example, according to **social learning** theory the punishing authoritarian parent **models** aggressive behaviour for his or her child, who in turn shows higher levels of aggression. Equally, the warm and fair authoritative parent provides a model who is low in aggression. Research on children's popularity has found that co-operation and lack of aggression were important factors. The popular children tended to come from families in which parents typically showed the authoritative parenting style – warmth, low in physical punishment, actively discouraging aggression.

INBORN

The way in which parents handle punishment is important because we have seen that punishment may create frustration, which may cause more aggression. In contrast, according to **psychodynamic** explanations the child of an authoritarian parent is likely to be harshly disciplined. The child will experience higher levels of frustration but because he is unable to express it this will create anxiety.

FIGURE 11.6 The way a parent handles punishment can affect the child's level of aggression

Based on his research, Gerald Patterson has advised that punishment should be very mild and take place as early in the sequence of 'wrong' behaviours as possible. If punishment is left until things have got out of hand it is more likely to be excessive, to be accompanied by hostility, and offer a bad model for the child. What a parent says, and the action he or she takes, will be more powerful when there is a warm, accepting relationship with the child.

COGNITION

Because the authoritative parent explains to the child why its behaviour is wrong, then this helps the child understand more about his or her world, it encourages them to take the other person's viewpoint and to think about the *consequences* of their actions. This relates to the child's **cognitive** development and should help them reduce or control their aggression.

There is a final but important point. Although we have focused on the parents' behaviour here, many psychologists propose that the individual's behaviour is not just a result of how they are treated but of their *interaction* with others. Much of the evidence we have looked at here is **correlational**, so we must not assume that parents *cause* particular behaviours in their children. There are many **variables** which can affect both the child's levels of aggression and the parenting style, for example:

INBORN

- the child's **temperament** – a child with a difficult temperament tends to respond negatively and vigorously to experiences; this temperamental style of responding will be seen as more aggressive than the typical response of the child with an easy temperament (see temperament p. 165). But each child will bring out different responses from the parent, the difficult child is not so likely to respond to reasoned discipline, and a parent may resort to harsher methods. So temperament can affect both levels of aggression *and* child-rearing style.

SOCIAL

- the **family circumstances** – social factors such as poverty or poor health may also have an impact on the behaviour of both parent *and* child.

Are there ways of reducing aggression?

Fortunately, the answer seems to be *yes*, so we will look at some proposals which are based on psychological evidence.

REWARDING NON-AGGRESSIVE BEHAVIOUR

LEARNING

Using the principles of **operant conditioning**, if the consequences of behaviour are pleasant, then it is more likely to be repeated. When behaviour which is *not* aggressive is rewarded, it should be strengthened. If two children agree to share a toy (rather than fight over it) and are told 'well done' or 'that's a very good idea', this rewards them for a non-aggressive solution to their conflict, and they are more likely to use non-aggressive solutions in future.

Sometimes children behave aggressively in order to gain attention from adults. In such cases, the adult who responds with anger and argument will actually be *rewarding* the child by giving attention. Psychologists propose that aggressive behaviour should be calmly stopped, but that the child be given that much-needed attention when it is *not* being aggressive.

PROVIDING NON-AGGRESSIVE MODELS

LEARNING

According to **social learning theory**, if we see models who are not aggressive then, through observational learning, we should be less likely to show aggression. This has been shown by many psychologists, including Robert Baron (1977), whose participants thought they were giving electric shocks to a 'victim'. He found that adults who saw a non-aggressive model gave fewer 'shocks' than those in a control group who did not see a model. It seems that when someone sees both aggressive and non-aggressive models *at the same time* then the influence of the aggressive model can be erased by the non-aggressive model. This shows the benefit of having non-aggressive models in society, even though aggressive models cannot be totally removed.

REMOVAL OF AGGRESSIVE CUES

LEARNING

According to Leonard Berkowitz' research on **aggressive cues** – whether guns or a boxing match – one way of reducing aggression is to remove cues. He related the levels of aggression in American society to the availability of guns in America, but similar cues come from what we see in films and on television as well as within our society. According to Berkowitz' proposals, demonstrators are more likely to be aggressive when police are dressed like those in Figure 11.7. If they were not wearing riot equipment there would be fewer aggressive cues and therefore less likelihood of aggression occurring.

COGNITIVE INTERVENTIONS

COGNITION

This means making people think about what they see and do. If people have a better understanding of their own and others' behaviour they may be less likely to be aggressive. In one study, psychologists asked children to write about how television is not like real life and why it was bad to imitate television violence. A week later the children were videoed reading their essays and taking part in a talk show about this topic. The **results** showed that not only did it change children's attitudes, but two years later they were still showing lower levels of aggression.

COGNITION

If someone pushes past you in the street, how do you react? Some people might see this behaviour as directed at them and respond aggressively. One way of helping them to show less aggression is to encourage them to see *another* cause for this behaviour – as due perhaps to clumsiness or being in a hurry. They may be less likely to respond as though the behaviour was a personal attack. Encouraging the use of these 'mitigating circumstances' has been shown to be very effective in reducing aggressive responses.

FIGURE 11.7 Policing a demonstration

COGNITION

Cognitive intervention helps us cope with the frustration which may cause aggression. If we take a different perspective on the problem or talk ourselves through it, this helps to dispel some of our frustration. Because frustration arises when we are blocked from reaching a goal, we can for example learn to find other ways of achieving a goal, or of making the goal less important, or using the 'block' to teach us something useful. As we talk to ourselves along these lines, we are finding ways of avoiding frustration in the future or at least finding new ways of coping with it!

FOSTERING EMPATHY

This means encouraging the aggressor to experience the emotions of the victim. Research which has looked at men's attitudes to rape has shown that when they receive information about the victim's experience, male participants are able to present arguments against rape and are more sympathetic to rape victims and less tolerant of sexual violence.

SOCIAL

A study which was designed to encourage empathy in children required them to take different roles. Sometimes they were able to give out sweets, then they would have to play the part of a child who is 'left out' when the sweets go round. Switching to the part of someone who receives bad treatment appeared to make them more sensitive to the emotions of others and lowered aggression levels. Techniques like this one can be used to combat bullying.

Summary

The explanations which we have considered in this chapter offer a variety of reasons for aggression. They are not mutually exclusive, for example several involve the role of environmental factors but they vary in the emphasis they put on these factors, and on which are the most imporant and why. One of the difficulties in testing these explanations is separating out the many variables involved. Because we cannot take children at birth and rear them in an environment with *no* aggressive influences, we cannot say with confidence that aggression is due to nature (innate factors) or to nurture (environmental factors). What does seem to be true is that other people have considerable influence in generating and in reducing aggression. It seems that aggression is reduced when people are encouraged to use their cognitive and emotional knowledge. The one factor we have not fully explored is the difference in aggressive behaviour between males and females. This is discusssed under gender differences on page 198.

Exercises

1 What is aggression?
2 Outline one psychological explanation of the origins of aggression.
3 Describe two psychological theories of aggression and explain one difference between them.
4 Explain how child-rearing styles might influence children's aggression.
5 Identify a child-rearing style and briefly describe the influence it might have on children's aggression.
6 Explain how parents might influence their child's aggression.
7 Using your knowledge of psychology, describe ways in which aggression in children might be reduced.
8 Give an example of an instinct and describe how it might affect aggressive behaviour.
9 How may punishment affect aggressive behaviour?
10 Give an example of the way in which social learning principles may reduce aggression.

INDIVIDUALITY AND IDENTITY

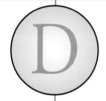

Each of the four chapters in Section D relates to a particular aspect of the individual – personality, intelligence, gender and the concept of self. We consider what these terms mean, how psychologists have studied these aspects of the individual, how they develop and the role that other people play in such development.

As we investigate individuality and identity in this way, we can examine the nature/nurture debate in more detail. By comparing the influence of heredity with the influence of the environment we are able to evaluate these competing views of human behaviour.

As you are reading, note the tabs alongside the text. These indicate definitions, core topics (which are explained in Chapters 1–4) and methodology (which is explained in Chapters 5–7).

The Development of Personality

Are you outgoing, careful, impulsive, friendly, pessimistic or easygoing? These are the kind of words you might use to describe the sort of person you are. They refer to those feelings and behaviours which you experience often, they are fairly permanent aspects of yourself – these words describe your personality. How do these personality traits originate? When parents say 'He's just like his father' or 'I don't know who she takes after' they are looking for personality characteristics which their children might have inherited. But our experiences also affect our behaviour, so what role does the environment play in the development of personality? Answers to these types of questions are provided by the topics in this chapter, which describes the development of personality from a variety of perspectives.

What is personality?

Personality is the word used to describe a person's characteristics or traits. The characteristics which form the personality are those which they show in many situations, and which are therefore seen as fairly stable. We tend to see these characteristics as forming a coherent whole. We could define personality as the pattern of individual characteristics which are relatively stable and which combine to make each person unique.

DEFINITION

This definition tries to encompass the debate between psychologists about:

SOCIAL

- how we identify and label these characteristics. For example, what is the difference between shy and timid? How can we measure them objectively?
- people show different behaviours in different settings so how can we decide what is relatively permanent and what is caused by the situation the individual is in, for example when performing a **social role** (see p. 212).
- to what extent does personality change throughout life, and why? This is a question related to the **nature/nurture** debate.

You need to be aware of these questions as you read through the chapter, which is concerned not with defining personality, but with explaining how it develops. We will look at four explanations, two of which provide an explanation from the nature perspective and two from the nurture perspective, as you can see in Box 12.1.

12.1

PERSONALITY DEVELOPMENT – THE NATURE/NURTURE DEBATE

- Explanations which stress the importance of **innate** factors (nature) are **psychodynamic** theory and **temperament**
- Explanations which stress the importance of **learned** factors (nurture) are **behaviourist** and **social learning theory**

Psychodynamic explanations for personality development

INBORN

There are a number of psychodynamic approaches, but we will focus on Sigmund Freud's **psychoanalytic** theory, which forms a basis for the psychodynamic approach. Freud proposed that instinctive drives underlie human behaviour. There are two groups of instinctive drives:

- **life instincts** (called eros) which are life preserving, life enhancing and creative, and include libido (sexual energy)
- **death instincts** (thanatos) which are destructive, the main one being aggression.

Our personality develops chiefly through the way we manage these instincts. However Freud argued that our instincts, motivations and anxieties are largely unconscious, as are the techniques we use to cope with them. By **unconscious** he meant they are inaccessible, so we are not aware of them, but nevertheless they affect our behaviour and attitudes and thus contribute to our personality.

Freud was working one hundred years ago in Vienna, and his theory was created from the material he gained through case studies of his patients. He did not see personality as a whole, but as having three parts. These three parts develop through stages, which we will examine shortly, but first we will focus on the three parts of personality.

THREE PARTS OF PERSONALITY

Freud proposed that personality has three parts – the **id**, **ego** and **superego**. They are quite different yet they are inter-related, as you will see below.

The id

INBORN

As we noted earlier, Freud claimed that human behaviour is based on instinctive drives. These are innate, so we are born with this 'package' of unconscious instincts (both life enhancing and destructive instincts) which Freud called the **id**. Because these instincts need immediate gratification, the id is demanding, selfish and impulsive, concerned only to satisfy its needs. It is seen as the 'demanding infant' in us and operates on the **pleasure** principle.

The ego

As the child develops it becomes aware that these demands cannot always be met or that what it wants is socially unacceptable. Children find that they have to wait to get home before they can go to the toilet. They have to share their mother's affection with their siblings. How do they cope with this? Freud said that by about three years of age a second part of personality develops which he called the ego. This is the *conscious* part of personality and it tries to find more realistic ways to gratify the id's demands, so it operates on the **reality** principle. It can be seen as the 'adult' part of us.

The superego

The child then starts to become aware of what it *should* do. This knowledge comes chiefly from parents, as we shall see shortly. By about six years of age a third part of personality then develops – the **superego**. This is *also* an unconscious part of personality and it judges the ego to see whether it is behaving in a moral way. The superego is seen as the 'parent' in us, checking that we do what is right and approving or disapproving of our behaviour. The superego operates on the **morality** principle and consists of two parts:

● the **ego ideal** relates to the kind of person we want to be, so we try to behave in accordance with our ideals – we feel pride and satisfaction if we do so.
● the **conscience** tries to stop us from doing things we know to be wrong, but if we do them we feel guilty.

These are the three parts of personality, but the ego is the only part of which we are conscious. The diagram in Figure 12.1 shows how the three parts of personality are related.

The ego has to manage the demands of the id in a way which will satisfy the

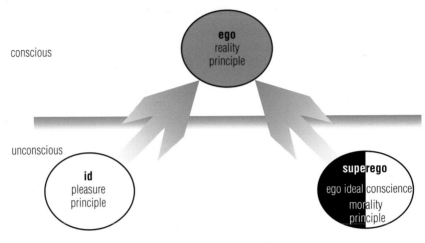

FIGURE 12.1 The three parts of personality

requirements of the superego. This may create conflict and anxiety, which the ego has to cope with. For instance, if you have to revise for a test tomorrow – your id wants to watch TV and eat a bar of chocolate, while your superego knows you should revise. This conflict creates **anxiety** and Freud proposed that people use several ways of coping with this anxiety, all of which are unconscious. One group of strategies he called **ego defence mechanisms**, which include:

- **repression** – forcing a threatening thought into the unconscious, such as sexual feelings for a parent
- **denial** – refusing to accept some aspect of reality because it creates too much anxiety, so a smoker refuses to acknowledge the risks of smoking
- **identification** – incorporating someone else into our own personality, adopting their behaviour and attitudes
- **sublimation** – channelling unacceptable impulses into acceptable activities, such as playing competitive sports as a channel for aggressive impulses
- **reaction formation** – behaving in the the *opposite* way to what we feel, such as being very polite and considerate towards someone against whom we are prejudiced
- **displacement** – transferring unacceptable feelings about someone towards someone or something which is fairly harmless or powerless and will not retaliate.

Each of these help us cope with anxiety – they help prevent the ego from being overwhelmed. They do so by distorting reality, but if they become a long-term solution to a problem they may prevent us from recognising and coming to terms with the problem itself.

These three parts of personality have developed by about six years of age so this is when the basis of personality is established, according to Freud. They form the structure of personality and they function throughout our lives as our inner, unconscious needs conflict with the demands of reality and our moral sense. Now we know the three parts of personality, we can look at how these parts develop.

PSYCHOSEXUAL STAGES AND PERSONALITY DEVELOPMENT

INBORN

Freud proposed that personality develops in distinct stages. At each stage one particular instinctive drive (the **libido**) is seeking gratification and as we cope with its demands the ego and superego develop. Our personality is shaped by how we cope with these demands.

The libido seeks sensual physical gratification and therefore, when the libido is focused on a specific part of the body, it becomes particularly sensitive and pleasure is produced by stimulating that part of the body. If there is not enough stimulation, or too much, then the libido may become fixated (or stuck) at that area. If fixation *does* occur it may have an effect on the child's later personality.

Freud proposed that as the individual matures the libido focuses on different areas of the body in a particular sequence. These sensitive areas, which he called erogeneous zones, represent the stages in the development of personality. We will look at the five **psychosexual stages** before we see what personality characteristics may result from fixation at any stage.

The oral stage (birth – 1 year)

At this stage the most sensitive zone is around the mouth. The baby gains pleasure from sucking, swallowing, biting and from putting things in its mouth. However, if it has too much, or too little, stimulation, it may become orally fixated. This means that it will continue to seek oral stimulation even when the libido has moved on to the next stage. An orally fixated adult may suck a pen or smoke.

The anal stage (1–3 years)

The libido moves to the anal area. The baby gains pleasure and satisfaction from emptying its bowels. Freud said that if the child is not allowed to gain enough satisfaction from emptying its bowels, then it may become anally fixated (for example, if an adult is always hurrying the child, or if the child always has to 'perform' whenever it sits on a potty).

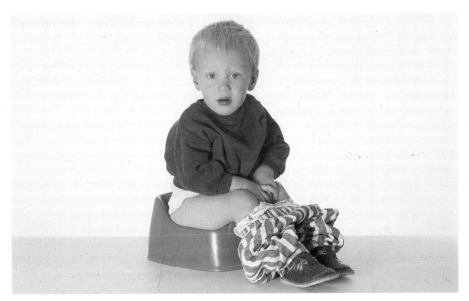

FIGURE 12.2 What happens to the child at this stage in its life could affect its later personality, according to Freud

This is the stage at which the ego starts to develop because the child has to control its desire to empty its bowels until the appropriate time. Adults who are anally fixated may enjoy getting their hands dirty, working with clay or with soil. Alternatively, because of reaction formation (an ego defence mechanism, see p. 154), the adult may be obsessed about cleanliness.

The phallic stage (3–6 years)

This is the most important of the stages for personality development. Pleasure seeking is focused on the genitals and Freud argued that the child begins to have unconscious longings for its *opposite* sex parent. In a boy this leads to conflict because he is frightened that his father (the same sex parent) sees him as a rival and will punish him. The boy is torn between desire for his mother and fear that his father will castrate him. This conflict – the **Oedipus conflict** – causes the boy anxiety. How does his ego manage this conflict?

Freud proposed that he adopts an ego defence mechanism – he **identifies** with his father. He tries to incorporate his father into himself so that his father will not harm him, and so that the boy can become more powerful and closer to his mother. All of these processes are **unconcious** in the child.

Through identification with his father the boy takes on the father's values, ideas, behaviours, morals and so on. It is in this way that the child comes to behave as a male, to parent and to develop a moral sense. Freud said this is how the superego develops, because the child **internalises** his father's values, which form the basis of his superego.

Freud was less clear about how a girl copes with the conflict which results from her unconscious longings for her father (the **Electra conflict**). Because she has no penis she thinks she has already been castrated. She therefore has less to fear from her mother so her identification with her mother is less strong. Nevertheless, this is how she too comes to behave as a female, to parent and to develop a moral sense – though Freud argued that because her identification was less strong her moral development and gender identity would be weaker than that of a boy.

Latency (5–12 years)

During this period the libido is diffused throughout the body and the focus is on social and intellectual development. Nevertheless the child continues to identify and interact with others of the same sex. During this period the relationship between the id, ego and superego is usually well balanced.

The genital stage (at approximately 12 years old)

As the bodily changes of adolescence take place the libido seeks satisfaction which can be provided by members of the opposite sex. The adolescent who has successfully accomplished each of the previous psychosexual stages should be able to form mature relationships and satisfy the id's needs realistically, but if there is **fixation** or **unresolved conflict**, this may hinder sexual relationships.

Psychosexual development and personality

We have noted that due to fixation and ego defence mechanisms certain personality traits may develop, a selection of which are shown in Table 12.1 below. In Freud's view, then, personality (which includes gender identity and

Oral stage	frustration – greedy, envious, pessimistic, cynical over-indulgence – trusting, optimistic, dependent
Anal stage	anal retentive personality – orderly, clean, miserly, obstinate, cruel anal expulsive personality – untidy, generous, impulsive
Phallic stage	vain, reckless, self-centred, ambitious, exploits others
Latency	normally there is no fixation at this stage
Genital stage	fixation here is normal

TABLE 12.1 Table showing personality traits resulting from fixation at each stage

moral sense) develops as a result of the way we manage instinctive drives. *How* we manage them depends on our ego and superego.

The evidence in support of Freud's ideas is contradictory. Research does suggest that traits such as generosity and impulsivity go together, but we need to establish that this is due to Freud's explanation. For example, if a link could be found between these traits and experiences at the anal stage, this would support Freud's theory. However, for the reasons given below, this is difficult to test.

EVALUATION OF THE PSYCHOANALYTIC EXPLANATION

Freud's ideas, proposed and developed over many years, have been very influential in Western thinking. We will look first at some of the criticisms before weighing up the overall value of psychoanalytic theory.

- It is difficult to test his theory because it is based on concepts, such as repression or the superego, which are not observable or measurable.

METHODS

- The theory was based on **case studies** of his clients. This is not a very reliable research method for a number of reasons (see methods, p. 39), including the possibility that the information gathered may be influenced by the researcher. Freud did not take notes for fear of damaging his therepeutic relationship with his clients; notes were written up when the session was over.
- Freud's explanation of the **phallic** stage is based on the child having two parents but does not explain what happens in single parent families (see gender development for more details, p. 190).
- His clients were not representative of people in general because they were mainly middle class Jewish women, living in Vienna, who came to him because of their problems. In addition, he did little work with children, yet childhood experiences are the keystone of his theory.

COGNITION

These are important criticisms, but the research which Freud's ideas have generated have led some psychologists to argue that whilst it is difficult to test *all* his ideas, research does provide evidence for some of his concepts. For instance, cognitive psychologists have found that stimulation of a specific part of the brain triggers very detailed memories of an individual's past. Because these memories had been 'forgotten', yet were still retained, this suggests that they resided in what Freud called the unconscious.

There is some acceptance of Freud's idea of the unconscious, the importance of early experiences on personality and the notion that there are reasons for our behaviour, though we may not be aware of them. His work regenerated interest in the emotional, as opposed to the rational, view of human beings

and led to the development of psychodynamic theories w'
developed his ideas.

Radical behaviourist explanations of personality development

Behaviourist explanations are quite different from psychodynamic explanations, as they propose that behaviour is shaped and maintained by its consequences. We learn to behave in particular ways through the processes of **reinforcement** and **punishment**. According to the behaviourist view, personality is learned, it is created through the application of reinforcement and punishment – through operant conditioning. This is described in detail in Chapter 2. Here we will look at how the main principles explain the development of personality:

LEARNING

- **Positive reinforcement** strengthens behaviour because it provides a reward. For example the child who is hugged after sharing its sweets or tidying its room is likely to become generous or tidy. The child who seeks attention and gets it (which is rewarding) by refusing to return a toy or drawing on the wallpaper will become selfish and destructive.

FIGURE 12.3 This child's father is rewarding his child's independence – according to behaviourists this is how she will develop an independent personality trait

- **Negative reinforcement** strengthens behaviour because something unpleasant is stopped. A boy whose sister is always spoiling his games may shout at her or attack her. If this stops her, he is likely to become more aggressive. If a girl is worried that the teacher will ask her a question, she may discover that sitting quietly and looking blank stops him asking questions. As a result she may become unresponsive and withdrawn.
- **Punishment** weakens behaviour, so a child who is reprimanded for being careless or reckless may become timid.
- Behaviour which is **partially reinforced** will take longer to become **extinguished** (see p. 12). This means that behaviour which is only rewarded *some* of the time is likely to continue for longer than if it is reinforced every time it occurs. This is just what happens in reality – very few behaviours are reinforced every time, perhaps because they are sometimes not seen by others, or because a behaviour is rewarded by one person but not by another. It is the behaviours which are partially rewarded which are most likely to persist and so be come personality traits.

EVALUATION OF THE RADICAL BEHAVOURIST EXPLANATION

This explanation is more straightforward to test because it concentrates on what is observable. It explains why a child may behave in a different way in different settings, for instance she may be helpful at school because the teacher reinforces helpful behaviour but not helpful at a home because the parent does not reinforce helpfulness when it is shown.

Research shows that it *is* possible to change people's behaviour by altering or removing reinforcers, but critics argue this is not an adequate explanation for personality development because:

- behaviour which can be changed so easily cannot be considered due to personality because these characteristics should be fairly permanent

INBORN
- it views the child as passive, there are no innate factors to influence personality, it appears to be little more than an accumulation of behaviours which have been created by reinforcement and punishment – in fact children play a much more active role in the development of their personality than the behaviourists accept
- it fails to explain why 'new' behaviour occurs

COGNITION
- it relates only to *behaviour* not to the reasons for behaviour, so it ignores the influence of the mind, of intention, emotion and understanding
- the principles of the behaviourist explanation are based on animal research, but humans are far more complex so we should not **generalise** from animals to humans.

Overall, then, the behaviourist explanation does not provide a comprehensive explanation for how personality develops, although behaviourist principles are incorporated into the explanation which we turn to next.

Social learning explanations for personality development

LEARNING

According to this theory, the child's personality develops as a result of observation and imitation. These ideas were proposed by Albert Bandura, a leading social learning theorist. Details are provided on p. 16, but here we will consider personality development in terms of his ideas about observational learning, reinforcement and punishment and self-efficacy.

OBSERVATIONAL LEARNING

Bandura (1977) proposed that the child learns not only through reinforcement and punishment, but also by observing others and **imitating** their behaviour. These others may be parents, siblings, friends, TV characters, teachers and so on. The child is more likely to imitate those who have particular qualities, such as being **nurturant** (warm and caring), **similar** or **powerful** (or effective). For example, someone of the same sex is more likely to be imitated than someone of the other sex.

As the child develops, different models will become more or less important. A three year old girl will imitate the behaviour of her mother but a 14-year-old girl might imitate the clothes and attitudes of a pop star. If the pop star is rebellious then the girl will be likely to imitate this behaviour and so develop a more rebellious personality.

REINFORCEMENT AND PUNISHMENT

Reinforcement and punishment are a part of social learning theory because:

- the child is more likely to imitate the behaviour of someone who is seen to be reinforced – this is called **vicarious reinforcement**. A child who is shy might be reluctant to speak out in class, but if another shy child speaks out and the teacher smiles with approval, then the child is more likely to imitate the behaviour – to speak out. In this way a shy child may become confident.

● if the child is rewarded when it imitates behaviour it has seen, it is more likely to repeat that behaviour. A boy playing football might shout at a referee – imitiating the behaviour of a professional footballer he has seen. If his father supports the boy's behaviour, this is rewarding for the boy, who is more likely to repeat the behaviour. He may develop a more challenging personality. If his father disapproves, the boy may become less challenging.

SELF-EFFICACY

Bandura (1977) argues that through the process of internalising a model's behaviour, learning which settings or circumstances are rewarding for which kinds of behaviour, the child achieves **self-efficacy**. This is when the child is able to predict outcomes of behaviour and to have certain expectations about itself. These expectations and standards form the core of the child's personality.

EVALUATION OF THE SOCIAL LEARNING EXPLANATION

This explanation is much richer than the radical behaviourist because it explains:

SOCIAL

● why each individual's behaviour varies – because it depends on the models it sees and in which circumstances it is reinforced
● why the individual's behaviour has some consistency – because only certain models will be of interest to it, and these will be the ones it imitates
● why 'new' behaviour occurs – because it is something the child may have seen in a different setting some time ago

COGNITION

● how factors such as cognition, motivation and intention shape the development of personality.

LEARNING

Nevertheless, it still proposes that the child's personality is learned as the result of its experiences and observations, so it does not explain why children differ so much when they are still young, before they have seen many models. It also suggests that personality is very dependent on the child's experiences, which undermines the notion of personality as something stable or based on innate factors.

So we have seen three explanations for how personality develops. There are differences between them yet they also have some common features, such as the important role of parents. Box 12.2 summarises the key features which we have examined, highlighting points of similarity and of contrast.

12.2

SIMILARITIES AND DIFFERENCES IN EXPLANATIONS OF PERSONALITY

	PSYCHODYNAMIC EXPLANATION	BEHAVIOURIST EXPLANATION	SOCIAL LEARNING EXPLANATION
Are there innate factors?	yes – libido	no	no
How important are parents?	both parents essential	important	very important
Is the child's role active?	not very – unconscious	fairy passive	very active
What social factors are important?	very few	other people	other people, media, experiences
Which are most important, emotional or cognitive factors?	emotional	neither	cognitive
Is there evidence for this explanation?	very little – hard to test	yes – but based on animals and humans	yes
Is personality consistent?	yes	no – it can be changed	fairly consistent

Temperament

When psychologists talk of **temperament** they are referring to the way we respond to our environment. Compare the babies in Figure 12.4, look at their toes and fingers. The baby on the left seems very active – vigorous and tense. The other looks relaxed and could be described as passive. These two babies may each have a different temperament, they have a different behavioural style.

DEFINITION

Temperament can be defined as the individual's behavioural style of responding to the environment, which is innate and persists over time. This definition is based on research (some of which we will examine shortly) which suggests that:

INBORN

● because a behavioural style is evident soon after birth and persists into adulthood, it is innate

FIGURE 12.4 Two different temperaments?

● it is based on the way in which our nervous system reacts to stimuli, which in turn affects how active and how emotional we are – our behavioural style
● our behavioural style affects our interactions with others.

Our concern here is not with the biological details of temperament, but with research to investigate patterns of behaviour, whether they persist over time and how they might affect our interaction with the environment. Such research poses difficulties because psychologists have to decide which behaviours to take as indicators of temperament, how to measure and how to classify them.

METHODS

We will discover how psychologists have investigated temperament using twin studies and have looked at the persistence of temperament by carrying out longitudinal studies.

INBORN

A LONGITUDINAL STUDY OF TEMPERAMENT

Alexander Thomas, Stella Chess and Herbert Birch followed the development of 136 children in the New York area over 12 years. Their aim was to define the characteristics of temperament in children and identify their role in the development of children's behaviour. The details now follow.

Thomas, Chess & Birch (1968)

The **method** involved interviews with parents and teachers, observations of the children and intelligence tests. Different researchers were used for different assessments, to avoid a 'halo' effect. For example, the researcher who observed the child in class did not interview the teacher. Interviewer and observer ratings were compared periodically, so as to check for reliability.

From the **results** the researchers identified nine dimensions of temperament, such as intensity of response, activity rate, mood, persistence, adaptability to new experiences. **Results** also showed a correlation between temperament scores of children when young and then in early adulthood, although the correlations were not high.

Thomas, Chess and Birch **concluded** that temperamental traits seemed to persist as the child developed which suggests that temperament is innate. They also **concluded** that, as the children's scores on each of these dimensions were linked in particular ways, three categories of temperament could be defined. In total 65% of their participants could be classified as belonging to one of these types, as shown in Table 12.2 below and in the pie chart on p. 62.

Category	% of sample in each category	Characteristics
easy	40	regular habits, approached new experiences positively, was adaptable and usually fairly happy
slow to warm up	15	passive, although not happy with new experiences it did not protest vigorously, but was usually happy once it adapted, it was mild in the way it responded
difficult	10	irregular habits, approached new situations negatively, responded very vigorously and was slow or unable to adapt, was irritable and cried more than children in the other categories
The remaining children in the sample (35%) fell into more than one category		

TABLE 12.2 Table showing the percentage of children falling into the three categories of temperament

There are some difficulties with this type of research which may have affected the results and therefore the conclusions. For example:

METHODS

- the measures of temperament vary in how useful they are at different ages, so the amount of crying is an important indicator at one year old, but not so valuable at 13 years old when the child is likely to have greater control of his or her feelings
- although overall there were some correlations, these were very low between one and five years of age and between one year old and early adulthood. Highest correlations were between about five years of age and early adulthood. Whether this reflects the difficulties in measuring behaviour or is an indication that there *is* considerable change in the first five years is unclear.

This research was concerned with identifying characteristics and measuring their persistence into adulthood. However research investigating the degree to which temperament is innate has also used twin studies, as we shall see now.

A TWIN STUDY OF TEMPERAMENT

There are two types of twins:

INBORN

- **identical** twins have exactly the same genes because they have developed from one fertilized egg which has split. They are called monozygotic (MZ) twins, meaning 'one egg'.
- **fraternal** twins have half of their genes in common and are as similar genetically as any two children of the same parents. They are called dizygotic (DZ) twins, meaning 'two eggs'.

Twin studies are useful for research which tries to identify the degree of influence of innate or environmental factors – to provide evidence in the **nature/nurture** debate. In relationship to temperament, Arnold Buss and Robert Plomin (1984) studied both types of twins using the following three dimensions of behaviour:

- **emotionality** – how easily a person becomes very upset or very excited – the more emotional a person is, the harder it is for them to calm down
- **activity** – how much energy a person puts into their activity – a person with high activity levels will talk rapidly and move about a lot
- **sociability** – how much a person wants to be with other people – someone scoring high on sociability will prefer to spend their time with others rather than alone as they seem to need interaction with other people.

Buss & Plomin compared the scores between each pair of twins. They wanted to see, for example, if a child who scored high on sociability had a twin who *also* scored high on sociability. If this was the case, then there was a strong correlation between the scores for this pair of twins. If temperament is genetic, then MZ twins (with identical genes) should have a higher correlation of scores than DZ twins (who have half of their genes in common). **Results** showed that there were much higher correlations between scores for identical twins than scores for fraternal twins. From these results Buss & Plomin **concluded** that temperament has a genetic basis, that it is innate.

METHODS

There are difficulties in this research which may have affected the results and therefore the conclusions. Yet again we come across the problems of separating the environmental factors from the genetic ones. Identical twins spend a lot of time together and are usually treated in a similar way, for example because they have the same genes they are always the same sex, size and have almost identical features, indeed other people often treat them as interchangeable because they are so alike. They are usually dressed in identical clothes, attend the same school and so on.

In contrast, fraternal twins are the same age, but may be of different sex, size or appearance. Their experiences will differ more, and it may be this which causes the lower correlation in scores for DZ twins, rather than the fact that they have only half their genes in common. This possibility weakens the evidence for the genetic argument.

TEMPERAMENT AND INTERACTION WITH THE ENVIRONMENT

The research which we have reviewed has provided evidence that there are differences between individual styles of responding. These differences are reasonably consistent, they are present at a young age and tend to persist. This suggests temperament does have an innate basis.

INBORN

Buss & Plomin have proposed that children who show extremes of a temperament type, such as children high in emotionality or very 'difficult' children, force their environment to adapt to them. In contrast, children in the middle range of a temperament type seem to adapt to their environment.

SOCIAL

Other psychologists have suggested that how the child's personality develops will depend on how well its temperament *fits* with its environment. For example, a 'slow to warm up' child will be more comfortable in a slow-paced, easy going home. But the demands of school, with a strict timetable and rapid change of activity, may be very stressful for the child. The way it responds will in turn affect the response of those around it. Michael Rutter (1978) proposes that the baby's temperament affects how it *interacts* with its environment and how others respond to it. The nature of this interaction will in turn influence the development of personality. In other words, the basis for traits such as optimism, shyness, flexibility or anxiety may be in temperament.

Summary

The explanations for the development of personality which we have considered here incorporate two of the recurring themes in psychology – the influence of nature and of nurture. We have seen that the interaction between the two is a common feature of the psychodynamic explanation and of temperament. The other two explanations consider that environment is the determinant of personality. We have noted some of the difficulties in investigations of temperament, which include how to define and measure behaviours. Indeed the definition of personality is widely contested, with disagreement about the extent to which it is stable, consistent, innate or learned. Regardless of these problems, it is an important area of study if we are to increase our understanding of human behaviour.

Exercises

1 What do psychologists mean by personality?
2 Choose two explanations of personality, and describe one way in which they are similar and one way in which they are different.
3 Compare and contrast two explanations of personality.
4 What do psychologists mean by temperament?
5 Describe one psychological study of temperament, including its main findings.
6 Why is twin research important in psychology?
7 Give an example of an instinct and explain how it might affect behaviour.
8 Outline the purposes of a longitudinal study and a cross-sectional study and say how they differ.
9 Describe two disadvantages in a longitudinal study.
10 What does the 'halo' effect mean in the Thomas, Chess & Birch study?

Intelligence

You might think that you know what this chapter is about, but psychologists would be less certain. This is because there is still no agreed answer to the question – what is intelligence? Someone who can speak several languages or play a tune they have heard only once, calculate complex sums, do several things at the same time, solve problems or remember the details of what they read would be called intelligent. Does this mean we have lots of different types of intelligences or do we have an underlying ability which is what we call intelligence? Are we born with a certain amount of intelligence or is it something which develops as we mature? These are the kinds of questions psychologists have been wrestling with for many decades and we will refer to them in this chapter. But first we are going to look at how intelligence is measured. We will then go on to consider research which has looked at the influence of heredity and of the environment on intelligence. This is an example of the nature/nurture debate in psychology.

What is IQ and how is it calculated?

DEFINITION

IQ means intelligence quotient and an IQ test is used to measure intelligence. IQ tests are examples of psychometric tests. A child taking an IQ test attempts a series of questions (known as items) which are age-related. This means that an eight year old taking the tests for eight year olds would do as well as most other children of that age. In this example, the child would therefore have a mental age (an MA) of eight. If she could get most of the answers right on the tests for *ten* year olds, her MA would be ten.

To calculate her IQ, the child's mental age is then divided by her age in years (her chronological age or CA), and the resulting figure is multiplied by 100. Below is the formula for calculating IQ, with an example of its use in calculating the IQ of our eight year old who successfully completed the tests for a 10 year old.

Formula: $\text{IQ} = \dfrac{\text{mental age (MA)} \times 100}{\text{chronological age (CA)}}$ Example: $\text{IQ} = \dfrac{10}{8} \times 100 = 125$

You can see that this child's IQ is 125, which is above average for her age. If she had only been able to complete the tests for eight year olds, her IQ would have been 100, which is the mean (or average) for her age. This formula is only useful up to 18 years of age, because after that intelligence is thought to change very little but age increases.

IQ tests for adults are designed so that the individual's score is compared to the norms for their age. One example is the Wechsler Scales: the test items are devised so that when a large number of individuals are tested, the mean score is 100. This represents a standard against which an individual's score can be measured. The items are also **standardised**, they are designed so that two-thirds of the scores from the population fall between the range 85–115 because research shows that on any measure (of intelligence, height or weight, for example) two-thirds of the population are within 15% of the mean.

The nature and uses of IQ tests

COGNITION

Modern IQ tests measure intelligence through sub-tests, for example:

- **performance tests** – such as identifying what is missing from pictures of familiar objects, putting blocks in order of size
- **verbal tests** – such as the meaning of words, categorising words
- **numerical tests** – such as number sequences, calculations (for an example see Figure 13.1 below)
- **spatial ability tests** – such as selecting patterns, visualising rotating shapes (for an example see p. 199)
- **reasoning tests** – using verbal or visual reasoning (for an example see Figure 13.1 below)
- **information processing tests** – devised to test abilities related to intelligent behaviour, such as memory or speed of processing information.

Tests may be given individually, as is the case when diagnosing problems. When given to several people at the same time, they are usually written tests, known as pencil and paper tests, and may be used to select people for employment or educational purposes.

The first test was devised to identify children who were slow in their intellectual development. Since then IQ tests have been used for a variety of purposes, some of which have been strongly criticised. We will look at four uses of IQ tests now.

EMPLOYMENT SUITABILITY

INBORN

Psychologists using the early IQ tests in the U.S. (the Stanford-Binet Tests) started from the view that intelligence is **innate**, so it cannot be developed. People could therefore be tested and fitted to a job which suited their intelligence level. An early example was the US Army Tests: the Alpha test was written and the Beta test was for those who could not read or write, so it was in picture form (see the extract in Figure 13.3, p. 175).

Tests today are not so simplistic. They are devised to find each individual's strengths and weaknesses and match them with a job which requires similar strengths or to match them with an appropriate career. These may be paper and pencil tests or use computers so that it is possible to test how fast people

COGNITION

respond to particular types of information, such as word meanings or numeracy skills. An example is the recruitment tests used by the British Army, which test a number of factors including numeracy, information processing and verbal reasoning abilities, as you can see in Figure 13.1.

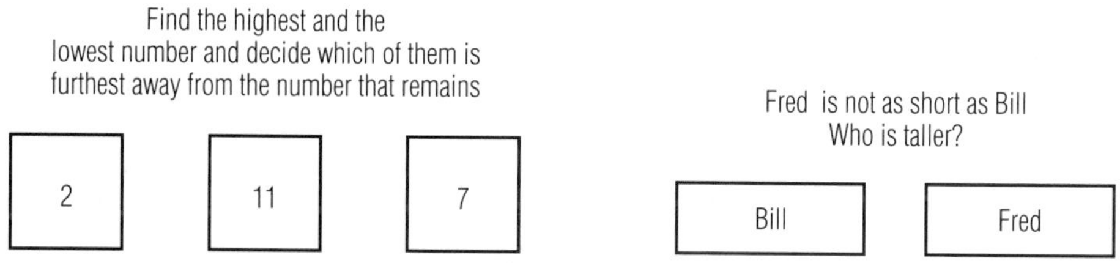

Find the highest and the lowest number and decide which of them is furthest away from the number that remains

| 2 | 11 | 7 |

Fred is not as short as Bill
Who is taller?

| Bill | Fred |

FIGURE 13.1 Extracts from British Army recruitment tests

SELECTION IN EDUCATION

COGNITION

The IQ tests used to select children for educational purposes are usually pencil and paper tests taken by groups of children all at one time. Research shows that there is a positive correlation between IQ scores and later educational achievement. This correlation may be due in part to the effects of labelling or the self-fulfilling prophecy.

An example of an IQ test which was used for selection purposes was the '11-plus' test which was taken by all 11 year olds in England and Wales during the 1950s and 60s. The purpose was to match the child's intelligence level with the most appropriate type of secondary school – grammar school (academic) or secondary modern school (technical). One of the major criticisms of the test was that it **labelled** children as failures at 11 years old, which in turn affected their self-image (see p. 219). This system of selection in education has been abolished in many areas of England and Wales.

ASSESSING LEVEL OF INTELLECTUAL DEVELOPMENT

METHODS

As you will see later in the chapter, IQ tests are used extensively in research. They have been used for instance to compare the intelligence level of twins and to assess a child's development at various stages of an intellectual enrichment programme. These tests must not be confused with achievement tests, which measure what the child has learned, although critics argue that most IQ tests depend on some learned abilities such as reading or an understanding of language.

COGNITION

Cognitive assessment tests are widely used in education to assess a child's ability in numeracy, reasoning and language comprehension in order to assess strengths and weaknesses in various types of mental abilities and provide appropriate learning experiences.

DIAGNOSING SPECIAL NEEDS

COGNITION

The first intelligence tests were devised by Albert Binet and his colleagues (1905) in France. Their purpose was to identify children who were below the level of their peers so that they could be provided with help in special schools. The diagnostic tests can be valuable in identifying where children have severe difficulties or unusual talents. IQ tests cannot be used on very young children, for whom the most commonly used test is the Bayley Scale of Infant Development. Its purpose is to identify major developmental problems and is used for children from a few weeks old to $2\frac{1}{2}$ years of age.

Diagnostic tests are usually given individually, for example the British Ability Scales (BAS) which were published in 1979 and can be used for children between the ages of $2\frac{1}{2}$–17 years of age. In the U.S.A. the Wechsler Intelligence Scale for Children is frequently used. Both of these tests provide a verbal, visual and 'general' IQ score.

Tests such as the Wechsler Scale are useful because they are not age related; instead the items range from very easy to very difficult. This allows a wide range of abilities to be tested, which is not the case with the more simple educational assessment tests. Because the Wechsler Scale has items for different types of intellectual abilities, they are more useful for diagnosing learning difficulties. For example a child usually shows some variation in scores for each ability, but where they are very inconsistent such as a high verbal and general score but a low reasoning score, this suggests the child may have a specific problem with reasoning. These tests are also useful for identifying the child who is far above the norm for his or her age – the 'gifted' child – who also has special needs.

FIGURE 13.2 The gifted child has special needs

The limitations of IQ tests

We have seen that IQ tests are used for a wide range of purposes, employing a variety of test methods. You might feel that if people have been using the tests for so long, for so many important things, then they must do the job well. However IQ tests have been criticised on the basis of their accuracy, fairness, validity and effects, all of which we examine below.

THE ACCURACY OF IQ TESTS

How accurate an indicator is the individual's IQ test score? Concerns relate to:

● **performance** – the individual may not do well in the test because of tiredness, lack of interest or confidence, an unfamiliar type of test, a hot or noisy room. In individual tests the tester may also have an impact. Children in particular can become shy, self-concious, inarticulate or exhibitionist when a stranger is present.

● **prediction** – sometimes IQ scores have been shown to be weak predictors of later scores. A test which was a good predictor would show a high correlation between the scores a child achieved at any two points in its development. Both the Stanford-Binet and the Wechsler Scales are quite good predictors for children's scores when tests are taken one or two years apart but the correlation gets weaker as children enter their mid-teens. Where a test is a fairly accurate predictor we could argue that this is due to the self-fulfilling prophecy. Where it is not, we can argue for the importance of personal qualities such as motivation and energy in later educational success.

THE FAIRNESS OF IQ TESTS

Criticisms about fairness focus on the way in which tests may penalise some people and advantage others. This may be because the tests:

COGNITION

● depend on **reading** and **writing** ability – this handicaps those who have difficulties with these skills. People who have difficulty processing written (as opposed to spoken) information or who are dyslexic may find these tests difficult and are likely to produce scores which do not reflect their intelligence.

SOCIAL

● are **culture specific** – an IQ test is not fair if it requires familiarity with a specific culture. In the first half of the 20th century, because of the notion that intelligence was inherited, immigrants to the U.S.A. were tested in order to filter out those who were, according to the testers, 'feeble-minded'. But the items were based on middle-class American culture, so immigrants who were unfamiliar with it were penalised. This point might become clearer if you look at Figure 13.3. The same criticism was directed at IQ tests administered in the early 1900s which showed that white participants had higher scores than black participants. Until the Stanford-Binet test was revised in 1973, it was standardised only on white children, yet it was used to test white and black children. Since then most psychologists have tried to eliminate bias in tests, an example being the Raven's Progressive Matrices Test. This is non-verbal, it uses patterns and shapes and is a test of abstract reasoning which is considered to be bias-free.

THE VALIDITY OF IQ TESTS

METHODS

If a test is valid then it measures what it is supposed to measure, but there is much debate about whether IQ tests actually *do* measure intelligence. One view is that they do because those who get higher IQ scores *also* do better at school and get better paid jobs (these two can be considered as indicators of intelligence). But you can see that this is a correlation – the higher the IQ score, the better the school work. We know that correlations can only show a

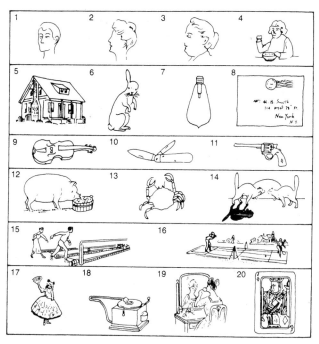

FIGURE 13.3 An extract from an early intelligence test. Can you say what is wrong with these pictures?

METHODS

relationship between two variables, we cannot conclude that one variable causes the other variable. Critics of the validity of IQ tests argue that:

● tests are said to be testing intelligence, not what the individual has learned. But they *are* testing learning if we need to know the meaning of words in order to answer some questions, or be able to understand the relationships between numbers. Some IQ tests may therefore be not so much tests of intellectual ability as tests of learned skills.

● we cannot test intelligence because we do not agree on what intelligence is. Many of the abilities which are widely accepted as intelligent, such as creativity, planning or adaptability are not measured by such tests. Current views of intelligence propose several intelligences – visual, musical, interpersonal, kinaesthetic and so on – each requiring particular abilities and using various parts of the brain. From this perspective, IQ tests do not measure intelligence because they do not measure all these abilities.

This brings us full circle – can we measure intelligence? The answer must be no. First of all, we do not know what intelligence is. Secondly, IQ tests are only ways of comparing people's performance on various tests of mental ability, which have been devised so as to produce a normal distribution of scores. This treats intelligence as though it was a physical attribute like weight or height.

So IQ tests have contributed to the false idea that intelligence is a 'thing' which is predictible, stable and can be measured. This is a view which began within psychology and quickly took hold in the public imagination. Most psychologists do not use IQ tests as a measure of intelligence, but as indicators or diagnostic tools. Unfortunately public perception is that intelligence is a 'thing' which is measurable.

Having said all this, we are now going to look at the influence which heredity and the environment twins may have on intelligence, and you will see that in researching these topics psychologists have used IQ tests widely. You need to remember these criticisms.

Intelligence and the influence of heredity

INBORN

According to the hereditarian view, the differences in intelligence between individuals are largely inherited. A supporter of this view was Cyril Burt (1958) who proposed that 80% of the variability which people showed in levels of intelligence was due to heredity and only 20% to environmental factors. The hereditarian viewpoint is that this is why bright children tend to come from bright parents and why there are differences between the IQ scores of black and white people. This was the dominant explanation for intelligence in the first half of the 1900s, but now has few supporters.

According to this view, the closer the genetic relationship between two people, the more similar their IQ scores should be. Critics argue that because people who are related genetically (such as a parent and child) usually share similar environments, this could explain the similarity of their IQ scores. In order to separate hereditary from environmental factors psychologists would have to remove children from their parents at birth and rear them in a very different environment. This is obviously impossible, but research alternatives have been provided by two unusual but naturally occurring situations, namely by studying twins and adopted children.

TWIN STUDIES

INBORN

Valuable information is provided by the unique situation of identical twins. Because identical twins (**monozygotic** twins or MZs) come from the same fertilised egg they have exactly the same genes. On the other hand, fraternal twins (**dizygotic** twins or DZs) are no more alike than any brother or sister – they share 50% of their genes. If identical twins have more similar IQ scores than fraternals, this would be evidence in favour of the **hereditarian** view of intelligence.

Comparison of identical and fraternal twins

Twin studies usually assess the IQ scores of pairs of twins to see how strongly they are correlated. A strong positive correlation means that if one twin has a high IQ score, it is very likely the other has. If one twin has a low score, so does the other. In 1980 Robert Plomin surveyed the results of several twin studies and two important points emerged:

- **results** consistently showed a stronger correlation between IQ scores for identical twins than fraternal twins: this supports the hereditarian view because MZ twins are genetically identical
- nevertheless MZ twins are usually dressed alike and treated alike by parents, relatives, friends and teachers; they also spend a lot of time together. This means that their environment is likely to be more similar than fraternal twins, and this may be an alternative reason for closer IQ scores.

Research on reared-apart identical twins

This type of research allows psychologists to try to separate the hereditarian from the environmental effects by studying people with identical genes who have been reared in different environments. An example of this is the Minnesota Twin Study, which started in 1979 and has been researching adult twins between 19 – 68 years of age. More than 50 pairs have been enrolled from several different countries using advertising and media coverage. The length of time for which twins have been separated varies from 1 year to 60 years. The **results** show a strong positive correlation between IQ scores, thus supporting the hereditarian view.

METHODS

However there are criticisms of methodology from psychologists taking the environmental perspective. The points made by Leon Kamin (1974) are typical of the criticisms of twin research:

- the majority of twins were brought up together for several years before they were separated – the criteria for 'separated' twins was at least five years in different homes
- in two-thirds of the pairs one twin was reared by its mother and the other by a grandmother or aunt and many of these pairs went to the same school
- the majority of the pairs studied had offered to take part in research so the sample was unrepresentative because it was self-selected
- some of the IQ tests were not properly standardised, thus making comparison of IQ scores inaccurate
- the factor which makes them unique (identical genes) *also* means they are not representative of the population as a whole, though they are treated as if they *are* representative in the **conclusions** from the research.

When **results** are examined from the smaller number of twins who were genuinely reared apart in different types of environment these show much lower correlations (and therefore more dissimilar levels) of IQ than those reared apart but in similar environments, so:

INBORN

- there was a positive correlation in IQ scores of MZ twins reared apart: this supports the hereditarian view as it shows environment has little effect on differences in intelligence, suggesting they are largely inherited

SOCIAL

- the correlations of IQ scores from twins reared in *very different* environments were lower: this supports the environmental view because it suggests that the environment does influence intelligence.

ADOPTION STUDIES

Another avenue of research has been to determine whether the IQ scores of adopted children are closer to the IQ scores of their birth parents (evidence for the hereditarian view) or their adoptive parents (evidence for the environmental view). **Results** show that:

INBORN

- the IQ of the *birth* parents is a better indicator of the child's IQ than that of the adoptive parents: this supports the hereditarian view
- there is no correlation between the IQs of two children adopted into the same family, and therefore genetically different but reared in the same environment. However evidence does suggest that their IQ scores are more closely related than you would expect as a result of chance: this is some evidence for environmental influence

SOCIAL

- the age of a child when adopted makes a difference – there is a correlation between the IQ scores of younger adopted children and their adoptive parents but this is not the case for those adopted in adolescence, suggesting that the environment is influential.

SOCIAL

Research such as that by A. Dumaret (1985) in France looked at children who were born to mothers from fairly poor or uneducated backgrounds. Using the Wechsler Scale to assess IQ, Dumaret's **results** showed that children who were adopted into upper class homes tended to have a higher IQ than their siblings who stayed with their birth mothers. Siblings who were reared in institutions or foster homes showed the lowest IQ score of all. This is evidence for the environmental view because although 50% of the genes were identical in *all* siblings, the difference in IQ scores was related to differences in their environment. You can see the comparative IQ scores in the bar chart in Figure 13.4.

Adoption studies have also been criticised. Weaknesses identified include:

- the IQ scores for young children are unreliable because they may change

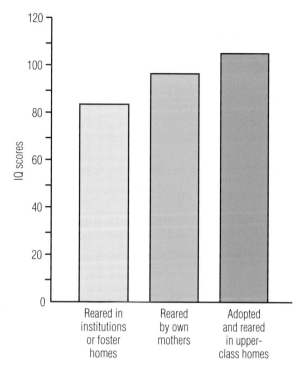

FIGURE 13.4 Bar chart showing IQ of siblings reared in different environments (from A. Dumaret, 1985)

considerably as the child gets older. Below two years of age the Bayley Scales are used to compare children's rate of development.

- children who become adopted may have experienced poor environments previously, and thus their measured IQ is artificially low when adopted.

SOCIAL

- there is variation in the type of families children go to. Some adoption agencies match the child to the family on as many factors as possible, whereas others tend to select families which are middle class with older well-educated parents, so adopting environments are not equally different for every child.

To sum up the research reviewed so far, there seems to be considerable evidence coming from twin studies which supports the hereditarian view. Nevertheless, it appears that environment may well play a part, and research from adoption studies suggests that the role of the environment may be considerable. Let us look more closely at research in this area now.

Intelligence and the influence of the environment

The environmental view proposes that variations in human intelligence are mainly due to environmental factors: we have already seen some evidence of this, particularly in the adoption studies. But what aspects of the environment are important? Researchers who have tried to answer this question have studied factors such as the three we will examine now – social class, family influence and special intervention programmes. We will look at research on these topics to discover whether it supports the environmentalist view that environmental factors are largely responsible for differences in IQ scores.

SOCIAL CLASS

SOCIAL

S. Broman and her colleagues (1975) produced a study of some of the variables which correlated with IQ. The **results** of tests of four year olds showed that:

● the higher the child's IQ the higher the mother's social class
● the higher the child's IQ the higher the mother's level of education
● there was no apparent difference between the scores of children below two years of age but differences become apparent soon after and *increase* with age. This finding could have been due to the difficulties of testing IQ in children under two: developmental tests are used instead.

Sara Meadows (1993), in her evaluation of the factors affecting children's cognitive development, notes that it is important to look at the variables which may affect intelligence rather than use class as a simplistic label:

● **biological** factors at the time of birth have been found to be related to lower intellectual development. These factors include maternal stress, poor diet and nutrition for both mother and child, smoking and birth difficulties. They are all correlated with lower class status and *also* with poorer intellectual development, although the reasons for this relationship are complicated.

COGNITION

● **language** is related to intellectual development and, according to Basil Bernstein (1961), to class. He argued that working-class children tend to hear less complex language and fewer abstract ideas than middle-class children and this affects their intellectual development. He called the difference between the two types of language **restricted** (which is brief and simple – 'Stop that!') and **elaborated** (longer and more complex – ('Don't do that because you'll get burned'). Although his work has received criticism he makes an important point about the link between language and education. Teachers tend to use the elaborated code which disadvantages any child who is not familiar with it, and Bernstein found these are likely to be children from working-class homes.

FAMILY INFLUENCE

Helen Bee (1982) has reviewed research into families whose children achieve high IQ scores and concluded that they shared five characteristics, all of which are discussed in other parts of this book:

FIGURE 13.5 Literature such as this has been produced for pregnant women because research has identified a correlation between their health and the intellectual development of their babies

COGNITION
- **appropriate play materials** for the child's stage of development were provided. It is their *appropriateness*, not the quantity, which were important. This links with Piaget's ideas on cognitive development (see p. 234).

SOCIAL
- **emotionally responsive and involved parents** answered questions, listened and encouraged the child. They spent time with the child, creating a warm environment (see attachments p. 77).

COGNITION
- **parents' language** when talking to their child was rich and accurate (see Berstein's work above).

SOCIAL
- **high expectations** were shown, parents expected their child to develop rapidly and do well in school (see self-esteem p. 210, and self-fulfilling prophecy, p. 221).

- **room to explore** and even make mistakes was allowed, excessive restriction or control was avoided.

INBORN
These results only show correlations; we cannot infer that one causes the other. One variable which could affect both IQ score and the child's family environment is **temperament** (see personality, p. 167). The child's temperament, or behavioural style, is likely to affect the way the parent interacts with the child, and the way the child responds to its environment. Parents will

find it pleasurable to play and talk to the 'easy' child, the child is likely to be happy playing with toys and exploring and will thus benefit from the intellectual stimulation this environment offers. The 'difficult' child has a short concentration span and tends to respond negatively, so it is less likely to have extended and pleasurable interactions with its parents, or gain from play or exploration sessions – thus its score on IQ tests may be lower.

SPECIAL INTERVENTION PROGRAMMES

In Chapter 8 of this book, where we look at childhood deprivation, there is evidence that IQ scores of children living in non-stimulating environments can be increased if the environment is enriched. This is the purpose of special intervention programmes: they aim to enhance the intellectual development of young children from non-stimulating environments, so that they will be able to benefit when they go to school. Many programmes were started in America in the late 1960s under Project Headstart. The children were generally three or four years of age, in some programmes teachers worked with the children at home and in others the children went to a centre which offered different types of stimulation.

COGNITION

Early results from Headstart programmes showed, on average, a jump in IQ of about 10 points for children in the first couple of years. Disappointment followed when it seemed that this effect 'wore off' when they started school. However by adolescence these children were doing better than those from similar backgrounds who had no enrichment. The reappearance of the early gains is called the 'sleeper effect' and is shown clearly in Figure 13.6.

These results were reported by Irving Lazar and Richard Darlington (1982) when they surveyed twelve longitudinal studies of the effects of enrichment programmes. They also found that children who had been part of the pre-school enrichment programs were less likely to repeat a year in school, or enter a remedial class. So although the scores appear similar in the early school years; the children may have been able to cope with school better.

Darlington is one of several psychologists to note that a possible reason for these results is less to do with the programmes themselves, and more to do with the difference the programme makes to the *parent's* attitude. Parents became more interested in their child's development, learning better skills to help the child, and Darlington says it is this factor which has the most impact on the child's improvement. Whether or not this is so, both factors (enrichment and parental attitude) support the **environmental** view of intelligence.

SOCIAL

In a study conducted by Craig Ramey and his colleagues (1981), children whose mothers had low IQs were monitored. The children attended a special

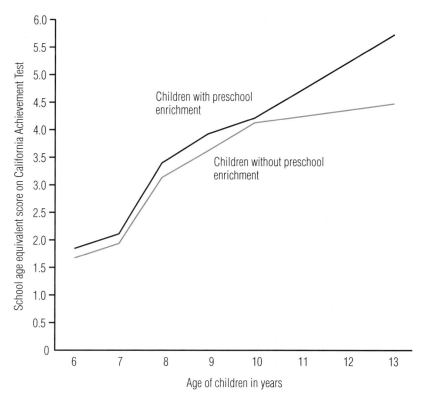

FIGURE 13.6 Graph showing scores of children from enriched and non-enriched pre-school programs. (from H. Bee 1992)

day-care enrichment programme from three months of age. The programme operated five days a week and provided an environment similar to that which Bee described as a good home environment – warm and stimulating. Results showed a considerable increase in IQ levels of the enriched children throughout the programme and into school, although this could be due to either of the factors noted in the previous paragraph.

So what have these studies told us about the influence of the environment? Because children's IQ scores can increase, and that increase persists, this suggests that the environment does have some influence. However, this is not sufficient evidence to support the environmental view conclusively because:

METHODS

- correlational studies again form the largest basis of evidence and these only show that a more stimulating and physically healthy environment is correlated with greater intellectual development, not that it causes intellectual development
- it *could* be that this is the reason for higher IQ scores, but if it is we need to tease out just which aspects of this type of environment are the most important

- a stimulating environment is one which also enables children to perform better on IQ tests, for example they are more likely to be able to name a familiar object or answer questions such as 'In what way are a pear and orange alike?'

Nevertheless, evidence from environmental studies is substantial enough to challenge the predominance of the hereditarian view of intelligence as largely fixed and stable.

The nature/nurture debate on intelligence – why is it likely to remain inconclusive?

It is clear from the evidence we have examined that we are still unable to identify how much heredity and how much environment contribute to individual differences in intelligence. The nature/ nurture debate on intelligence is likely to remain inconclusive for the following reasons.

DEFINING INTELLIGENCE

Yes, this is still a problem! Donald Hebb (1949) said this was because intelligence has two meanings:

COGNITION
- one meaning is that intelligence is an 'innate potential', the capacity for development, which is due to qualities of the brain and how it functions: this is innate and not measurable

SOCIAL
- the other meaning is that intelligence is the result of interaction between this innate potential and the environment.

Hebb's point, with which other psychologists agree, is that when we talk of differences in intelligence we are referring to the second meaning, and that is what IQ tests measure. However, more recent research on infomation processing has enabled psychologists to incorporate the first meaning into measurements of intelligence.

SOCIAL
Another difficulty is that intelligence is a concept, it is abstract, so the only way we can measure it is to look at intelligent *behaviour*. But this depends on culture – behaviour which is intelligent in one culture is not necessarily viewed as intelligent in another. Therefore intelligence is developed in and defined by the culture in which it operates. Indeed, there is an argument that measuring intelligence is not particularly useful, but we are concerned about it because it is important for our individualist and competitive Western cultures.

METHODOLOGICAL DIFFICULTIES

METHODS

Investigations of intelligence are hampered by a number of methodological difficulties which may, in turn, affect their results. These difficulties may account for some of the conflicting evidence we have seen, and are likely to continue. For example:

- it is impossible to completely separate the two factors, for example intellectual abilities are not fully developed at birth, they mature and develop by exposure to the environment, but it is difficult to test how important environment is. Even if psychologists were able to separate identical twins at birth and rear them in completely different environments (which is **unethical**), they would not be representative of the normal population and the conclusions would be of limited **validity**.
- because the variables being examined are naturally occurring, much of the research is correlational, which is unable to identify cause and effect.
- IQ tests beg the question 'What is intelligence' – they only measure some aspects of intelligent behaviour and they require some element of learning.

THE INTERACTIONIST POSITION

Today the nature/nurture debate in psychology is no longer dominant. Psychologists largely adopt the interactionist view because the evidence suggests that *both* innate abilities and environmental factors are crucial. The interactionist view is that both have a role to play, but it is how they interact which is of most interest. Thomas Bouchard (1990) suggests that our innate abilities and dispositions direct us to those aspects of our environment which interest us and are relevant to us. We may therefore pay little attention to experiences which are not useful to us.

One way of viewing this interaction is to think of intelligence as a rubber band: the innate aspect of intelligence determines how *long* the rubber band will be and the environment determines how *far* it will stretch. Some interactionist researchers have called this the 'reaction range', which is the extent to which intelligence can vary as a result of environmental factors. They propose that a child may have an IQ score of 83 but this can vary by 20–25 points depending on the environment to which the child is exposed. Therefore, because interactionist research is not concerned whether intelligence is due *either* to nature or nurture, it is unlikely to be able to resolve the nature-nurture debate.

Summary

This chapter started with a review of IQ tests and considered the problems of defining the concept of intelligence, and the limitations of IQ tests. Though some early tests were used to discriminate against particular cultural groups, IQ tests are now predominantly used as indicators of intelligence, to diagnose problems or for occupational purposes. Our review of the evidence for the hereditarian and environmental basis for individual differences in intelligence has underlined the difficulty of coming to any conclusions about which has more influence. Indeed, psychologists have largely retreated from efforts to discover which is more influential, and are now investigating how heredity and environment influence each other and how it is possible to help people maximise their potential.

Exercises

1 What is IQ and how is it calculated?
2 Describe one use for IQ tests.
3 From your study of psychology, describe and explain one limitation of IQ tests.
4 Why do psychologists study twins?
5 How has evidence from research on twins contributed to the view that intelligence is inherited?
6 Describe and explain the evidence which suggests that intelligence is mainly influenced by inheritance.
7 How have studies of social class contributed to the view that intelligence is influenced by environmental factors?
8 How has evidence from special intervention programmes contributed to the view that intelligence is influenced by environmental factors?
9 Describe and explain the evidence which suggests that intelligence is mainly influenced by environmental factors.
10 From what you have learned in psychology, why is the nature/nurture debate on intelligence likely to remain inconclusive?

The Development of Gender

14

When a baby is born one of the first questions we ask is – 'is it a boy or a girl?' The answer to this question will become a central part of how we see the baby. But the baby does not know what it means to be a boy or a girl. How does it find out? Are there real differences between the abilities and behaviours of males and females or do we just learn differences as we grow up? Some people who have been reared as males say they don't feel like a male, they feel as though they are a female. What do they mean? Answers to questions such as these have intrigued psychologists for decades. This chapter reviews some of their research and the theories which have been proposed to explain how we develop a sense of being male or female, with all that this entails. It is important to note that most of this material comes from Western societies – chiefly Britain and the United States. When we talk of what is 'typical' or 'appropriate' for males or females, we are referring to these societies.

Gender concept

In the study of gender, psychologists have used a bewildering variety of terms. You will see 'sex' used in contrast with 'gender' but some psychologists use these terms as if they mean the same thing. They argue that they refer to different things which are so closely related that it is difficult to distinguish between them. Nevertheless it is valuable to know this distinction, namely:

DEFINITION
- **sex** refers to biological aspects of the individual. For example, a child's sex is identified at birth by whether or not it has a penis – this is a sex difference.

DEFINITION
- **gender** refers to the psychological or social aspects of maleness or femaleness, which we acquire as we grow up. Our interest in this chapter is how

the child acquires these psychological and social aspects of maleness or femaleness, in other words how we acquire our **gender concept**.

Our gender concept is part of our self-concept – our knowledge and feelings about ourselves. This develops in part through our experiences in the social world, and in part through the way our thinking develops. Our gender concept includes:

DEFINITION

- **gender identity** – the clear understanding of ourselves as female or male, including the understanding that this stays the same, for ourselves and others, throughout our lives.

DEFINITION

- **gender role** – the behaviours, attitudes and beliefs associated with males and females. There is much discussion as to whether gender roles reflect real differences between males and females or simply reflect **gender stereotyping**. Gender stereotypes are the rigid ideas which society holds about what is typical of males and females. We consider them in more depth later in the chapter.

As you will see, each of the following explanations propose different relationships between gender identity, gender role and gender concept.

GENDER AND CHILDREN'S BEHAVIOUR

We are going to look at four explanations of how gender is acquired, but in order to evaluate them we need to know something about children's behaviour as they grow up. Research indicates that in relationship to gender, most children show the following patterns of behaviour.

- by two years of age children know their own sex 'label' and play more with gender-typed toys (girls with dolls, boys with guns) and they are more sociable with playmates of the *same* sex
- by three and a half years of age they can say which behaviours are shown by boys and which by girls as well as awareness of some of the characteristics of males and females ('Mummies are ladies')
- between three and five years of age children much prefer gender-typed toys and same-sex playmates, have more accurate knowledge of the characteristics of both genders but think that it can change – a man who puts on a dress may be called a lady. Those children who could 'label' themselves at a young age had more knowledge about gender than late labellers but both preferred same-sex activities.
- by five to six years of age children also know that gender is permanent, they show very strong preferences for same-sex activities and friends, they gender stereotype (boys stereotype more than girls: they make other boys conform to 'appropriate' boy behaviour but girls show less concern about another child's cross-sex behaviour)

- by seven or eight years of age the stereotypes for both sexes start to weaken: children begin to understand and accept non-stereotypical information such as men being nurses or women being soldiers
- differences in **family styles** seem to have little effect: children raised in one-parent, two parent or homosexual homes show no evidence of difficulties with their gender identity.

Now that we have noted some gender-related behaviours in children, they will help us evaluate the following explanations of how gender is acquired: psychodynamic, social learning, cognitive developmental and gender schema theory.

The psychodynamic explanation of gender

INBORN

According to Freud's psychoanalytic theory, **instinctive drives** underlie human behaviour. The way we cope with one of these drives – the libido – is what underpins our acquisition of gender identity and our adoption of the appropriate gender role (see personality p. 156). Freud argues that:

- at about four years of age the child enters the **phallic stage** of psychosexual development and experiences conflict between its unconscious desire for the opposite sex parent and fear of what will happen when the the same-sex parent finds out about these feelings.
- a boy experiences the **Oedipus conflict** because of his desire for his mother and fear that his father will castrate him. To resolve this conflict the boy identifies with his father – he adopts his father's behaviours, speech, and attitudes. His father is therefore less likely to harm him, and the boy feels closer to his mother. Through identification with his father the boy **internalises** male characteristics, he starts to perform his male role and his gender identity is formed.
- a girl experiences the **Electra conflict**: she has unconscious longings for her father and fears loss of her mother's love. She thinks she has already been castrated by her mother and is not so fearful of her as the boy is of his father. Her identification, in order to reduce the conflict, is therefore less strong than it is for a boy. Nevertheless she adopts her mother's characteristics and these form the basis for her female role and female identity.

FIGURE 14.1 This boy has identified with his father and is adopting his behaviours

EVALUATION OF THE PSYCHODYNAMIC EXPLANATION

INBORN

According to the psychodynamic view, gender differences are inevitable because they are based on an innate drive. These differences in gender identity and gender-related behaviour should be evident by about six years of age. The evidence we looked at earlier shows that gender-related behaviour *is* more apparent from about five years old onwards. Nevertheless children do show clear preference for sex-typed toys and friends a long time before the phallic stage is reached, which Freud's theory cannot explain.

Evidence for stronger stereotyping by males is explained by Freud – it is because the boy's identification with his father is stronger than the girl's identification with her mother. The reason for tomboyish girls is poor identification with the mother. However he is not able to explain why stereotyping for both sexes weakens as the child approaches adolescence.

A final criticism is that, according to Freud's explanation, children brought up in a single parent or homosexual families would have difficulties developing their gender role and gender identity, yet there is no evidence of this. Overall, then, the psychodynamic explanation does not provide an adequate explanation for the acquisition of gender.

The social learning explanation of gender

LEARNING

According to **social learning** theorists, children learn by **observing** and **imitating** others, and by **reinforcement** (see p. 16). These processes explain the acquisition of gender in the following way:

● Children are more likely to imitate the behaviour of same-sex models, whether parents, peers, cartoon characters or celebrities. This is why they prefer gender-typed toys: girls like make-up because they see women using it, boys prefer playing football because that is what men do.
● Someone who is seen to be reinforced for a behaviour is more likely to be imitated. A boy who sees a man congratulated for his bravery is more likely to act bravely himself than if the model had not been congratulated. A girl who hears a young woman being told what a good mother she is, is more likely to imitate 'mothering' behaviour.

FIGURE 14.2 These toys encourage the child to adopt gender-typed behaviour

● If the consequences of behaviour are rewarding it is more likely to be repeated. Adults often reward gender-typed behaviour, so a girl will receive approval when she plays at doing housework but not when she plays at being a gangster. Children's peers provide reinforcement and punishment – boys make fun of other boys when they do not conform to 'boy' behaviour (for instance when they cry or play with dolls). Toys, and the difference between them, give children messages about adult expectations and help the child imitate gender-typed behaviour.

● Through imitation and reinforcement the child gradually adopts appropriate **gender role** behaviours. As the child continues to perform this role it becomes internalised and the child acquires its **gender identity**.

COGNITION

● In the last ten years research on social learning has included more cognitive aspects. Research shows that children learn what behaviour is appropriate not simply by imitation but by noting how *frequently* behaviour is performed by those of the same sex. This indicates to them what is typical of their own sex, as well as of the other sex. K. Bussey and A. Bandura (1984) proposed that gender-typed behaviour is *initially* shaped by the responses of others, for example reinforcement such as 'what a big strong boy you are', but as the child gets older he constructs his own personal understanding based on his cognitive abilities and past reinforcement.

EVALUATION OF THE SOCIAL LEARNING EXPLANATION

This theory proposes that gender is learned and gender differences merely reflect what the child sees in society and could therefore be changed. By imitating and being rewarded for the appropriate gender role behaviours, children acquire their gender identity. Social learning theory explains why children play with gender-related toys (because adults provide them and play is modelled on adult behaviour). It also explains why boys are more concerned about cross-sex behaviour – it is because their fathers show disapproval of sons who show cross-sex behaviour.

LEARNING

The theory is unable to explain why children show such early gender-typed preferences, and why same-sex models are more important. Reinforcement and modelling are, by themselves, unlikely to produce such strong preferences at a very young age. This explanation predicts that children reared in single parent or homosexual families may have problems with gender identity if there is no same sex adult in a traditional role, but there is no evidence of this.

COGNITION

The newer cognitive element of the theory links with evidence for the increase in stereotyping at about six years of age but does not fully *explain* the reason for stereotyping. It also explains individual differences in gender behaviour, such as feminine boys or tomboyish girls. Overall this theory explains several features of gender development, but not all of them.

Cognitive developmental explanation of gender

COGNITION   Lawrence Kohlberg (1966) believed that the most important factor in the development of gender identity was the child's level of cognitive development which in turn depends on maturation (see p. 227). Once the child understands that gender is constant she will then start to take notice of same-sex models and adopt sex-typed behaviours and so her gender role develops. Kohlberg proposed that gender constancy develops through the following three stages.

STAGE 1 – GENDER LABELLING (UP TO THREE YEARS OLD)

By about 18 months of age the child knows what 'label' it is – boy or girl – and by the age of two and a half years old it can 'label' other children and adults. However its understanding is based largely on appearances and the child thinks a person's gender can change, so a man who puts on a dress would become a lady.

STAGE 2 – GENDER STABILITY (THREE TO FIVE YEARS OLD)

Gender stability is achieved when the child understands that it will be the same sex throughout its life – a girl will know that she will become a woman when she grows up. However, she can still be deceived by appearances (see conservation p. 230). Sandra Bem (1989) showed photographs to children who were between three and five and a half years old. The photographs were of a male and a female toddler with no clothes on the lower part of their bodies. It was clear which sex they were because their genitals were visible. However, on the *top* part of their bodies they wore clothes for the other sex, so the cultural definition of sex (clothes) was in conflict with the biological (genitals).

METHODS   Bem had to be very careful about the **ethics** in this study, for example the parents of the participants and of the toddlers who appeared in the photographs all saw the photographs first, and gave their written consent to their children's participation. In addition, when children were shown the photographs, it was in their own home, with at least one parent present.

Results were that 60% of the children were not sure whether the child was a boy or girl, indicating they were still at the stage of **gender stability**.

However, in another study of the same age group, children saw photographs of their classmates dressed in opposite sex clothes and almost *all* knew their classmates were still the same sex. This certainty could have been because they knew their classmates well, but Bem's photographs showed children who were not known to the participants.

STAGE 3 – GENDER CONSTANCY (FROM FIVE YEARS OLD ONWARDS)

COGNITION

In Bem's study the 40% of children who correctly identified the sex of the toddler had achieved **gender constancy**. Kohlberg proposed that once the child has this full understanding of gender, she has developed gender identity and will pay more attention to information related to females, copy same-sex models and thus adopt the appropriate gender role. This is demonstrated in research by Diane Ruble and her colleagues, who compared children who had high gender constancy with those whose gender constancy was low or weak.

Ruble, Balaban & Cooper (1981)

The **method** was that participants were assigned to one of three conditions, each having an equal number of participants who were either high or low in gender constancy.

The **procedure** was that in the two experimental conditions children saw a cartoon which was interrupted by a commercial. In one condition the commercial showed two boys playing with a gender-neutral toy, in the other condition two girls played with the same toy. In the control condition the participants only saw the cartoon. Afterwards each child had the opportunity to play with the toy and the researcher asked questions about whether the toy would be suitable for a little girl, a little boy or both.

The **results** showed that only those children who showed high gender constancy were affected by the sex of the children in the commercial. They avoided playing with the toy when the other sex models had been playing with it and said it would be an appropriate toy for that sex.

The **conclusions** were that once a child has achieved gender constancy it becomes active in searching out gender-appropriate toys and behaviour. Until then, says Ruble, the child is only passively influenced by reinforcement and information relating to gender.

EVALUATION OF THE COGNITIVE DEVELOPMENTAL EXPLANATION

SOCIAL

This theory proposes that once the child develops gender identity it starts to adopt appropriate gender role behaviour, so it explains why there is a sudden increase in children's concern about gender-appropriate behaviour and in stereotyping at about six years old. It also explains why gender identity is not affected by family style, because development depends in part upon the wide range of information the child receives from its environment, of which the family setting is only a part.

This theory is unable to explain why there are individual differences in conformity to gender roles and boys show more concern about conforming than girls. Neither does it explain why children show differences in choice of toys and playmates *before* gender constancy has developed. Attempts to address these weaknesses are incorporated into the next theory.

The gender schema explanation of gender

COGNITION

The gender schema explanation was developed through the 1980s and is cognitive, like the previous one. A schema is a mental framework, a way of organising our knowledge about our experiences. We use schemas to make sense of the world using what we already know, we notice information which is related to our schemas and they act as a guide for future action (see mental representation, p. 29). The **gender schema** explanation proposes that:

- the gender schema is very simple initially, it is based on the label boy or girl.
- the child starts to organise its experiences around these labels because our society uses them so much. Society says in effect 'these are useful ways of sorting out much of the information you receive'. Because the schema directs our attention to information which is relevant to us, the child notices more information relating to its own gender and less relating to the other.
- by about six years of age the child has developed gender identity (as proposed by Kohlberg) and pays much more attention to information which is relevant to its own gender. The child is testing the concept of gender and has rather fixed ideas about what is appropriate for its gender – it stereotypes, and this is a normal part of cognitive development. This rule testing is also one of the ways we form concepts (see p. 31).
- from about eight years of age onwards as the child's thinking becomes more abstract so its schema becomes more complex and flexible – children will say that a boy who likes to play with dolls may also like to play at

FIGURE 14.3 These young women belong to the Tamil Tigers in Sri Lanka. When shown this picture a 5 year old girl might say 'Ladies can't be soldiers', whereas a 9 year old might say it's OK for a girl to be a soldier, its just that I don't want to'.

dressing up, but they know he is still a boy. This flexibility develops initially in relation to their own gender schema because they have richer information about their own gender.

This explanation proposes that society tells children about gender – girl or boy, he or she, mummy or daddy – from birth. This helps the child, constantly faced with a bewildering amount of information, to organise its experiences in accordance with these schemas. According to this view, gender identity and gender-typed behaviour is not inevitable, it is a reflection of society's interpretation of the world.

EVALUATION OF THE GENDER SCHEMA EXPLANATION

Because gender schema theory incorporates the ideas of the cognitive developmental explanation, it has the same strengths. It also explains why a young child knows its own sex but is still confused about others and why children show considerable gender knowledge *before* gender identity at six years of age.

There are similarities with social learning theory, for example the schema develops as a result of the information provided by parents and others.

Gender schema theory also explains why, in social learning theory, the child attends to same-sex models: it is because the schema directs the child to notice information relevant to its own gender. Individual differences in gender-role behaviour are explained by individual differences in the way we organise and interpret information.

Overall, this is the most comprehensive explanation of how a child acquires its gender. Where it is weakest is in the early years because it still fails to explain fully why children show such strong sex-typed preferences at a very young age, although some answers to this are explored in the following section. Box 14.1 provides a summary of similarities and differences which will enable you to compare and contrast these four explanations of gender.

14.1

SIMILARITIES AND DIFFERENCES IN EXPLANATIONS OF GENDER

	PSYCHODYNAMIC EXPLANATION	SOCIAL LEARNING EXPLANATION	COGNITIVE DEVELOPMENTAL EXPLANATION	GENDER SCHEMA EXPLANATION
Are there innate factors?	yes – libido	no	yes – maturation	yes –maturation
How important are parents?	both parents essential	very important	fairly important	fairly important
Will one parent/ gay parent families affect gender development?	yes	possibly	no	no
Which are more important, social or cognitive factors?	neither (apart from parents)	social and some cognitive	cognitive and some social	cognitive and some social
What is the sequence of gender development?	identification ↓ gender identity + gender role	imitation ↓ gender role ↓ gender identity	gender constancy ↓ gender identity ↓ gender role	schema ↓ gender identity ↓ gender role

What evidence is there for gender differences?

We have already looked at explanations of why gender differences occur, but how different are males and females? This question has generated a huge quantity of research and sometimes the results conflict, one study showing a significant difference but another study showing very little difference. Eleanor Maccoby and Carol Jacklin (1974) published the **results** of their survey of more than 1,500 studies of research on sex differences. They noted few consistent differences, and these were not great. When looking at such research, it is valuable to remember that:

METHODS

- differences in the type of study, size of sample or methodology will produce differences in results which are difficult to compare
- researchers still debate what terms such as masculinity and femininity mean, partly because they are dependent on the social norms of a particular period

METHODS

- research which does show differences is more likely to be published than that which finds no differences, so the bias in published research gives an exaggerated impression of differences.

So published research tends to emphasise the *difference* between men and women whereas there is considerable overlap in abilities and characteristics. With these points in mind, we will look at some of the differences identified by Maccoby & Jacklin, namely aggression, play styles, visual-spatial ability and attributions for success and failure.

AGGRESSION

This is one of the most widely reported differences – males (boys and adults) show higher levels of aggression than females. J. Langlois (1980) studied pairs of children whilst they were playing. Some pairs were of the same sex and others were boy and girl. Their play and interactions were observed, and **results** showed little difference in levels of aggression at three years old. By five years old, however, boys consistently showed more aggression than girls – but only towards other boys.

LEARNING

A study of 10–12 year olds showed that children differ in their attitudes to aggressive children: aggressive boys got more attention than non-aggressive boys and were liked by their peers more. This is an example of boys rewarding their peers for aggressive behaviour. Aggressive girls were not liked by their peers, they spent more time in mixed-gender groups than other girls and tended to retaliate more.

The research of aggression by Albert Bandura which is reported on p. 139 provides evidence that boys show higher levels of aggression than girls. Boys also initiate more conflicts than girls, use heavy-handed tactics to get their way (such as physical aggression and threats), they tend to be more oppositional and likely to escalate conflict. This is related to the gender difference which we will consider next.

STYLES OF PLAY

SOCIAL

Research on play styles offers an explanation why very young children prefer to play with others of the same sex. **Results** show that girls spend more time than boys in face to face interaction and relatively quiet activities with one or two friends. Boys spend more time in large scale motor activity in a group.

Eleanor Maccoby (1988) reported an **observational** study of three year olds who were using a trampoline. Pairs of girls took turns jumping up and down on the trampoline, whereas boys tended to jump up and down on the trampoline and on each other, without thought for taking turns. This shows the higher levels of physical activity and lower level of concern for others which boys show – because these differences are evident at only three years of age they are unlikely to be learned. These differences in play styles may explain why girls and boys choose same-sex playmates and activities.

VISUALISING SPATIAL RELATIONSHIPS

COGNITION

Research suggests that males are generally better at visualising spatial relationships than females, which is one of the abilities assessed by intelligence tests. As part of the standardisation of the Wechsler Scale (see Intelligence Tests, p. 170) in the mid-1960s, over 2,000 6–16 year olds were tested in America. Results showed that, up to adolescence, boys were slightly better at visual-spatial tasks than girls. However, by the mid-teens, boys scored higher than girls on all types of visual-spatial tasks, an example of which is shown in Figure 14.4.

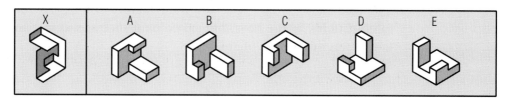

Look at figures A–E. Which of these shows figure X viewed from a different angle?

FIGURE 14.4 An example of a visual-spatial task

ATTRIBUTION FOR SUCCESS OR FAILURE

Some research has suggested that males and females tend to give different reasons when asked why they succeeded or failed at a task. Males are more likely to say they are responsible for their success ('I'm fairly good at this') but not for failure ('That was difficult'), whereas females tend to say they are responsible for their failures (I'm not very good at this') but not for their successes ('I was lucky').

David Burgner and Miles Hewstone wanted to see whether this difference was apparent at a young age. They provided a task which a participant could do easily (successful outcome) and one which was extremely difficult (unsuccessful outcome – failure), as described below.

Burgner & Hewstone 1993

Participants were boys and girls with a mean age of five and a quarter years.

The **materials** which were to provide a successful outcome were an easy seven-piece jigsaw. For the unsuccessful outcome there was a small loop which had to be moved along a twisted wire – if the loop touched the wire a buzzer sounded. A third task was provided which was similar to the wire and loop task, but was very easy. The results on this last task were not part of the experiment. The tasks were completed on a small table with the experimenter and child sat either side. A tape-recorder was hidden underneath the table to record the child's responses.

The **procedure** was that the experimenter demonstrated the jigsaw puzzle, then broke it up and asked the child to complete it. When the child had finished it was asked "Why did you think you could do/not do that?" The same sequence was repeated with the difficult loop and wire task, and then the easy task.

The **results** followed the expected pattern. Boys took credit for success and blamed something else for their failure. Some girls followed the same patterns as the boys, but others said success was due to luck and failure was due to lack of ability.

The researchers **concluded** that the differences in attributions that are given by adults are evident at five years of age. One possible explanation for this difference is that females do not want to boast. In a study which asked teenagers to rate successful characters in stories, half the characters were male and half female, and some boasted about their achievements whereas other characters were modest. **Results** showed that boasting characters were liked less, particularly if they were female. This may be the reason, rather than a different *perception* about their own abilities, why females are modest about their reasons for success.

To summarise, we have looked at only a fraction of the studies of gender differences, noting that results frequently contradict each other and looking at the reasons why this might be so. In addition, results of more recent research suggest that differences which were evident 30 years

SOCIAL

ago are less evident today. This is probably due to changing cultural expectations of men and women as well as greater sensitivity to gender stereotyping.

How are gender differences promoted and reinforced?

SOCIAL

Our social environment provides us with endless information about other people and, through our interaction with it, about ourselves. In this final section we will look at ways in which the social environment promotes and reinforces gender differences.

THE MEDIA

LEARNING

The media includes television, films, newspapers, magazines, radio, books, computer games and the internet. They are influential because they provide models as well as examples of vicarious reinforcement (as in social learning theory) and provide information which the child draws on as its gender concept and gender schema develop (as in cognitive theories).

COGNITION

One concern is that sometimes this information is biased, that males and females are portrayed stereotypically. Gender stereotypes are the rigid ideas which society holds about the typical behaviours, attitudes and beliefs of males and females, so stereotyping in the media promotes differences between males and females. It also reinforces differences when models are themselves rewarded for sex-typed behaviour. This topic can be studied using the **content analysis** technique, as in A. Manstead & C. McCulloch's study (see p. 202).

METHODS

Manstead & McCulloch's **results** confirm other research on gender stereotyping in the media, namely that males are frequently portrayed as authorities, workers, independent, active; females are portrayed as dependent, home-based, consumers, passive.

In children's fairy stories (Snow White, Sleeping Beauty, Cinderella, Rumpelstiltskin) there are beautiful helpless heroines who are rescued by strong adventurous princes. History books are filled with males who are heroes, kings, explorers, adventurers, scientists – with little mention of women. In computer games and cartoons males perform 'action' roles; even where women take the lead they are attractive as well.

Are children aware of the gender differences being promoted? Aletha Huston (1984) noted that adverts for boys' toys were loud and fast, whereas those for

Manstead & McCulloch (1981)

The **sample** comprised all advertisements transmitted by Granada Television beteween 6 and 11.30 pm over seven days in July 1979, except for repeats and those portraying only children or fantasy characters. The total sample was 170.

The **procedure** was that each advertisement was analysed independently by two investigators who coded the central figures (no more than two in an advert) in terms of various characteristics, such as role (e.g. parent, homemaker, professional, interviewer); location (eg. home, occupational setting); whether they were product users or authorities on the product; reasons for using the product (eg. opposite sex approval, self-enhancement, saving effort, career advancement).

The **results** showed that 70% of the figures seen to give authoritative information about products were male but 65% of product users were females; females appeared much more frequently in dependent roles and men in autonomous roles; 64% of figures seen at work were males, whereas 73% of figures seen at home were females; females were more likely to use a product for reasons of social approval or self-enhancement.

girls' toys were soft and fuzzy. When six year olds were shown adverts for a 'neutral' toy, but in either the 'fast' or the 'fuzzy' style, they could tell whether it was aimed at a girl or a boy by the style it used. Other research has shown a positive correlation between the amount of time children spent watching television and how stereotypical their views were.

Critics argue that media influence might not be so extensive because:

METHODS
- content analysis research, like Manstead & McCulloch's, does not give a complete picture. For instance an advert may be designed to make fun of the stereotypes by exaggerating them or by using them inappropriately with a product, which the content analysis may not allow for.

COGNITION
- children are active in selecting information and developing their own understanding (as we have seen in social learning and cognitive explanations), so evidence that children can differentiate between adverts does not mean that they accept the images they project.

SOCIAL
- everyday experiences with family, school and friends provide the child with information which may not conform to stereotypes.

- the media also provide non-stereotypical information, the characters in children's books are less stereotyped, increasingly women are seen in positions of authority and performing non-stereotypical roles in TV programmes. This could be one reason for the popularity of 'Absolutely Fabulous', in which the female characters go *against* the stereotypes for mothers, daughters and middle-aged women.

FIGURE 14.5 Absolutely Fabulous – challenging female stereotypes

PARENTS

Research suggests that parents actively promote and reinforce gender differences, for example:

COGNITION

- Jeffrey Rubin (1974) and his colleagues found that parents *expect* gender differences because within 24 hours of their baby's birth they described their girls as softer and smaller than parents of boys, who thought their boys were more alert, stronger and better co-ordinated. Fathers tended to see greater differences between the sexes than mothers, though there was no apparent physical difference between the male and female infants.

- Babies are treated differently depending on what sex they are *thought* to be. Observations of experienced mothers interacting with a 'stranger' baby revealed that when the baby was dressed as a boy it was handled more vigorously and given toys such as a hammer-shaped rattle. When the *same* baby was dressed as a girl it was held and talked to more and given soft toys to play with. So parents may be stereotyping the baby from birth and the growing child will learn these expectations from the way it is treated.

- Parents respond differently to their child's behaviour. Robert Sears (1977) and his colleagues found parents tolerated aggression in their sons much more than in their daughters and parents were more likely to punish a boy if he hit a girl than if he hit another boy. Research shows that fathers are more concerned that children show appropriate behaviour, particularly their sons. They will discourage boys from 'girls' activities but are less troubled if girls play 'tomboy' games.

LEARNING

- Through the process of the self-fulfilling prophecy (see p. 220), parental expectations can promote and reinforce differences. The expectations a father has of his son when he kicks a ball around are likely to be different when his daughter is kicking a ball. These expectations will be conveyed in the amount of time and encouragement he gives each child. Some studies have shown that mothers have lower expectations of their daughter's achievement in maths, as have some maths teachers!

What if parents do not promote or reinforce gender differences? Recent research on six-year olds whose parents tried to treat them the same, regardless of their sex, shows that they were not much different from conventionally reared children in their choice of friends and play activities. However, they *did* hold less stereotyped beliefs. This suggests parental influence on their understanding may be stronger than the influence on their behaviour.

SCHOOL

SOCIAL

School is an important social setting for children. It gives them opportunities to negotiate relationships with others: peers and teachers provide models and reinforcement (or punishment) for behaviour. Ways in which gender differences can be promoted and reinforced in the school environment include:

- If children are separated on the basis of gender – 'Boys line up here and girls over here' – or are prohibited from studying certain subjects at school, this promotes and reinforces gender differences.
- Research in the 1970s showed differences in the way teachers treated children – they spent more time talking to boys than girls. This seemed to be partly because boys were more disruptive in class, but also teachers were found to have higher expectations of boys than of girls.

LEARNING

- The role models which teachers provide are also influential. The majority of primary teachers are female, yet a greater proportion of headteachers are male. In secondary schools there are more males than females teaching science and maths and holding senior positions. This tells children what sort of jobs males and females do.

Summary

We have seen various explanations for how children develop their ideas of what it means to be male or female in their society, although none of the theories explain fully how it occurs. As social learning theory develops a much stronger cognitive content, its explanation bears a close resemblance to the gender schema explanation. Apart from Freud's explanation, they all suggest that social factors play a major part in promoting gender differences. Evidence for gender differences is changing, but most marked and persistent is levels of aggression, and even that varies from culture to culture. Society itself is also changing. In the 1950's, only men had short hair and wore trousers, only women had ponytails and wore earrings – now these differences have disappeared. Stereotyped ideas of the male as breadwinner are less strong and many of the gender-typed jobs, such as typists or shipwrights, are obsolete. This makes it harder, and perhaps less useful, to study gender differences.

Exercises

1 What do psychologists mean by gender?
2 Explain the difference between sex and gender.
3 Explain what psychologists mean by gender concept.
4 Describe one psychological explanation of the development of gender.
5 Outline two psychological explanations of the development of gender. Include one point of similarity and one difference between them.
6 Give one example of a gender difference that has been supported by the findings of psychologists.
7 Describe a study which provides evidence that females and males behave differently.
8 Describe how the media influence gender development.
9 Explain how the media reinforce and promote gender stereotypes.
10 Describe one way in which others, for example teachers, promote and reinforce gender differences.

Towards a Concept of Self

In this chapter we are going to look at the idea of 'self'. Philosophers and psychologists have discussed the peculiar situation which results from thinking about ourselves. When we study ourselves we are both the *object* being studied *and* the person doing the studying. Imagine you have a dilemma – will you go out tonight with friends or stay in and study? As you make your decision you can, at the same time, observe how you are responding to your friends' persuasion, deciding whether to spend money now or wait till the weekend. As you will see in this chapter, this self-observation is one way in which we learn about ourselves – about the kind of person we are and how we feel about ourselves. We will also find out how other people help us to know about ourselves, how they provide us with information and provide the opportunity to 'play' at being different kinds of people. This information contributes to our understanding of who we are – our concept of self.

What is a concept of self?

When you have developed a concept of self, you have developed a sense of what it means to be you, of yourself in relation to others. In Western societies the self is seen as separate from the society in which the individual lives, whereas in many other societies the self is part of society as a whole. Even in the West, our understanding of self depends crucially on the society in which we live – it develops as we find out more about ourselves through our social experiences.

SOCIAL

In order for a concept of self to develop, you first have to see yourself as separate from the rest of the world, to recognise yourself as a separate physical entity. This is fairly well established by the age of 15–18 months, then the toddler starts to gather information which relates to itself, of what makes it special. Let us just run through three of the ways in which we gather this knowledge, before we look at self-concept in more depth.

- **Information from others** – toddlers hearing 'Aren't you a good boy?' or 'That's a clever girl' receive information about what gender they are and how people feel about them. Charles Cooley (1902) used the term 'the looking glass self', which means that we see ourselves as others see us. However not everyone sees us the same way: your parents' view is different from your teacher's which is different from your friend's view. Each reflects back a different 'self' to us, though the views of some people are more important than others.

- **Self-observation** – according to **self-perception theory**, we find out about ourselves by observing our own behaviour. When we are not sure about our abilities or feelings, we watch how we behave, we notice the outcomes of our actions and how we feel about them. For example, if you regularly get good marks in your studies you think of yourself as a good student and, if this is what you want to be, you will be pleased with yourself. Thus, by observing your behaviour and feelings you gather information for your self-concept.

- **Comparison with others** – we compare ourselves with others in order to find out about ourselves. Even the young child notices that people are big or small, men or women, old or young: they try to find out where they 'fit' in these categories. We also look to others to see how we are doing compared to them. If most people get a 'C' grade for homework and you get a 'B' then you think you are doing fairly well.

Throughout the rest of this chapter you will see how we use information from these three sources in order to develop our self-concept – our knowledge of what it means to be 'me'. Let us now look at what the self-concept is composed of, and how others contribute to it.

The components of the self-concept

DEFINITION If I want to understand what it means to be me, I need to have developed knowledge about 'me' (or myself) as distinct from others. This knowledge forms my self-concept, which has been defined as the set of views or beliefs which the individual has about him or herself. It consists of the following parts which we will consider in turn now:

- **self-image** refers to how you see yourself, what you know about yourself.
- **ideal self** refers to the kind of person you would like to be.
- **self-esteem** refers to how you feel about yourself, your evaluation of yourself. One way in which we evaluate ourselves is to compare our **self-image** with our **ideal self** – the closer they are the higher our **self-esteem** is.

SELF-IMAGE

Psychologists investigating **self-image** (the knowledge you have about yourself) have asked people to describe themselves. Children typically give answers such as 'I'm Jon, I'm eight, I like football, I'm tall, I've got a sister, I go to Rivermead School'. The self-image of children usually consists of facts and external or physical features. An adult might say 'I'm female, a mother, a hairdresser, an Aquarian, fairly shy, Welsh'. The adult's answers include more

social roles and traits: this reflects the adult's more complex social experiences and understanding.

The way others treat us provides information for our self-image. If several people **stereotype** or **label** us (see the last two sections in this chapter), this may become a central aspect of our self-image. Information which we acquire when young becomes more central to our self-image, and seems to remain so. For example, Michael Argyle (1983) showed how distinctive features may persist as part of our self-image. He found that girls who were taller than average at 13 years of age still saw themselves as taller later in life, even though they were average height then.

Self-image varies from culture to culture, reflecting different attitudes to the individual and the society in which the individual lives. In a study asking American and Japanese participants to describe themselves, **results** showed that the Americans cited personality traits four times as often as the Japanese, but the Japanese cited social roles and situations three times more often. We can **conclude** that Americans think of themselves as autonomous entities, whereas the Japanese consider themselves in terms of social contexts.

IDEAL SELF

Our **ideal self**, is the kind of person we would like to be. We may want to look like someone else, be as talented, be popular with the opposite sex, be a good student. We choose our 'ideals' but they are also provided for us by others such as teachers, the media and of course parents – 'Why can't you keep your room tidy like your brother does?'

SELF-ESTEEM

Self-esteem refers to our evaluation of ourselves. How much do you like the kind of person you think you are? Do you accept yourself as you are? Do you think you are worthwhile? Our self-esteem comes from a number of sources – we will look at three of these now.

FIGURE 15.1 For some people Kate Moss and Michael Owen represent ideals

Comparison of self-image and ideal self

We compare our **self-image** (what we know of ourselves) to our **ideal self**, and the greater the gap between them, the lower our **self-esteem**. If we set our ideals too high – we cannot all be a Kate Moss or a Michael Owen – then we are likely to experience low self-esteem. Alternatively, the closer we think we are to our ideal self, the higher our self-esteem, so one way to avoid low self-esteem is to have a realistic ideal self.

We know that physical attributes are part of our self-image, so satisfaction with our appearance increases our self-esteem. For example, in our society muscle strength is a characteristic of the 'ideal' man: research with males has shown that the greater the muscle strength, the higher the man's self-esteem.

Those traits which are highly valued in our culture provide ideals by which to judge ourselves and will be more important to us than less valued traits. For instance, high achievers living in a competitive culture are more likely to have high self-esteem than if they lived in a culture stressing mutual co-operation

Information from others

SOCIAL

Our self-esteem also depends on what others think of us, whether they value us or feel we are worthwhile. Once again, information received in the early years has a powerful effect. Stanley Coopersmith (1967) investigated self-esteem and its relationship to parental influence. This **longitudinal** study followed white middle-class boys in the USA from 10 years old up to adulthood. As a result of **questionnaires**, tests and **interviews** with teachers, parents and the boys, Coopersmith identified high self-esteem and low self-esteem boys, although there was no difference in intelligence and physical attractiveness between the two groups.

METHODS

Results showed a positive correlation between high self-esteem boys and parents who created a warm accepting environment, gave responsibility but created firm guidelines. These parents also had high self-esteem and high expectations of their sons. High self-esteem boys were more popular and more successful as adults than the low self-esteem boys. We can **conclude** that parenting style is related to self-esteem, white middle-class boys.

FIGURE 15.2 Giving children responsibility should increase their self-esteem

In order to avoid loss of self-esteem, we manage our behaviour in a way which produces the kind of response we want from others, we create a 'self' to present to others. If we misjudge our 'audience' and they see through our act then we will suffer embarrassment and loss of self-esteem. We are more likely to manage this self-presentation in front of those who are important to us. This varies, for instance one study found female college students relied more on evaluations by their peers, but males on evaluation by their parents.

SOCIAL

Evidence that the way others treat us can affect our self-esteem comes from research on adolescents. Adolescence is a time of rapid physical change and research with boys suggests that those who are late maturing have less self-confidence than those whose physical maturity starts early. This can be explained through the self-fulfilling prophecy (see p. 220). **Results** showed that early maturers were treated in a more adult way, were seen as more confident and given more responsibility than later maturers. We can **conclude** that the self-esteem of these boys was influenced by other people's expectations.

Social identity

SOCIAL

Another source of self-esteem is provided by the groups to which we belong. According to Henri Tajfel (1978) they give us our **social identity**. He argued that we enhance our perceptions of our own group and devalue other groups in order to increase our self-esteem (see p. 118). For example, if the school or college you attend has a good reputation then this increases your self-esteem. However, if it has a poor reputation, this could lower your self-esteem so you might claim that other colleges are even worse.

Sometimes we cannot leave a group to which we belong, we cannot change our gender or race and this is why these groups are called 'closed' groups. Research shows that if we belong to a 'closed' group with low status we will boost our self-esteem by comparing ourselves with those in the group who we see as inferior to us in some way because this makes us feel better about ourselves. However consistent efforts to raise the status of groups has been shown to have a significant impact on the individual's self-esteem and behaviour. This was one aim of the Black Power and Feminist movements (see p. 128).

Protecting and enhancing self-esteem

As we have just seen in social identity theory, individuals act to protect and enhance their self esteem. We try to see ourselves in a good light, for example if given a list of adjectives and asked which apply to us, we tend to choose the positive ones. One study found that people even put a higher value on the letters which appear in their name when compared to others in the alphabet! We value activities we are good at more than those we are not and consider

COGNITION

our negative aspects to be less important than our positive ones. Diane Ruble (1987) found that children consciously avoid situations which might lower their self-esteem and create an environment which is likely to raise their self-esteem.

Social roles

We have seen that we need others in order to develop self-concept, and Erving Goffman (1959) proposed that we have a core self which originates in the social roles we have learned to play. He proposed that we are like actors, performing roles in front of an audience (others). He describes the three stages through which the role, and therefore the core self, develops:

- **First stage** – we imitate those around us. In early childhood we imitate without knowing the meaning of what we do. As adults when we take on a new role we imitate the behaviour of others who perform this role – we wear a 'mask'.
- **Second stage** – the child acts out roles performed by others who are important. By playing these roles we start to understand the context in which different roles are played, what is appropriate and how others react to our performance. A child feeding his teddy-bear or a group playing at hospitals are acting out adult roles. We perform the role until others accept the identity we project and we feel comfortable in it, then *we* can accept it.
- **Third stage** – we accept the role and integrate it with our other roles into a coherent whole – what Goffman calls our core self (our self-concept).

FIGURE 15.3 Some of the abilities which this little girl brings to her nurse role may become important to her self-concept

Researchers studying self-concept have asked people to give 20 answers to the question 'Who am I'. Results show that seven year olds mentioned five roles on average and undergraduates averaged ten. This reflects the number of roles we take on as we move out into the world, as well as the importance of roles in our self-image. Four types of role mentioned frequently by adults are:

- family roles (such as father, mother, sister, grandparent)
- occupational roles (such as shop assistant, nurse, student)
- marital roles (such as single, married, divorced)
- religious roles (such as Catholic, Muslim).

SOCIAL

Social roles bring expectations, these are called the **norms** of the role. For example a mother is expected to be loving and protective of her child. Equally, when we are performing a role we expect that others will treat us in a certain way. A teacher expects her students to sit fairly quietly and listen when she speaks, students expect the teacher to help them understand the subject.

We learn the expectations of these roles by watching and listening to others. Sometimes our observations are deliberate (such as watching what others do on your first day at college) but for other roles we learn what the expectations are without any conscious effort, for example the role of son or friend.

One very powerful study of the influence of roles was carried out by Philip Zimbardo and his colleagues and is described on page 214. He commented on the 'frightening' results of this study, which is often called the Prison Simulation Experiment. Within six days 'prisoners' had become withdrawn and obedient, 'guards' had become aggressive and punitive. 'Prisoners' who attempted to rebel were punished by denial of food, being deprived of sleep and verbal abuse. Several 'guards' commented on the 'high' they felt at having power, and a few were disappointed when the study ended abruptly. Even the less hostile 'guards' never challenged the aggressive ones, a high level of aggression was the **group norm**. Zimbardo **concluded** that this showed the power of social forces to affect people's behaviour.

HOW DO SOCIAL ROLES CONTRIBUTE TO SELF-CONCEPT?

Social roles contribute to our self-concept because they enable us to find out:

- about the kind of person we are as we perform a role (our **self-image**)
- how to perform a role by using others as models (for our **ideal self**)
- how we feel about ourselves in the performance of a role (our **self-esteem**)

Zimbardo et al (1973)

The **aim** of the study was to see whether the dehumanising effects of prisons was due to the nature of prisoners, the nature of prison staff or the prison environment itself.

The **sample** comprised 21 participants who were selected as a result of an advertisement. All were white middle-class males who were randomly assigned to one of two groups, either a prisoner or a guard.

The **procedure** was that a mock prison was built in the basement of Stanford University. 'Guards' met to receive uniforms and basic instructions on their duties, and were explicitly directed that there was to be no violence. 'Prisoners' returned to their homes but did not know when the experiment was to start. They were 'arrested' early one morning, taken to the prison, stripped, dressed in loose gowns and put in cells.

Observers watched and recorded the behaviour of prisoners and guards over the next few days. The experiment was terminated before it was half-way through due to the extreme reaction of the prisoners.

We will look at examples of each of these as we consider how social roles contribute to self-concept.

Social roles and self-image

COGNITION

Performing a role gives us information for our self-image. It gives us an opportunity to observe ourselves in various settings and **infer** what kind of person we are. In Zimbardo's study, a 'guard's' **self-image** may have changed when he discovered 'I am the sort of person who could treat someone very badly', or perhaps even more importantly 'I am someone who *enjoys* treating people badly'.

If the role is new we may not feel comfortable in it and, like the newly qualified cadet in Figure 15.4, it may be a while before our self-image incorporates this new role. We may indeed try to reject an unwanted role when it is thrust upon us. Becoming unemployed creates a new social identity which you may not want to take on because of the negative affect on your self-image and your self-esteem.

Goffman notes that our core self is formed as we incorporate and integrate new roles, but integration can be difficult when we take on several new roles at once. This is especially true when the roles are associated with very

FIGURE 15.4 The way this cadet is treated when performing his new role will affect his self-esteem

different behaviours. Teenagers, for example, try out many new roles in a short period of time, which can cause confusion in their **self-image**. Their parents might continue to treat them as children, but in new roles as students or part-time workers others may treat them as equals, give them important responsibilities or freedom to make their own decisions. The expectations of these roles conflict, yet teenagers have to integrate the various 'selves' which they discover as a result of performing these roles.

Despite this rather fragmented view of self, it seems that we are able to maintain a consistent self-image. These are the **conclusions** from a study of middle-aged women's self-concept and their roles. They were asked to describe themselves in the role of worker, wife, friend and daughter in terms of qualities such as competence and dependability. **Results** showed that they differed across roles, but were highly consistent from role to role. For example, one might say she was very dependable as a worker but not so dependable as a daughter, nevertheless overall she saw dependability as a part of her self-image.

Social roles, self-esteem and ideal self

SOCIAL

We use others to provide us with information about how to perform the role – they represent an 'ideal' model for the role. We internalise these ideas about what a good mother, or a successful student, or a 'real' man is like – they become part of our ideal self. When we perform the role, we judge ourselves against these ideals. For example a mother who is often impatient with her child may feel this is not the way a 'good' mother would behave. The difference between her ideal self and her self-image may lower her self-esteem.

Social roles, self-esteem and others

Performing roles give us an opportunity to evaluate ourselves and be evaluated by others: we use their feedback to tell us how well we are doing. If other people treat the cadet in Figure 15.4 in accordance with his new role, this means he is successfully approaching his 'ideal' for a cadet, which will increase his **self-esteem**. In contrast, for example, a teacher who cannot control a class of children may develop low self-esteem – the children show by their behaviour that he is not performing the role well.

SOCIAL

We saw earlier that if we have traits which our society values, we are more likely to have high self-esteem. This is also true for roles, for example if you perform a highly-valued role (such as a doctor), this role enhances your self-esteem. Many feminists have argued that the child-care role, which is mainly performed by women, is not valued in western societies and that this is why house-bound mothers experience low self-esteem.

Other people tend to treat us in accordance with the social roles we perform, but sometimes we may not want to be treated in this way. We may try to distance ourselves from a role, though this can cause problems because a professional role such as a nurse or police officer brings constraints on behaviour (despite the police officer pictured in Figure 15.5!). The role of mother or friend is less subject to formal constraints, but still you may risk rejection by others if you deviate too far from the norms of some roles. This may be true, for example, of boys who fail to conform to their gender role (see p. 192).

Labelling

DEFINITION

Labelling is the term used when we classify someone and make the label explicit to them, such as 'difficult', 'clever', 'schizophrenic', 'foreigner'. Labels may be applied to individuals by people who have more power, such as a parent or an expert. The label becomes:

COGNITION

● a way of **organising information**, for instance we use labels in the acquisition of gender (see p. 195). The label boy (or girl) is given to the child

FIGURE 15.5 This police officer is trying to distance herself from her role

from the moment it is born and the child uses the label to categorise the behaviours, dress, attitudes of other people in order to find out what being a 'boy' or 'girl' means.

COGNITION

- a way of **explaining behaviour**, for example a pupil who frequently interrupts a teacher with questions might have been labelled 'bright' – the behaviour will be interpreted as evidence of curiosity. If the pupil has been labelled 'difficult' the interruptions will show how disruptive she is.
- the **basis for our judgement** and treatment of others. For example, when faced with the questioning pupil our teacher is likely to treat the' clever' child patiently but to discipline the child who has been labelled 'difficult'. When the individual knows the label which has been given them, they too may interpret their behaviour in accordance with the label and it becomes part of their self-concept.

A study by David Rosenhan provides evidence that if others have a label for us, they will use it to explain our behaviour and as a basis for their treatment of us. He arranged for eight researchers to request admission to mental hospitals throughout the USA on the basis that they were hearing voices (which is a symptom of schizophrenia). However, from the moment of their admission they acted normally and said that they no longer heard voices. Rosenhan was interested to find out how each of these 'patients' were treated.

Results showed that they were diagnosed as schizophrenic and kept in from between 7–52 days. None of the staff challenged this label, though genuine

COGNITION

patients said 'You're not crazy, you're a journalist or a professor'. Researchers observed that the hospital routine and lack of activity led to behaviours that were quite normal (for example frustration) in the patients, but the staff perceived such behaviours as evidence of mental disorder. In other words, this label was used to interpret the patient's behaviour.

HOW DOES LABELLING INFLUENCE SELF-CONCEPT AND BEHAVIOUR?

Arnold Sameroff (1983) proposed that this tendency to interpret an individual's behaviours in the light of the label can have a profound effect on the individual's self-concept and behaviour. Imagine a girl who has been labelled 'difficult' by her parents or teacher:

COGNITION

● her **self-image** includes the knowledge that she is 'difficult' because she is told she is difficult, is described to others as difficult and is treated as difficult. As we saw earlier, a teacher may interpret frequent questioning in class as disruptive behaviour and reprimand the child. Through self-observation she notices what behaviour is labelled as difficult and **infers** that being 'difficult' makes her distinctive from others, so it becomes part of her self-image as she gradually internalises this label.
● her **self-esteem** is affected because she receives more punishment and blame, she may feel others do not value her and knows she is failing to meet the standards set by them (her ideal self): all of this may contribute to low self-esteem. However, being difficult gets attention and makes her **distinctive** – if this is important to her then her self-esteem may be enhanced by this label.
● as the label is incorporated into the child's self-image, it becomes one of the ways the child defines herself and is thus important to her sense of self. She is more likely to behave as though she *is* 'difficult' because she thinks this is the kind of person she is. The child is constantly seeking information from others in order to build up a picture of who and what she is – this label provides that information.

SOCIAL

Thomas Szasz (1974), has argued that when we want to exclude others we give them negative labels – foreigner, criminal, mentally ill and so on. Such labels are used for people who do not conform to the **social norms** of their society. The label acts as a stigma and allows us to treat others with less respect, concern and humanity. As we have already noted, such treatment is likely to lead to low self-esteem which in turn affects behaviour. Those with low self-esteem may become withdrawn and depressed, a condition which may persist and affect many areas of their lives.

In the Zimbardo prison study we looked at earlier, the label 'prisoner'

FIGURE 15.6 A scene from 'One Flew Over the Cuckoo's Nest' – a film which provides many examples of labelling and its effects on individuals

allowed the guards to treat prisoners badly. After the failed rebellion they became withdrawn and passive: the experiment was stopped in order to prevent further deterioration in the prisoners' mental well-being. Nevertheless, their treatment and the knowledge that they behaved in this way may have become part of their **self-concept**.

COGNITION

Labels help us to organise and interpret information and thus make sense of the world. For example, a boy's gender schema includes information for the **ideal self** ('boys are strong', 'boys play football', 'boys grow up to be men'). The boy wants to meet these ideals so he does 'boy' things and imitates same-sex models. As he performs 'boy' behaviours his knowledge of himself (his self-image) develops and the greater the match between his **self-image** and his ideal self, the higher his **self-esteem**.

In Chapter 13 on Intelligence we noted that in the 1950s and 1960s children took the 11+ test (see p. 171). 'Passing' or 'failing' the 11+ test became a label which affected the child's self-concept. We have seen that early information about the self seems to persist in the individual's self-concept, so the child who 'passed' would be more likely carry into adulthood the image of himself as clever and successful. The child who failed would be likely to have low self-esteem which would lead him to think 'I can't do that', 'I'm not clever enough to be an accountant', 'I'm not the type of person who goes to university'. Their **self-image** could affect their future behaviour.

The self-fulfilling prophecy

DEFINITION A **self-fulfilling prophecy** is the process by which someone's expectations about another person come true. If you have expectations of someone, you treat them in accordance with those expectations. In turn *they* respond to the way you treat them, so that in fact their behaviour fulfils your expectation of them – they behave as you thought they would. Your expectations are not made explicit (as they are in labelling); here it is what is *implied* in your behaviour which affects the behaviour of the other. These stages in the self-fulfilling prophecy are illustrated in Figure 15.7

Evidence for the self-fulfilling prophecy comes from Mark Snyder (1977) and his colleagues. Male students conducted phone conversations with female students who the males thought were either attractive or unattractive. The males were much livelier when they thought they were talking to the 'attractive' females rather than the 'unattractive' females. Judges listened to the female sides of the conversations and the females who shared in the lively conversations were judged as being more attractive. From these **results** we

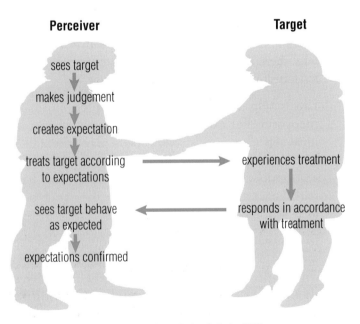

FIGURE 15.7 The self-fulfilling prophecy process (from Darley & Fazio 1980)

could **conclude** that their responses were affected by the way the male callers conversed with them, so the callers' expectations were fulfilled.

The Snyder **experiment** took place in a laboratory, but what about real life? Children are particularly vulnerable to the self-fulfilling prophecy because as we have already noted, they depend on others to provide information for the development of their self-concept. Robert Rosenthal and Lenore Jacobson investigated this because they felt that teachers unwittingly conveyed their expectations to students, which then affected students' performance (see p. 222).

Rosenthal noted that the treatment towards the 'bloomers' transmitted the teacher's expectations to the child in several ways. The teacher used more eye contact, smiling and nodding; they gave more accurate feedback about their work, perhaps saying where they could improve it rather than just a general 'well done'; they pushed these students more and gave them more chance to answer questions in class.

Rosenthal & Jacobson **concluded** that it was the teachers' expectations which had caused the increase in IQ scores and therefore that the self-fulfilling prophecy did occur in a real-life setting. They suggested that it was most evident in the early years because the teachers had not formed expectations of the children, so they were more influenced by the false IQ information. Also because younger children are more vulnerable to the opinions and treatment of others they tend to be more easily influenced.

COGNITION   The self-fulfilling prophecy may also occur when we stereotype someone because the stereotype will trigger certain expectations. These expectations may be confirmed through the process of the self-fulfilling prophecy, as the other person behaves in accordance with our expectations. This is why the self-fulfilling prophecy is closely related to the maintenance of prejudice and discrimination (see p. 128).

HOW DOES THE SELF-FULFILLING PROPHECY INFLUENCE SELF-CONCEPT AND BEHAVIOUR?

The self-fulfilling prophecy influences our self-concept because if, for example, someone sees us as friendly, we fulfil this expectation by our behaviour. Through self-observation we see ourselves behaving in a friendly way and this provides information for our **self-image**.

The self-fulfilling prophecy also affects **self-esteem** because the way others treat us tells us how valued we are. Consider Snyder's research and imagine how the self-esteem of the 'attractive' female students might have been

Rosenthal & Jacobson (1966)

The **procedure** was that at the beginning of the school year the researchers gave IQ tests to children aged 6–12 years old in one school. The test was unfamiliar to the teachers, who were told that it was a way of identifying 'bloomers' – children who were about to show a rapid increase in their learning abilities. The researchers let slip the names of the students who had come out in the top 20%. This information was false, the names had been randomly selected from each class by the researchers. At the end of the academic year all the children in the school were tested again.

The results are displayed in Figure 15.8

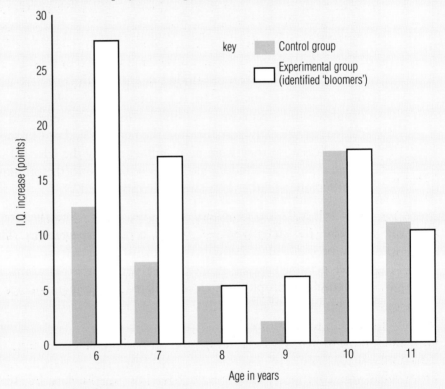

FIGURE 15.8 Bar chart showing percentage increase in IQ score for students in each year (from R. Rosenthal & L. Jacobson 1966)

The **results** indicate that children in the first two years of school showed roughly twice the increase in IQ scores when compared to the control group, as did the 9 year olds. However there was no difference in the increase in IQ scores for the other children, in particular the older ones.

affected by their treatment: imagine how the 'blooming' students felt about themselves in the Rosenthal and Jacobson study. Equally, our self-esteem may be low because the way others treat us makes us feel we are not valued – we saw this earlier in the study of boys who were late maturers.

Summary

This chapter has shown the extent to which our self-concept is created by society and needs social support to maintain it. It has also shown that the expectations generated by labelling and by the self-fulfilling prophecy contribute to our self-concept and affect our behaviour. Although most cultures value both collectivist and individualist characteristics, Western societies tend to value individualism more than other cultures. In this chapter much of the earlier research reflects a concept of self which tends to be individualistic and bounded, whereas more recent research incorporates notions of self which are related to the culture in which the individual lives.

Exercises

1 What is self-concept?
2 What is meant by self-image and self-esteem?
3 How does a person's self-image contribute to their concept of self?
4 Give one example of a social role and explain how it might affect an individual's self-concept.
5 What is 'labelling'?
6 Give an example of labelling. Explain how this may affect a person's self-concept and behaviour.
7 What is a self-fulfilling prophecy?
8 Give an example of how a self-fulfilling prophecy might affect someone's self-concept and behaviour.
9 From what you have learned in psychology, how might parents affect a child's self-concept and behaviour?
10 Devise a study to test whether the self-fulfilling prophecy does occur. Briefly describe the research method and procedure you would use. Do not replicate the Snyder or Rosenthal & Jacobson studies.

COGNITIVE AND SOCIAL COMPETENCE

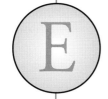

Section E examines the development of cognition and social behaviour. In Chapter 16 we look at two aspects of cognition – intellectual development and the development of visual perception.

The remaining three chapters consider various aspects of cognition in a social setting – which is known as social cognition. We look at how moral behaviour and understanding develops and at when and why we help others. We see how our own understanding can be affected by our mental processes, by the media and by other people.

As you are reading, note the tabs alongside the text. These indicate definitions, core topics (which are explained in Chapters 1–4) and methodology (which is explained in Chapters 5–7).

Cognitive Development

Imagine that your teacher showed you two pieces of string side by side, of the same length, and then scrunched one up. You would know it was still the same length as the other one, but a four year old child would not. This shows that our understanding of the world changes as we grow up, we think about things in a different way. How we see, think, remember and make sense of our world is known as cognition and by the end of this chapter you should have a clearer idea of what cognition means. We start by looking at an explanation for the child's developing cognition, and the second part of the chapter considers another aspect of cognition – how we make sense of what we see. This is called visual perception, and we focus on the role that heredity and the environment play in its development.

Piaget's theory of intellectual development

Jean Piaget was interested in how humans adapt to their environment. In his early work with children he asked them questions, and was interested to find that when children gave the wrong answers they were often the same *kind* of wrong answers. As a **result** of extensive investigations into children's thinking Piaget **concluded** that children were actively trying to make sense of the world – he called them little scientists because of the way they explore and test it.

COGNITION

Piaget proposed that children's knowledge is *structured* differently from adults and it changes from infancy to adulthood in the same way in most children. The changes in understanding are due to **maturation**, so they are determined biologically although experience is necessary for changes to develop fully.

INBORN

Piaget proposed that the child's understanding develops through four stages – these are described below along with their characteristics.

SENSORY MOTOR STAGE (BIRTH–18 MONTHS)

The baby explores its world using its senses (sight, sound, taste, touch and so on) in combination with body movements. Initially these movements are reflexes, such as the grasping or sucking reflex, and they form the basis for its exploration. For example the infant watches a moving object, reaches out towards it and after many attempts is able to grasp the object. The baby will then bring the object to its mouth, and explore it using its sense of taste and smell. Characteristics of the sensory motor stage are:

INBORN

- **Reflexes** – the new born infant's reflexes are evident – sucking, rooting, grasping. The baby starts to use these purposefully, as the basis for exploration, by about four months of age.

DEFINITION

- **Object permanence** – this is Piaget's term for the child's understanding that an object still exists even when it is not visible. For instance if you shake a rattle in front of a five month old it will reach out for it. If you cover the rattle with a cloth, the baby loses interest, as though the rattle never existed. If you do the same thing with a one year old, the baby will

COGNITION

continue to reach for the rattle, and may show distress that it has disappeared. From this behaviour Piaget inferred that the child has achieved **object permanence** – it has a **mental representation** of the object.

FIGURE 16.1 This child is using its sensory and motor skills to understand its world

PRE-OPERATIONAL STAGE (18 MONTHS–7 YEARS OLD)

During its second year the toddler starts to use symbols or signs to represent things. This includes the use of language, which enables the child to talk about things and express ideas. Characteristics of this stage include:

- **Symbolic thinking** – this is evident when the child makes something 'stand for' something else. For example, it will use a cardboard box as a house, car, boat or a shop. Language is evidence of symbolic thinking, because the child knows that when you say 'table' the word 'stands for' an actual table – he could draw one, or point one out in the room or tell you how you could use a table.
- **Animism** – children up to about four years old think that inanimate objects have feelings like they do (this is animism), saying for example 'the flowers are tired' when flowers are wilting. A possible explanation for animism is described in the next characteristic, egocentrism.
- **Egocentrism** – have you ever played 'hide and seek' with a three year old who hides by standing in front of you and covering her eyes? Because she cannot see you she thinks you cannot see *her:* this is an example of egocentric thinking (or egocentrism). Piaget argued that from birth the child has understood the world only from her own viewpoint. She thinks others have the same views and experiences as she does – it is her own view which dominates her understanding.
- **Centration** – this refers to the child's tendency to take notice of only *one* feature of a situation so she is unable to notice or understand two different features of a situation. This may be because she cannot represent these two features to herself, so it leads to errors in the child's understanding. Centration explains **egocentric** thinking (see above point).

CONCRETE OPERATIONAL STAGE (7–11 YEARS)

Piaget found that between five and seven years of ages children's thinking showed some major changes. We will look at two examples of this research – the 'three mountains task' and conservation experiments – before we identify the characteristics of this stage.

The three mountains test of egocentric thinking

Piaget and his colleagues devised the 'three mountains task' to test children's egocentric thinking (see Figure 16.2). The child sits at a large, table-top model of three mountains and is asked what he can see from his side of the table. A doll is then placed at various positions around the table. The child is shown photographs of the mountains taken from these different positions, and asked to indicate which of them shows the doll's view.

Results showed that four and five year old children thought the doll's view would be the same as their own, which indicates **egocentrism**. However most seven year olds identified the doll's view correctly. Piaget **concluded** that the child understands that it is possible for there to be two different views of the same thing at the same time – he is able to **decentre**.

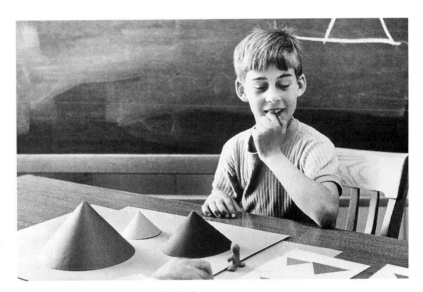

FIGURE 16.2 A child doing the 'three mountains' task

Conservation tasks

In what is called a conservation task, Piaget showed a child two identical glasses, each filled with liquid to the same level: the child agreed that there was the same amount of liquid in each. However, when the liquid was poured from one glass into a *different* shaped glass, the four year old child said that there was now a different amount of water in the new container. Because the *appearance* of the liquid is transformed, the child thinks the *amount* has changed.

However a seven year old would tell you the amount was the same – this indicates they are able to **conserve** because they are not deceived by appearances. When asked why they think the amount is the same, seven year olds often answer that if you poured it back into the original glass, it would be the same level – this shows **reversibility** in the child's thinking.

To summarise then, characteristics of the child's thinking at the **concrete operations** stage are:

● **Decentring** – the ability to take into account more than one feature of a situation at one time (which also explains the next characteristic).

- **Conservation** – the understanding that although the *appearance* of something changes, the thing itself does not. The child is not deceived by appearances because he can remember the initial state of the liquid *and* the process by which its appearance was changed. This understanding develops slowly, with conservation of liquid being apparent early in the concrete operations stage, but conservation of area appearing two or three years later. Conservation relates to other topics, for instance research on the child's understanding of gender shows that once children can conserve, they know that a man is still a man even if he puts on a dress (see p. 193).
- **Reversibility** – the ability to reverse one's thinking which is evidence that the child can use abstract reasoning, can represent information to himself and therefore manipulate it, although, as we can see below, the child may need concrete experience first.
- **Logical thinking** – reversibility in the child's thinking is evidence that it can think in a logical sequence. However the child first needs the opportunity to work through sequences with actual objects (which is why this is called *concrete* operations): they can then understand the sequence and can reverse it mentally. Children also start to create their own rules during this stage, and these became more complex as the child advances through the stage (see moral development p. 256 and empathy p. 267).

FORMAL OPERATIONAL STAGE (11 YEARS AND OLDER)

The child has entered the formal operational stage when its thinking is:

- **abstract** – which means it can manipulate ideas in its head, without any dependency on concrete manipulation. It can do mathematical calculations, think creatively, imagine the outcome of particular actions.
- **logical** – it is able to think and to work through problems in a logical, rather than haphazard, way.

According to Piaget, once the young person has achieved **formal operational** thinking, there is no further change in structure, only in the complexity, flexibility and level of abstraction.

How do children progress through these stages?

Although more recent evidence indicates children reach these stages at a younger age than Piaget proposed, the characteristics of each stage are still evident. Piaget also explained how and why children move through these stages. This explanation involves four concepts – schema, assimilation, accommodation and equilibration, which we will examine now.

SCHEMA

COGNITION

Piaget saw the schema as a basic building block of intelligent behaviour – a way of organising knowledge. He proposed that the infant has innate schemas which are their **reflexes** and these form the basis for how it understands the knowledge it gains through interaction with its environment. So for example the infant's grasping schema develops as it grasps objects of different sizes. As the infant matures and interacts with its environment, the schemas develop and become more complex through the processes of **assimilation** and **accommodation**.

ASSIMILATION

DEFINITION

The baby will use its grasping schema for getting hold of fingers, rattles or blankets – Piaget called this **assimilation**, the use of a schema to operate on the environment. Assimilation is the process of incorporating experiences into already existing schemas. However, there are times when the schema is inadequate for what the baby is trying to do, such as trying to grasp a large object for the first time. For this the schema needs to be modified.

FIGURE 16.3 This baby has developed a schema for holding

ACCOMMODATION

DEFINITION

Piaget called the process of *modifying* a schema **accommodation**. This occurs when the schema has to be changed because it cannot cope with the new experience or information. Sometimes the new information may be so different that the child creates an entirely *new* schema. If the baby is unable to grasp a large object, it will, through the processes of accommodation find that these objects can be held with two hands. It will then have a schema for holding. As it uses the schema for holding things of various sizes and textures (assimilation) the child's holding schema develops.

EQUILIBRATION

We noted at the start of the chapter that Piaget stressed how active the child was in exploring its environment – what drives the child like this? Piaget proposed that when the child has assimilated the schemas for all its experiences, it is in a state of **equilibrium**, or cognitive balance. But because of its continuing exploration of its world it will come across new experiences which will create cognitive *imbalance*. The need to regain equilibrium is what drives the child to restructure and modify its **schemas**. Piaget called this process equilibration. It also ensures that when accommodation occurs, the new information is consolidated through the process of assimilation.

DEFINITION

An evaluation of Piaget's theory

Piaget represents the view that intelligence develops as we adapt to meet the needs of our environment – successful adaptation is evidence of intelligent behaviour. For Piaget, intelligence was not a quantity which you could measure, but a process of adaptation. Piaget was devising and testing his ideas from the 1940s onwards and his work has generated considerable research. Critics of his ideas argue that:

- the changes in intellectual development which he identified occur at a much younger age than he claimed.

SOCIAL
- he failed to take sufficient account of the child's social environment.
- these first two criticisms are related, and critics have shown that we must take account of the child's social understanding when testing their abilities. For example Susan Rose and Marion Blank (1974) argued that when a child gives the wrong answer to a question, we repeat the question in order to hint that their first answer was wrong. This is what Piaget did by asking

METHODS
children the same question twice, before and after the liquid was poured into another glass. When Rose & Blank replicated this but asked the

question once, after the liquid had been poured, they found many more six-year olds gave the correct answer. This shows children can conserve at a younger age than Piaget claimed.

- Piaget's research demonstrates the difficulties in finding out what children understand – they may have understood but be unable to demonstrate it in the kind of tests psychologists devise. This is a challenge for developmental psychologists!

Despite these criticisms, the abilities which Piaget identified have been largely substantiated, although he did underestimate the ages at which they develop. His ideas have been widely used to enrich children's cognitive development and we will look at some examples now.

The influence of Piaget's ideas

Piaget's ideas have been used in many areas of child rearing such as in toys, playgroups and schools. Below we consider toys and activities which are designed to match the child's abilities at various ages. In the section after this we look at ways of helping the child move through each stage.

TOYS AND ACTIVITIES FOR EACH STAGE OF DEVELOPMENT

Sensory/motor play

Examples of toys which aim to develop **sensory** and **motor** skills are those which attach to a cot and have knobs or handles for manipulation. This in turn may produce the sound of a bell or the movement of a dial. As it gets older, the baby needs toys which give it opportunity to manipulate objects, to recognise shapes and move things about. Examples of these are putting shapes through matching holes into a box, stacking toys, carts with wheels.

Pre-operational play

Toys and activities at this stage should have a number of characteristics:

- **Constructive play** – from about two years old the child's ability to put things together can be developed with building blocks and lego. Play with water and sand help the child experiment with quantities, movement and change, encouraging the development of conservation. This type of play involves sensory and motor skills, but also the understanding of cause and effect and use of imagination.

- **Imaginative play** – the child's ability to think symbolically enables it to create its own world, so it should have plenty of materials for dressing up and imaginative play: blankets make houses, boxes become cars, chairs become trains. Imagination is also expressed through drawing and painting, so children need to have lots of paper and crayons or paints. This kind of play also develops sensory motor skills.
- **Problem solving and rule games** – as 'little scientists', children like to solve problems. Toys which give them this opportunity will develop their problem solving skills. Jigsaw puzzles, picture dominoes and other simple rule games will also encourage the development of sensory skills, such as matching colours or shapes.

Concrete operational play

Activities which encourage problem solving and rules should be available. In school, children should be able to use materials so that they can, for example, work out mathematical problems in a concrete way. These may be small coloured blocks for counting or different lengths and colours of rod for measuring.

FIGURE 16.4 Problem solving play

TOYS AND ACTIVITIES WHICH HELP DEVELOPMENT THROUGH THE STAGES

Piaget argued that learning was best achieved through interaction with the environment, and this learning occurs through assimilation and accommodation. Below we look at how opportunitites can be provided to use these processes, and how the social environment can itself contribute to intellectual development:

- **Assimilation** – there should be a few toys or activities which are of a similar level of difficulty, such as two or three jigsaws with about the same number of pieces, similar in size and with pictures that are equally complicated. This allows the child to assimilate its schema for jigsaws.
- **Accommodation** – there should also be variety and challenge in the range of toys available to the child so it has opportunities for new experiences which create **disequilibrium**. A child who is competent with a five-piece jigsaw will be challenged by a 12-piece jigsaw with straight edges. She will have to modify her existing schema for doing jigsaws because it does not 'fit' this new experience. As she incorporates the new information accommodation has occurred.
- **Decentring** – Decentring can be encouraged by giving the child the opportunity to hear or see things from other people's perspectives. When a group of children work together they have to take account of other ideas. Adults can also play an important role by pointing out another feature of a situation and encouraging the child to consider it.
- **Discovery learning** – learning by exploration and testing has been widely adopted in schools. Rather than learn by being told or doing exercises, children are encouraged to explore, ask questions and test out answers. This is an opportunity for groups of children to learn from each other (see decentring) by working together.

We have seen here how Piaget's ideas have influenced toys and the experiences from which children benefit. By watching children at play we can assess their level of cognitive development and so provide appropriate toys and experiences to encourage it.

The development of visual perception

DEFINITION

Perception is the process of interpreting, organising and elaborating on sensory information. So when we study visual perception we look at how we make sense of the information which comes into our brain through our eyes. As you look at this page light waves enter your eye, but it is your visual perception which enables you to organise them into a pattern of black and white marks which you understand as letter shapes.

FIGURE 16.5 An opportunity for decentring and discovery learning – these girls have devised and tested a parachute

Visual perception is another topic which is relevant to the nature/nurture debate. According to these two perspectives, our perceptual abilities are mainly either:

- innate because we are born with certain abilities and their development depends largely on maturation – the **hereditarian** view
- learned through our experiences – the **environmentalist** view.

You will see as we review the evidence for these two perspectives that psychologists have used a variety of approaches, all of which pose difficulties for the researcher. These will be considered in more detail as we assess the research evidence at the end of the chapter.

Evidence for the hereditarian view

INBORN

Psychologists have studied newborn infants to find out what they see and understand. Anything which is evident in newborns must be innate, and the sooner an ability appears after birth, the more likely it is to be due to innate factors. The new born infant has several basic visual skills:

- they can focus on objects approximately 20 cm away, but they cannot vary this focal length

- they can differentiate between light and dark, because they fixate on the *edge* of objects, which are defined by the contrast between light and dark.
- they can differentiate between form and background, because when they scan their environment they can fixate on a slowly moving object – this is defined by a shape (which does not change) as it moves across a background (which disappears and reappears behind the object).

These indicate innate visual abilities, thus supporting the hereditarian view. However, psychologists have investigated the extent to which more complex visual abilities are innate. We will look at three of them – pattern recognition, face recognition and depth perception.

PATTERN RECOGNITION

The ability to recognise pattern was investigated in a series of studies by Robert Fantz.

It can be seen that infants spent more time looking at the more complex pattern in the pair. Where patterns were similar, or the same, in complexity there was little difference in the time spent looking. Fantz **concluded** that:

- infants could differentiate between two patterns and thus showed pattern recognition
- infants preferred looking at the more complex pattern
- because these abilities were present very soon after birth they are therefore likely to be innate.

FACE RECOGNITION

Fantz (1961) also tested the development of the infant's ability to recognise faces. He used three face-size patterns in pink and black, as shown in Figure 16.7: a. is face-like, b. has the same features scrambled, and c. is a blank face containing the same areas of dark and light. This was a **cross-sectional** study because he presented various combinations of these patterns to infants between four days and six months of age. A graph illustrating the fixation time for each stimulus is shown in Figure 16.7.

INBORN

Results showed that infants slightly preferred the organised face over the scrambled face, and much preferred these two when compared to the blank face. Fantz **concluded** that infants have an innate preference for faces.

Critics have argued that there is very little difference in fixation time between the organised and scrambled face, so evidence for innate face recognition is weak. Others argue that these conclusions may be incorrect because both

R. Fantz (1961)

The **aim** of the study was to see whether infants preferred a complex visual stimulus more than a simple one.

This was a **longitudinal** study over 15 weeks, using the **experimental** method.

The **participants** were 30 one-week old infants. Each week the infant was shown a set of patterns which were presented in pairs. The length of time the infant looked at (or fixated on) each pattern was recorded.

The **results** of the experiment are shown below.

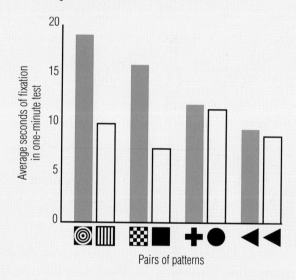

FIGURE 16.6 Bar chart showing amount of fixation time for each pattern (from R. Fantz 1961)

these faces are much more complex than the blank face, and it is the *complexity*, not the face-like nature of the stimulus, which infants prefer.

DEPTH PERCEPTION

Depth perception is the ability to judge how far the ground drops away, as it does when you look down a flight of stairs or look over a cliff. Eleanor Gibson and Richard Walk (1960) used the visual cliff apparatus to test depth perception. This consists of a board which goes across the centre of a large

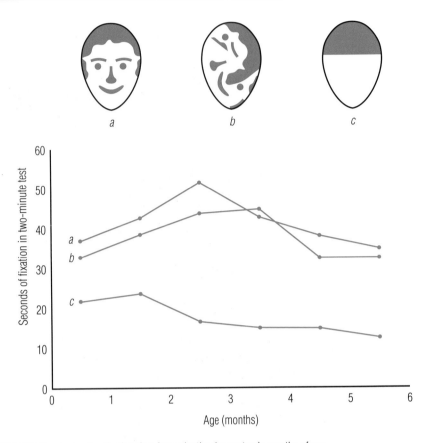

FIGURE 16.7 Graph showing fixation time for each stimulus up to six months of age

sheet of glass. Immediately under the glass on one side of the board is a check pattern (the 'shallow' side). Under the glass on the other side of the board the check pattern 'drops' several feet (the 'deep drop'). Gibson & Walk placed participants on the centre board and encouraged them to move off it and onto the glass which was over the 'drop' (see Figure 16.8).

INBORN

Results showed that very young animals, such as chicks and kittens, would not move over the deep drop but would readily move over the shallow side. If they were placed on the deep side they *froze* – they could not move. Gibson & Walk **concluded** that these animals have innate depth perception. New born infants cannot move about by themselves, but six-month old babies would move over the shallow side towards their mothers although they would not move over the deep side. This could be evidence for the hereditarian view, however:

LEARNING

- as the babies were several months old they might have learned the visual cues (such as an abrupt change in the pattern size) which indicates that the ground 'drops away'. This possibility supports the environmental view.

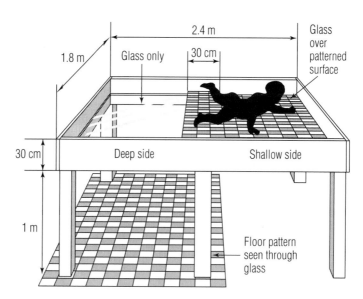

FIGURE 16.8 Gibson & Walk's visual cliff apparatus

INBORN

● this experiment does not allow us to find out whether depth perception is due to learning or to maturational changes. If due to **maturation**, this supports the hereditarian argument.

In an investigation to clarify these points, Joseph Campos and his colleagues (1970) studied babies on the visual cliff by attaching heart-rate monitors to them. If heart-rate slows, it is an indication of interest, if it speeds up it is an indication of fear. Campos found that heart-rate changed, depending on the age of the baby. Their **results** are summarised in Table 16.1.

Age of baby	Change in heart rate	Conclusions
under 2 months	none	no perception of depth
2–9 months	slows	interest, so depth perception
9 months +	increases	fear, so implications of depth perception

TABLE 16.1 Table showing age and change of heart-rate in babies on deep side of visual cliff apparatus (after J. Campos et al 1970)

We could **conclude** from these results that very young infants cannot perceive depth because there is no change in heart rate under two months of age, but those over two months can perceive depth because their heart rate slows.

INBORN

Because they are still very young, this suggests depth perception is innate. However, because the *implications* of depth do not appear until nine months of age (heart rate increased) the baby was likely to have learned that depth

LEARNING

means danger through experience in its environment.

So the visual cliff experiment shows depth perception is innate in animals and possibly in humans, which supports the hereditarian view. However, the *implications* of depth may be **learned**, supporting the environmentalist view.

We have seen, through the results of the research in this section, some of the evidence that infants are born with basic visual abilities. A number of the more complex abilities, even if not present at birth, are certainly evident at a very young age. In all, this is strong evidence for the hereditarian view, although we have revealed evidence which suggests the baby needs exposure to its environment before these abilities can fully develop.

Evidence for the environmentalist view

In order to consider the role of environmental factors on the development of visual perception we will look first at the experiences of adults who have gained sight for the first time, then at efforts to discover if visual abilities can be changed and finally at **cross-cultural** studies of visual perception.

NEWLY SIGHTED ADULTS

Adults who have gained their sight for the first time can be seen as similar to infants, in that they have 'unused' visual abilities. They are particularly interesting to researchers because they can *say* what they see, which infants cannot. If newly sighted people are unable to make sense of what they see, this suggests they need experience, so we might conclude that the environment is the main factor in the development of visual perception. On the other hand, if they can correctly interpret what they see once they gain sight, this suggests that most of our visual abilities are innate.

INBORN

In the early 1930's von Senden brought together evidence from 65 studies of people who had gained sight for the first time as adults. It appeared that most showed the same abilities as infants, such as the ability to separate form from background, but most were unable to recognise simple objects or shapes which they knew by touch. Some people learned to do this, suggesting that exposure and interaction with the visual environment is necesary for the development of visual perception. However this required effort – those who gave up did not 'learn' to make sense of what they saw.

LEARNING

METHODS

These findings are reflected in a detailed **case study** done by Richard Gregory and Jean Wallace of a man known as S.B. (remember **ethics** and anonymity?). S.B. could see for the first time after an operation at 52 years of age. He was able to recognise and judge the distance of objects he was familiar with by touch, but had difficulty with unfamiliar objects. He could recognise people's emotions by the sound of their voice, but never learned to recognise emotions from facial expressions. He was too frightened to cross a busy street on his own, but had confidently done this when he was blind. He liked bright colours, but became depressed when light faded. Despite his initial excitement at gaining sight, he eventually became depressed and died three years later.

Despite this apparent evidence that the environment is the dominant factor in the development of visual perception, we would be unwise to draw that conclusion from the above studies. This is because:

METHODS

- they are case studies, so we should not generalise from them
- the adult patient's visual system is not the same as an infants – it may have deteriorated from *lack of use*, not because of lack of stimulation from the environment
- after years spent using *other* senses to compensate for lack of sight, newly sighted people become very dependent on other senses, touch and hearing for example. This may hamper their ability to use their new visual abilities. For example, S.B. preferred to spend evenings sitting in the dark, even when he could see!

CAN VISUAL ABILITIES BE CHANGED?

If an ability is innate then it cannot be altered so if visual perception can be altered this suggests that it is not innate. Several psychologists have devised ways of altering the visual information a participant receives, to discover whether humans are able to readjust their perception.

A century ago Stratton devised a lens which made his visual world appear upside down and left to right. He wore this all the time for several days and kept his other eye covered. He gradually learned to adjust to the 'upside down' information he received – imagine drinking a cup of coffee wearing this lens! He reported seeing a fire in one place, but the sound of its crackling came from another point, so clues in his environment could have helped his

INBORN

adjustment to the new world. He never saw his world the right way up so as his perceptions did not alter this suggests visual abilities are largely innate. He was able to function because he could adapt his movements, rather than change his visual perception. When he removed the lens he soon saw things as 'normal'.

A more recent study by I. Kohler (1962) related to colour. He wore lenses which were half green and half red. He found that soon after putting them on, he had adapted and colours seemed 'normal'. When he took them off again, though, he saw red where the lens had been green, and green where it had been red – his brain had been compensating for the colours.

Kohler's **results** indicate that his visual abilities did change and thus supports the environmentalist position. However these are the opposite of the conclusions from Stratton's work. Overall then, it is difficult to draw firm conclusions from work with newly sighted adults.

EVIDENCE FROM CROSS-CULTURAL STUDIES

Cross-cultural studies help us separate innate and learned influences. If research shows that the same visual abilities are evident in many cultures then they are probably innate. If differences in ability are found from culture to culture, then visual perception is likely to be learned. The research we will consider has highlighted some of the difficulties in cross-cultural research.

William Hudson (1960) investigated three-dimensional depth perception with various tribal groups in Africa using the picture in Figure 16.9. The picture includes depth cues to help the viewer understand it, for example:

- relative size (smaller means further away)
- height in the visual field (the elephant is higher in the picture than the antelope so it must be further away).

COGNITION

Results showed that members of African tribes were unable to understand this picture, for example they thought the man was about to spear the elephant. Researchers **concluded** that they did not have three-dimensional depth perception.

FIGURE 16.9 A picture to test depth perception (from Hudson 1960)

Richard Gross (1990) has summarised criticisms of this research. He notes that Hudson used the conventional ways of indicating depth in Western cultures, which we learn from a young age. See Figure 16.10 for an example.

FIGURE 16.10 In Western cultures, children learn depth cues from an early age, as in this illustration of Postman Pat

Gross adds that later researchers amended Hudson's test picture by adding *other* depth cues – texture gradient and distance haze – as in Figure 16.11. When these cues were added there was a marked increase in participants' ability to interpret the picture.

METHODS

Where has this point taken us? It underlines the difficulty of studying people of other cultures, because we are bound by the conventions of our own culture. Therefore studies may not be valid, for example researchers think they are testing depth perception, whereas they are actually testing cultural conventions of how to represent depth in two dimensions. This is not to say that **cross-cultural** studies have no value, but that psychologists should be aware of their weaknesses and try to compensate for them.

FIGURE 16.11 Hudson's test picture with additional depth cues

The nature/nurture debate on visual perception – why is it likely to remain inconclusive?

It is clear from the studies we have looked at that the development of visual perception is the result of *both* hereditarian and environmental influences. Some abilities appear to be innate and others learned. Many abilities develop only after time, but whether this is due to environmental factors or to maturational factors is less clear. As examined below it seems that the nature/nurture debate on visual perception is likely to remain inconclusive.

ETHICAL LIMITATIONS

One of the major ethical concerns in psychology is protecting participants from physical and psychological harm. This limits psychologists' control over research, for example:

METHODS

- in order to separate out **innate** and **learned** factors psychologists would need to deprive infants of any visual experiences over a period of time (perhaps by keeping them blindfolded), and then compare their visual abilities with infants reared normally. Obviously this is unthinkable.
- psychologists cannot deprive or give adults their sight in order to do research. This is why they have experimented on themselves or have studied newly sighted people. Because these are people who are undergoing traumatic experiences, concern about their physical and psychological well-being constrains what psychologists can ask and do to them.

METHODOLOGICAL DIFFICULTIES

METHODS

A number of methodological difficulties may affect research results. These difficulties may account for some of the conflicting evidence we have seen. For example:

- the influence of heredity is strongest when the child is new born, but newborns make very poor participants. They may be sleepy, bored or unwell, temperamental differences may affect responses. These difficulties are reduced as the baby gets older, but by then the environment will have started to have an effect.
- babies cannot speak so researchers can only *infer* their abilities.
- changes which appear through the first few months of life may be due to maturation or environment.
- the results from cross-cultural studies may be affected by bias in the test materials and the method of testing.

INCONCLUSIVE RESULTS

We have just reviewed some of the reasons why the results of visual development research has so far produced no clear answers. Furthermore, we cannot conclude that because a newly-sighted adult *can* do something it is innate: we have seen that visual recognition was related to what had been already learned by touch. Equally, an innate ability may have deteriorated due to lack of use, so it will not be apparent. Findings tend to be contradictory, or they provide some evidence for *both* explanations. Will new research provide any clear answers? This appears to be unlikely, because more recent research has moved in a different direction, as we will see in the final point.

THE INTERACTIONIST POSITION

Today the nature/nurture debate in psychology is no longer dominant. Psychologists largely adopt the interactionist view, because the evidence suggests that *both* innate abilities and environmental factors are crucial. The interactionist view is that both have a role to play, but it is how they interact which is of most interest and most difficult to tease apart. Because interactionist research is not concerned whether visual perception is due *either* to nature or nurture, the debate is unlikely to be resolved by interactionist research.

Summary

This chapter has considered some aspects of cognitive development. Piaget's theory identifies stages in intellectual development whereas the research on visual perception has been unable to identify anything as distinct as stages. Both topics have highlighted the importance of innate factors (such as heredity and maturation) and the necessity of the environment for their development. This chapter has provided us with an opportunity to consider the work of psychologists by including a variety of research methods, with their accompanying strengths and weaknesses. It has also pointed out that even experienced psychologists design studies with weaknesses, and these may seriously affect their results and the conclusions they draw.

Exercises

1 According to Piaget, what is a schema?
2 What is object permanence and in which of Piaget's stages does it develop?
3 Describe two characteristics typical of children in the concrete operational stage.
4 Explain the difference between assimilation and accommodation.
5 Describe how Piaget's ideas have influenced aspects of child-rearing.
6 What is perception?
7 Describe one study which supports the idea that visual perception is innate in humans.
8 Describe one study which suggests visual perception develops through experience.
9 Explain why psychologists cannot agree whether perception is learned or innate.
10 From what you have learned in psychology explain why the nature/nurture debate on visual perception is likely to remain inconclusive.

The Development of Moral Behaviour and Moral Judgements

Moral behaviour is what we do and moral judgements are the decisions we make about an action – is it right or is it wrong, fair or unfair? Consider someone who cheats in an exam – cheating is the behaviour and in this case we would say it was wrong, i.e. immoral. If I asked you *why* it was wrong, then you would be giving your moral judgements. How does this sense of right and wrong develop? We will start by looking at three different theories, each of which attempts to answer this question, and then look at the part other people play in moral development.

Explanations of moral development

Explanations of moral development should be able to say how we develop a sense of what is right and what is wrong, as well as explaining how this relates to moral behaviour. They should give reasons why moral judgements and behaviour change as we get older. Each of the following explanations do so, but they explain it in different ways, as you will see. They are the psychodynamic, the learning and the cognitive-developmental explanations of moral development.

Psychodynamic explanation of moral development

An example of a psychodynamic explanation is Freud's theory, in which he proposed that the moral part of the personality was the **superego**, which is

INBORN

explained in detail under personality (p. 156). Freud proposed that during the **phallic** stage of psychosexual development the **libido** (one of our instinctive drives) is focused on the genitals. As a result, the boy experiences unconscious longings for his mother which conflict with his fear of his father – the Oedipus conflict. He **identifies** with his father in order to avoid the father's anger and become closer to his mother. Through this identification the boy adopts his father's attitudes, behaviours and moral standards – what is right, wrong, good, bad.

Freud claimed this 'internal parent' was represented by the superego. He divided the superego into two parts:

- the **ego-ideal** represents the kind of person the child *wants* to be: it is the rewarding and approving parent, the source of pride when we do the right thing.
- the **conscience** watches the child's behaviour, stops it from doing the wrong things: it is the punishing parent, the source of guilt when we do the wrong thing.

According to Freud, then, once the boy has identified with his father he will *think* and *behave* in a moral way. He no longer needs an external influence to make him behave morally – the influence is internal. Freud felt that once the boy had left the phallic stage successfully, by about seven years old, he was morally mature.

The girl experiences the Electra conflict: she does not fear her mother so much, although she does fear loss of her mother's love, so identification with her mother is weaker (see p. 157). Freud claimed that as a result of weaker **identification**, females have a weaker moral sense than males.

However there are criticisms of the psychodynamic explanation, for example:

- children younger than five years of age show moral behaviour
- children are not morally mature by seven years old – moral development continues well beyond this age
- research which has compared girls and boys suggests that girls are morally *stronger* than boys, opposite to what Freud's explanation would predict
- children who are reared in single-parent families have no cause for identification, so they should have poor moral development: there is no evidence of this
- SOCIAL research suggests that there are many other influences on a child's moral development, such as other adults, siblings, peers, the media
- since Freud, other psychoanalysts have stressed the importance of the ego in the individual's moral development, rather than instincts as Freud did. They say that the development of the ego (or self) takes place over many years, and depends not only on parents but on 'significant others' such as teachers or peers.

Learning theory explanations of moral development

LEARNING

Learning theory explanations focus on the child's environment and its effect on moral development. We will look at the contributions from classical conditioning, operant conditioning and social learning theory.

CLASSICAL CONDITIONING

Classical conditioning can create moral behaviour if wrong behaviour is associated with something unpleasant. The principles of classical conditioning are provided on page 11, but here we will relate them to moral development.

Imagine that a five year old has just stamped on her little brother's toy. If her mother shouts at her or gets angry this creates anxiety (a fear response). Shouting is the unconditional stimulus and anxiety is the unconditional response. If the mother responds in similar ways to other naughty behaviour,

LEARNING

the child begins to associate the naughty behaviour with anxiety. In other words, anxiety becomes the conditional response to the naughty behaviour. So even when the child *thinks* about being naughty she feels anxiety: this is what stops her being naughty again.

However, classical conditioning is a very limited explanation of moral development because it can only say why children stop doing things which are wrong. It cannot explain why children behave in a moral way, nor can it explain the evidence that there are consistent patterns in children's understanding of right and wrong.

OPERANT CONDITIONING

LEARNING

The operant conditioning explanation says that moral behaviour is like any other behaviour, it is shaped and maintained by its consequences. Behaviour can be strengthened by **reinforcement** and weakened by **punishment**. Details of operant conditioning are provided on page 13, but here we will relate them to moral development.

- **Positive reinforcement** strengthens moral behaviour. Giving the child rewards such as approval, thanks or attention when it has behaved in a moral way should encourage the child to behave in a moral way in the future. Also, according to learning theorists, behaviour which is *not* reinforced should become **extinguished**. Therefore if the child does something wrong, make sure you do not reward the behaviour!

● **Negative reinforcement** *also* strengthens moral behaviour. When a child sees another child who is upset it may experience distress, which is unpleasant, and one way to relieve it is to make the other child stop crying. If the distressed child offers a toy or a sweet to the child who is crying, and the crying stops, the child's own distress is reduced. This is an example of negative reinforcement, because offering comfort has stopped an unpleasant experience, so the child is more likely to offer comfort to others in future.

FIGURE 17.1 This little girl is receiving two types of reinforcement – positive reinforcement from her mother, and negative reinforcement by giving her spinach to her little brother

● **Punishment** is anything which weakens behaviour, however attempts to use punishment to develop moral behaviour are not very effective because they show the child what it *should not* do, not what it *should* do. It may also be ineffective if a child is naughty in order to gain attention. Subsequent punishment gains the child attention (which is what it wants), so in this case punishment is *rewarding*. More importantly, certain kinds of punishment may give messages to the child about hostility and rejection which create those feelings in the child itself (see aggression p. 144).

Although reinforcement and punishment may be effective, nevertheless there are a number of important criticisms of operant conditioning, such as:

- operant conditioning provides an explanation of how moral *behaviour* develops but fails to explain how moral *thinking* develops.
- research in the last decade shows that adults do not reinforce moral behaviour very often, but they punish *wrong* behaviour more frequently. How then does moral development occur if unsuccessful methods are widely used but successful ones are not?
- punishment *does* appear to work in some circumstances
- the effectiveness of reinforcement varies enormously, for instance some children do continue to behave unkindly and selfishly even when they are reinforced for the right kind of behaviour
- the child's moral behaviour will reflect its experiences so there will be no consistency in children's moral development, yet research indicates there are consistent patterns in moral development

SOCIAL LEARNING THEORY

LEARNING

Social learning theory proposes that moral development occurs as a result of the child **observing** and **imitating** the behaviour of others and being rewarded for moral behaviour. The main principles of social learning theory are that children are more likely to imitate **models** who are important to them, perhaps because they are similar to the child, powerful or nurturant, or when the model is reinforced (see p. 16). Children therefore learn moral behaviour by:

- observing the behaviour of people such as parents and teachers (who are powerful and nurturant), for example when they make sure everyone has an equal size piece of cake, help someone to push a car that won't start, or say why we should help others.
- observing those of the same sex or age, such as peers and same-sex siblings. The child may imitate their moral behaviour, such as lending a pencil to another child or copying an older brother when he tidies up at home if parents are tired.
- being reinforced for imitating the behaviour. If a boy lends his pencil to another child, who offers a sweet in return, the boy's behaviour has been rewarded and he is more likely to offer help in the future.
- imitating a model whose moral behaviour has been reinforced – **vicarious reinforcement**. In Figure 17.2, the model is being reinforced by the big smile of the lady collecting money.

Social learning theory explains how moral thinking develops from moral behaviour. Through these processes of observation, imitation and reinforcement the child learns new behaviours and when to perform them. These behaviours gradually become **internalised**, and the child performs

FIGURE 17.2 This model may affect the child's moral development

appropriate behaviour without it being modelled. So, through *behaving* in a moral way, the child's sense of right and wrong becomes internalised. Albert Bandura (1977) called this **self-efficacy**, which is the feeling of competence and appropriateness about our behaviour and abilities. Behaving in accordance with these internalised standards is rewarding – it increases our self-efficacy.

Critics of the social learning theory explanation point out that:

METHODS

- it is based on research which is artificial, for example using films of adults modelling behaviour which children watch. This is not like real life, where children may have other distractions or may interact with models.
- if children learn moral behaviour from their experiences, there will not be a consistent pattern. Research shows that there *is* a general pattern in moral development.

Cognitive developmental explanations of moral development

COGNITION

These explanations propose that children's moral development is related to their cognitive development. Because cognitive development follows a consistent pattern, so does moral development (although the patterns occur a little later). We will consider the explanations offered by two theorists in this area: Jean Piaget and Lawrence Kohlberg. You will see that their explanations are based on what the child *says*, which they take as evidence of the child's understanding and thinking about moral behaviour.

PIAGET'S RESEARCH ON MORAL JUDGEMENTS

METHODS

Piaget used several techniques to discover the basis of children's moral judgements. In his research to find out how children understand rules he used the **clinical interview** method. He played marbles with children whilst asking questions about the rules they created, and what would happen if they were broken, or did not work very well.

Another method was to ask questions about the behaviour of children in stories. For instance in one story a child breaks a cup whilst stealing some jam, in another the child breaks lots of cups by accident. Piaget then asked the child questions such as 'which child was the naughtiest? which child should be punished more? why?'

Results showed that children under about eight years of age said the child who broke all the cups was the naughtiest, so he was the child who should be punished more. These children were making moral judgements on the basis of the consequences of actions. By eight years old, children were able to make the correct judgement, and take the *intent* into account as well.

PIAGET'S THEORY OF MORAL DEVELOPMENT

COGNITION

From this research, Piaget (1932) proposed that up to about three or four years old the child is unable to make moral judgements because she does not understand rules, so she cannot understand breaking rules. Once she understands rules her moral development begins. There are two stages:

- **Stage 1: heteronomous morality** (morality imposed from outside). The child sees rules as coming from 'outside' – they are made by parents, teachers, God, and are unchangeable. Moral judgements are based on rules – if you do something wrong you will be punished. The child is at the pre-operational stage of development, so his thinking shows **centration** – he can only attend to one aspect of a situation, the consequences of the action. The child judges the rightness or wrongness of behaviour on the consequences. Piaget called this moral **realism**, and children show it up to about eight years old.
- **Stage 2: autonomous morality** (morality based on your own rules). This develops when the child is able to **decentre**, so she can judge the *intent*

behind the action as well as the consequence. Children now understand that rules can be flexible to suit the situation, they make up their own rules, for example when playing hide and seek the small child will be allowed to count to a lower number. The child's thinking shows **moral relativism** because it is more flexible, and can take account of other people's perspective. Piaget argued that because males play in larger groups than females, this opportunity to take account of others' views and negotiate rules leads to higher levels of moral reasoning in males.

Piaget's theory was based on children's *actual* behaviour, and although children's moral development does seem to follow this general pattern, there have been criticisms of Piaget's theory, for example:

COGNITION

- research has shown that when the *intention* is emphasised, even three year olds can make correct judgements. This echoes criticism that his theory under-estimates children's cognitive abilties (see p. 233).
- as noted in regard to the psychodynamic explanation, research suggests that *girl's* moral development is actually more advanced than that of boys.
- the stages are too general and suggest there is no significant change in moral thinking beyond early adolescence, although research shows that there is. This criticism is addressed in Kohlberg's research.

KOHLBERG'S RESEARCH ON MORAL REASONING

METHODS

Kohlberg's theory was based on Piaget's, so it is cognitive, but it identifies more stages in the development process, and continues into adulthood. Kohlberg was interested in **moral reasoning**, and to assess people's moral reasoning he told them a story – a moral dilemma – and then asked them questions. One example is the story of Heinz, as shown on p. 257.

KOHLBERG'S THEORY OF MORAL DEVELOPMENT

COGNITION

Having analysed the answers, Kohlberg (1969) proposed that there were three levels of moral reasoning, each having two stages.

- **Level 1: pre-conventional morality** (authority is outside the individual and reasoning is based on the physical consequences of actions). The **first** stage relates to punishment of actions – if it is punished it must have been wrong. People are obeyed who have greater power. The **second** stage of reasoning is determined by behaviour which brings personal gain such as a reward or to get help from someone else – 'the pharmacist should have let Heinz pay later, because one day he might need something from Heinz.'

Heinz' dilemma

Heinz' wife was dying of cancer. Doctors said a new drug might save her. The drug had been discovered by a pharmacist in Heinz' town but he was charging a lot of money for it – 10 times what it cost him to make. Heinz couldn't afford to buy the drug, so he asked friends and relatives to lend him money. But still he only had half the money he needed. He told the pharmacist his wife was dying and asked him to sell the drug cheaper, or asked if he could pay the rest of the money later. The pharmacist said no, Heinz got desperate so he broke in to the pharmacy and stole some of the drug.

Sample of questions:

Should Heinz have stolen the drug?

Would it change anything if Heinz did not love his wife?

What if the person dying was a stranger, would it make any difference?

- **Level 2: conventional morality** (authority internalized but not questioned and reasoning is based on the norms of the group to which the person belongs). At the **first** stage answers are related to the approval of others, saying that people like you when you do good, helpful things. The **second** stage reasoning is based on respect for law and order – not the authority of specific people like parents, but a generalised **social norm** of obedience to authority and doing one's duty.
- **Level 3: post-conventional morality** (individual judgement based on self-chosen principles and moral reasoning is based on individual rights and justice). Reasoning at the **first** stage says that although laws are important, to be fair there are times when they must be changed or ignored. For example in Heinz' dilemma the protection of life is more important than breaking the law against stealing. In the **second** stage people assume personal responsiblity for their actions, based on universal ethical and moral principles which are not necessarily laid down by society. Kohlberg doubted few ever reached this stage.

Kohlberg proposed that the individual's reasoning progresses through each stage, and therefore cannot 'go backwards' from Level 2 to Level 1. He did not tie the levels to a specific age, although research has suggested that Level 1 is up to about 10 years old, Level 2 is 10 years up to adulthood, and that very few adults show Level 3 reasoning. He found that generally males achieved higher levels of moral reasoning than females.

Kohlberg's theory does provide more detail than Piaget's and reflects changing levels of morality in adulthood. However it has been criticised on a number of points, for example:

METHODS

- his studies only used male participants, although some recent research has shown similar results with girls' moral thinking

METHODS

- it is very difficult for participants to put their reasoning into words when they include abstract ideas of justice; they may have an *intuitive* understanding relating to the higher levels, but be unable to express it

METHODS

- the dilemmas were unrelated to the lives of most of his participants
- his theory has been criticised because it is **ethnocentric** which means he viewed morality from the viewpoint of his own, Western, society. Other cultures have different values which would lead to different types of reasoning and judgements on these moral dilemmas, whereas Kohlberg saw the values in his research as *the* moral standards
- the theory is about reasoning and not behaviour.

SOCIAL

There are also some general criticisms of the cognitive-developmental theories of moral development. One is that although the child's *social* context is acknowledged, these explanations do not say *how* the social context influences moral reasoning. Another is that despite evidence which generally supports this pattern of moral thinking, we do not always behave in accordance with our knowledge of what is right or wrong! So far then, we have discussed three types of theories which offer explanations for moral development, none of which are complete explanations. Box 17.1 summarises some points of similarity and difference between them.

Pro-social reasoning

EISENBERG'S STAGES OF PRO-SOCIAL REASONING

Many of the ideas we have looked at so far have examined what children think about doing *wrong*; more recently psychologists have looked at the judgements children make about *good* (or pro-social) behaviour. Psychologists studying pro-social reasoning are studying the explanations people give for why we should help others.

METHODS

As an example, Nancy Eisenberg (1986) used dilemmas which were more realistic than Kohlberg's because she wanted to find out whether her participants would put their *own* interests before someone else's interests. This is

17.1 SIMILARITIES AND DIFFERENCES IN EXPLANATIONS OF MORAL DEVELOPMENT			
	PSYCHODYNAMIC EXPLANATION	LEARNING EXPLANATION	COGNITIVE-DEVELOPMENTAL EXPLANATION
Are there innate factors?	yes – instinctive drives	no	yes - reflexes and maturation
How important are parents?	both parents essential	important as models and providers of reinforcement	not very important
Is the child's role active?	not very – unconscious	conditioning – fairly passive; social learning – active	very active
Which are more important, social, emotional or cognitive factors?	emotional	social; some cognitive in social learning	cognitive and some social
Does explanation predict that moral judgements will be consistent with moral behaviour?	yes	conditioning – no; social learning – eventually	Piaget – probably Kohlberg – not necessarily

another example of a clinical interview. One dilemma asks the child to imagine he is walking to a friend's birthday party but passes a child who has fallen over and is hurt. If he stays to help, he might miss the fun of the party. What should he do?

COGNITION

Eisenberg noted the children's answers, and from these **results** she proposed six stages of **pro-social reasoning**, which are related to age:

- **Stage 1 – self-focused** (up to six years old): the child is concerned to satisfy its own needs or only help if the other could help them. 'I'd help because she'd help me next time'.
- **Stage 2 – needs of others** (up to 10 years old): the child shows awareness of the other child's needs. 'He needs help'.
- **Stage 3 – approval of others** (up to 13 years old): the child behaves pro-socially because he thinks others will like him, or he should do it. 'He'd like me more if I helped'.
- **Stage 4 – empathic orientation** (adolescents): the reasons for helping show empathy with others' feelings. 'I know how he feels'.

- **Stage 5 – transitional** (adolescents and some adults): reasons for helping show some evidence of acting on internalised norms or responsibilities. 'I'd feel good if I helped'.
- **Stage 6 – strongly internalised** (usually seen only in adults): reasoning shows a clear relationship between behaviour and the need to act according to one's principles. 'I'd feel bad if I didn't help'.

These six levels are similar to Kohlberg's six stages but the reasoning seems more advanced. Eisenberg suggested this was because the ideas were about pro-social (or helping) behaviour, and not about what you should *not* do. Is she right? Another explanation for her evidence of pro-social reasoning at a younger age is because of the kind of dilemma the child is given. The stories are easier to understand because they are related to the child's own experience.

STUDIES OF THE DEVELOPMENT OF PRO-SOCIAL REASONING

J. Youniss (1980) conducted a **cross-sectional** study in which he gave stories to children about the behaviour of a child of the same age towards its friends. His participants gave these types of responses:

- 6–8 year olds talked of giving and sharing with others and 'playing nicely'
- 9–11 year olds said you would help others out to make things fair
- 12–14 year olds said friendship involved things like encouraging friends or consoling them when they were disappointed.

COGNITION

Youniss points out that the child's reasoning moved from moral concern on the physical level to the psychological level. We can see here how children's knowledge of how to behave towards friends echoes cognitive developmental ideas. Increasingly they show awareness of the other's situation, and consideration of more abstract ideas. The **conclusions** drawn from this study therefore echo the conclusions from Kohlberg's and Eisenberg's work.

Carol Gilligan (1982) criticised the male bias of Kohlberg's research, in particular his focus on justice and fairness. Gilligan asserts that females are more concerned about caring and responsibility for others because they are socialised into an **ethic of caring** whereas Kohlberg's classification rates justice more highly than caring.

She investigated the responses which females gave to real-life dilemmas, and from the **results** she **concluded** that women go through three stages of pro-social reasoning:

- caring for self
- caring for others
- balancing the requirements of care for self with care for others.

FIGURE 17.3 Why does this child care for his little brother like this?

She also **concluded** that females and males show similar levels of pro-social reasoning, which is supported by other research. However she *did* find a difference in the emphasis, namely that the pro-social reasoning of females is based on caring rather than justice.

Other research has shown that parents can help to speed up their child's development of pro-social reasoning. **Results** showed that children advanced through the stages faster when they were shown how to give and take from an early age, using games which involved exchange, and when they were encouraged by their parents to do so.

The role of others in moral development and behaviour

As we have examined each of these explanations for children's moral development and behaviour, we have come across the part that others play. Here we will discuss the role of parents and peers.

THE ROLE OF PARENTS IN MORAL DEVELOPMENT AND BEHAVIOUR

This section focuses on the influence which parents may have on moral development and behaviour, considering the effect of punishment, internalised and externalised moral behaviour and parents as models.

The effect of punishment

LEARNING

Punishment, which should weaken behaviour, has been found to be more effective when:

- a **warm relationship** exists between parent and child, making reinforcement and punishment more effective. Why should this be? A warm affectionate relationship suggests a strong attachment. Punishment may increase feelings of guilt, or may include withdrawal of affection, both of which are more likely to be effective in a strongly attached child. The result of this may be that the relationship between parent and child influences the strength of the child's moral development.

COGNITION

- an **explanation** is given with punishment. This suggests that increasing the child's *understanding* of its behaviour will affect the parents' behaviour (they will not need to use punishment very often) and the child's moral behaviour (because behaviour which is wrong is less likely to occur).

Internalised and externalised moral behaviour

Martin Hoffman (1970) investigated the relationship between a child's moral behaviour and the way the parent used discipline. He asked children, their classmates and parents a variety of questions relating to helpful behaviour and to discipline. From the **results** he proposed three types of discipline:

LEARNING

- **power assertive discipline** where the parent used threats or force or withdrew privileges. Hoffman suggests this style creates hostility.
- **love withdrawal** which involved ignoring or isolating the child.

COGNITION

- **inductive discipline** which meant reasoning with the child, encouraging the child to think about its behaviour, the consequences and how his or her parents felt. This encourages empathy for others and a sense of personal responsibility for actions.

We have already noted other research which supports Hoffman's findings and there seem to be two types of moral behaviour which result from these styles:

- **internalised moral behaviour** is shown by children who behave morally even when there is no external pressure to do so. They show greater consideration of others and express more guilt when they do wrong. This behaviour is related to the inductive and, to a lesser degree, the love withdrawal styles.

- **externalised moral behaviour** is shown by children who behave morally in order to avoid punishment. They tend to show less concern about others and this behaviour is related to the power assertive style of parental discipline. Hoffman suggests this style provides a model which shows the child they should direct hostility outwards and that the morality of actions is controlled from the outside.

METHODS

These results are **correlational**, however, as they are in most studies examining parental discipline and moral behaviour. We cannot conclude, therefore, that a parent's disciplining style causes particular moral behaviour, only that the child's moral development is related to parenting style.

Parents as models – how influential are they?

LEARNING

Social learning theory presents a strong case for the importance of parents as models. However, their influence can be affected by the following factors:

- **consistency** – research shows that the more consistent the parent's behaviour, the more likely the child is to imitate the moral behaviour

COGNITION

- **what is done and what is said** – when an adult says one thing but does another, the child will copy what is *done* not what is *said*. Children who are at Piaget's first stage of moral development are only able to attend to one aspect of a situation, and what they see dominates their understanding.
- how **influential** are parental models? Judith Smetana compared children who were suffering from physical abuse with some suffering neglect and another group who were not maltreated. In all three groups she found the children gave similar decisions on what was right and what was wrong. It seems that different parental models had little effect on their children's moral sense.

THE INFLUENCE OF PEERS ON AN INDIVIDUAL'S MORAL BEHAVIOUR

Once children start at playgroup or school, their social context becomes much larger and richer. They move from the family environment, where there is adult supervision and few other children, to a place where they are surrounded by others with less adult protection. They have to negotiate with their peers – to learn to give and take and to have mutual respect. Peers may affect moral behaviour, as models and as part of a social group.

Peers as models

LEARNING

Peers can be particularly influential as models because they are similar in age. In their **cross-cultural** work, Beatrice Whiting and Carolyn Edwards (1988) studied children in Kenya, India, Mexico, Japan and the United States. They found a consistent pattern in their results – that early responsibility for the care of others is related to more concern about others. This was true for both boys and girls. Whiting & Edwards described how the older child behaved as adult carers would towards the younger children. They were modelling moral behaviour for younger children and this was true even between four year olds and two year olds.

Research shows that boys tend to be more likely to imitate their peers than girls are. They are more likely to copy the behaviour of older or more influential boys, and to respond to approval from other boys.

Peers and group norms

SOCIAL

Both boys and girls respond to the **norms** and values of their peers. The importance of the social group increases as children approach adolescence (see friendships p. 97) and with it comes the pressure to conform to the norms of the group in order to win acceptance or approval. If the individual's peer group condones behaviour which is illegal or unfair, it is difficult for the individual to reject the behaviour so he or she is likely to conform. If the group condones behaviour which is pro-social then the individual is likely to conform for just the same reasons.

In order to conform to the group norms the individual may behave in ways which they know to be wrong – so their behaviour is not consistent with their thinking. This is an example of **normative** influence (see conformity, p. 108).

Psychologists have discovered that disputes between parents and children were about breaking house rules (such as being untidy) or social rules (such as saying 'please'). In contrast, disputes between peers and between siblings tended to be about moral issues such as sharing and ownership. This suggests that it is childrens'relationships with peers which have an important influence on children's moral behaviour.

THE RELATIONSHIP BETWEEN MORAL DEVELOPMENT AND MORAL BEHAVIOUR

It is one thing to know what is right, but another to actually *do* it. Below is a summary of some of the factors which affect whether our moral behaviour is in accordance with our moral development:

COGNITION

- **level of moral reasoning** – the higher the level of moral reasoning, the greater the likelihood that the individual behaves in accordance with his reasoning. Evidence comes from research by Kohlberg, who gave participants the opportunity to cheat: those whose reasoning was at the pre-conventional level were the most likely to cheat.

FIGURE 17.4 Children's moral behaviour is greatly influenced by their peers

- **taking personal responsibility** – although you may be able to provide sound moral reasons for a course of action, you may not feel that it is something you personally should do. You may feel that the costs of sticking to your principles are greater than the benefits.
- **the presence of others** – those who show **externalised moral behaviour** are likely to behave in a moral way simply to avoid punishment, so the presence of others, or at least the possibility of others finding out what they have done, will determine whether behaviour is moral or not. Those with **internalised moral behaviour** are likely to behave in a moral way regardless of whether anyone else is present.
- **the need for approval from others** – if this need is strong, then we are more likely to behave according to group **norms** or imitate the behaviour of others, rather than according to our own moral reasoning. The others may be parents, peers, teachers, other adults or people who are important to us. This need for approval can therefore make our moral behaviour *higher* or *lower* than our level of moral reasoning.

SOCIAL

Summary

In summary then, the explanations proposed in the first part of the chapter emphasise the role of parents, yet research indicates that parents may not be as influential as these explanations suggest. They are sometimes inconsistent in their behaviour, they punish more than reward, they show less concern over moral transgressions than social ones. Despite this, children make moral choices at quite a young age, in some circumstances children's moral development may occur with little reinforcement, or even when they experience parental abuse. Jerome Kagan (1984) has proposed that morality is a universal human competence, like memory or language. This is why you can see evidence of it in two year olds. How it develops depends on the child's environment and cultural notions of right and wrong. In studying these factors, research which concentrates on how children understand their social worlds shows us the complexity of the interaction between the child and its world.

Exercises

1 Explain the cognitive-developmental theory of moral development.
2 Describe the role of parents in learning theory explanations of moral development.
3 Outline two explanations of moral development. Describe one point of similarity and one point on which they differ.
4 What is pro-social reasoning?
5 Outline how pro-social reasoning develops in most children.
6 Describe the results and conclusions of one study of the development of pro-social reasoning.
7 Describe a study of pro-social reasoning in children.
8 Describe how parents may influence their children's moral development.
9 Describe two ways in which peers may influence an individual's moral behaviour.
10 Explain one way in which a person's moral development might affect their behaviour.

⟨18⟩ Pro-Social Behaviour

In this chapter we are going to look at behaviour which helps other people – a student who offers to share revision with a classmate, a little boy who tries to comfort his crying sister, a teenager who gives up her seat on a bus to an old lady or someone who dives into the sea to rescue a drowning child. Psychologists call this behaviour, which helps another, pro-social behaviour. Helping others often causes us inconvenience, requires time and perhaps risk to ourselves, so why do we do it? One reason may be empathy for the suffering of others, so we will start by looking at how empathy develops in children. We will continue by looking at studies of altruism and then what makes bystanders help (or not!) in an emergency. Finally we consider how society's expectations, or social norms, influence helping behaviour.

The development of empathy

DEFINITION **Empathy** has been defined as an emotional response to someone else's feelings or situation. There is disagreement as to whether your emotions have to be identical to the other's, or just similar. Because empathy with the plight of others seems to be an important reason for helping them, psychologists have studied how empathy develops. Martin Hoffman (1982) proposes that it is linked to **cognitive development** and that empathy develops in four stages.

HOFFMAN'S FOUR STAGES IN THE DEVELOPMENT OF EMPATHY

Stage 1   Global empathy

During the first year of life an infant shows empathy through its behaviour, such as crying when it hears another baby crying. This could be because the infant is still **egocentric**, and therefore is unable to distinguish between itself and others. Hoffman says this empathic response is due either to inborn human tendencies towards empathy or to early classical conditioning.

LEARNING

According to **classical conditioning** principles, the empathic response is created by association. When a baby is hurt it feels pain, it cries, it may see blood. In other words it feels distress. As these experiences are repeated it learns to associate a cry of pain, or the sight of blood, with a feeling of distress. Because of this association, it will come to feel distress when it hears *others* cry, or when it sees blood.

In Figure 18.1 below you can see that the baby's unhappy expression is imitated by the mother. She is comforting the child by showing she knows his feelings, in other words she is showing empathy. This baby is not aware of

LEARNING

what he looks like, but he is learning from his mother that his feelings of unhappiness are associated with this particular expression. In classical conditioning terms, seeing this expression in others will automatically trigger his feelings of unhappiness.

Stage 2   Egocentric empathy

From about one year old, toddlers respond to the feelings of others, so they will try to comfort a crying child, or show fear when another child is fright-

COGNITION

ened. However, because they are still **egocentric** they cannot understand

FIGURE 18.1 Giving comfort and encouraging empathy

what may relieve the other's distress, so a toddler may offer a favourite toy to her mother who has a cut finger. The child is showing an empathic response but is not able to understand the cause of the other's distress.

Stage 3   Empathy for another's feelings

COGNITION

From two years of age children start to show they can identify other's feelings, and respond in the appropriate way. They may try to mend a broken toy, or wipe up spilled juice. As egocentricity reduces the child is increasingly able to take the perspective of someone else – this ability is called **role-taking**. Research has shown that there is a positive correlation between role-taking and helping behaviour. However this is only apparent from about seven years or older, when role-taking has started to develop.

At this stage, children will respond less to what they see and more to what they *infer* from what they see, so for example they know *why* Mum will be more unhappy when she tears a favourite dress than when she tears a tea-towel. As they get older they may show a real effort to understand the other's emotions in order to relieve the other's distress.

Stage 4   Empathy for another's general plight

From about ten years of age children begin to recognise the implications of someone else's situation – poverty, for example, as well as immediate distress. They may also understand the plight of large groups of people – such as victims of war, famine or earthquakes. This is possible because they child has developed the ability to understand other people's experiences, so for example they know that people do not always show the emotions they feel.

COGNITION

By the time the child has reached late adolescence, empathy should have fully developed. We can now look at how empathy explains helping behaviour, in particular altruism.

What is altruism?

DEFINITION

Altruism is defined as voluntary unselfish helping behaviour which involves personal cost and is performed without thought of reward. Let us examine this definition in more depth in order to understand what altruism is:

- **voluntary** – done willingly, without expectation or pressure from anyone else (in contrast to the **social norms** for pro-social behaviour detailed at the end of the chapter)
- **unselfish** – done without thought of one's own well-being
- **helping behaviour** – any behaviour which helps another person
- **personal cost** – involving costs such as time, effort, safety, expense, reputation

● **no thought of reward** – done without thinking of possible benefits, though some argue about whether *any* action can be pure altruism, because altruistic behaviour brings the helper benefits such as increased self-esteem or public approval.

FIGURE 18.2 The men rescuing this child are showing altruistic behaviour, according to the definition above

Altruism is of interest partly because so much psychological research has gone into aggression and other forms of *anti*-social behaviour, and partly because whether or not they gain benefit, people do indeed put others' safety and well-being before their own. In addition, in an increasingly anonymous world, it is important that we know how to develop and encourage altruism. Below we will look at some psychological studies of altruism, including research on empathy, arousal and ways of encouraging altruism in children.

STUDIES OF ALTRUISM

Empathy

We have noted that altruism differs from other types of pro-social behaviour in that it is done without thought of self-benefit, so why do we do it? One explanation is that we feel empathy for the other person, making us act. The research by C. Daniel Batson, described below, makes this distinction clearer.

C.D. Batson et al (1983)

The **method** was an experiment comparing one group who were high in empathy and another who were low in empathy. This was an **independent measures** design using female participants who were divided into two groups. One group was told they were about to watch a woman who was similar to them (high empathy condition), the other group thought they were very dissimilar (low empathy condition).

The **procedure** was that each participant was asked to watch a woman (a confederate) on closed circuit TV who was apparently receiving shocks in a learning experiment. As the shocks got worse, the woman told the researcher that due to a childhood experience she was very sensitive to shocks. The researcher then proposed that the participant, who was watching, might like to take her place. The length of time the participants had to watch the suffering was varied.

Results showed that even when they did not have to watch the suffering for long, participants high in empathy still volunteered to change places.

METHODS

This appears to be an example of true altruism, although the participants may have felt pressured to help when the researcher suggested it. Batson amended this weakness in a later study, in which participants were rated as high or low in **empathy** from a questionnaire they completed. Even when it was easy for participants to *avoid* changing places with the victim, those high in empathy did not take that opportunity. They preferred to change with the victim and take her shocks.

These **results** show that participants who were high in empathy preferred to relieve the suffering of others rather than walk away, while those low in empathy were more likely to avoid changing places. Batson **concluded** this could be due to arousal, which is the topic we turn to next.

Arousal

INBORN

There is good evidence that empathy is a major factor in altruistic behaviour – there is a correlation between empathy and altruism in children and adults. Psychologists have proposed that the link between empathy and altruism may be **arousal**. Arousal is excitement in the nervous system, and it can be easily identified by an increase in heartbeat or sweating, for example.

An experiment which demonstrated a link between empathy, arousal and altruism was conducted with 20 year olds. Each participant was linked with a 'performer' (who was a confederate of the experimenter) who played roulette. Participants were told that performers were rewarded, or punished with an electric shock, depending on whether the ball fell on an odd or even number. Participants were also monitored for measures of arousal – heartbeat and sweating. Half of them thought they were *similar* to their partners, the other half thought they were *different*. Similarity increases empathy, so this is how the researchers manipulated empathy.

Results showed that participants who thought they were similar to performers (therefore high in empathy) showed high arousal in their response to their partners success or failure. When the researchers gave participants the chance to share the rewards, or shocks, with their partners, they found those high in empathy were more likely to take their partner's shocks.

Batson and his colleagues offered this explanation. They argued that when we see someone who is suffering this causes arousal, which is uncomfortable. The action we take to reduce it depends on whether the arousal is due to:

- our own **personal distress** (such as guilt, anxiety, fear of public disapproval), in which case we can reduce this type of distress by rationalising that it isn't our fault, it's none of our business, walking away or, of course, by helping
- **empathic concern** about the distress of others which can *only* be reduced by trying to reduce the *other's* suffering. Once their suffering is relieved our own arousal will be reduced.

Encouraging altruism

Psychologists studying the roots of altruism have found that parents have considerable influence, for example research shows that:

- parents who are loving, nurturant and thoughtful have children who are more likely to show the same qualities – in other words there is a positive correlation between parent's and children's behaviour
- LEARNING
- parents who *behave* altruistically, as well as preaching altruism, had children who were more altruistic. An explanation for this, and the previous point, could be the parent's role as a model
- COGNITION
- mothers who told children the consequences of their actions and who explained the rules clearly had children who were more likely to be helpful or sympathetic to others. Similarly, when older children are given reasons for being helpful, and encouraged to focus on how others feel, this increases their altruistic behaviour This shows how cognitive factors can affect altruism.

In summary then, altruism does appear to exist and is *different* from general helping behaviour. It seems that the link between empathy and altruism may be arousal. There is still no answer to the question – is there true altruism? We could argue that taking someone's electric shocks to reduce our own arousal means we are benefitting from our 'altruistic' action so it cannot be pure altruism. Perhaps it is more important to put this question to one side and focus on the ways altruistic behaviour can be encouraged.

Bystander intervention

Psychologists have looked at helping behaviour in public. What makes, or stops, people from helping others? Much of this work stems from concern that when there is an emergency, sometimes people are slow to help. There are a few vivid examples of someone being murdered or a child abducted with no-one stepping in to help. The focus of research on bystander intervention is to study how people who witness emergencies behave. We will look first at studies of the situations which encourage bystanders to go to help others, then we will look at personal factors which affect bystander behaviour.

WHEN IS A BYSTANDER LIKELY TO HELP OTHERS?

Three aspects of the situation which affect bystander intervention are the reaction of other bystanders, the number of bystanders and whether others act as models.

Reaction of other bystanders

Other people help us to interpret ambiguous situations (see conformity, p. 109), so when an incident is ambiguous we are particularly likely to take note of the way others respond.

Bibb Latané and Judith Rodin (1969) conducted an **experiment** in which participants sat in a room completing a questionnaire. In one condition the participant was alone, in the other they were with another person (a confederate of the researcher). The female experimenter went in to an adjoining room, then there was the sound of her falling, crying out and moaning. The confederate had been instructed to ignore these sounds.

SOCIAL

Results showed that of the participants who were alone 70% went to help, and when the participant was with the confederate 40% went to help. After the experiment participants said they felt anxious but looked to the other person in the room to see how they responded. As they seemed quite calm, the participants decided that there was no emergency. Latané & Rodin claimed this is what happens when large numbers of people witness an emergency: they all define it as 'safe' because no-one else seems to be concerned. This is called **pluralistic ignorance**.

Number of other bystanders

John Darley and Bibb Latané (1968) were interested to find out what people would do when they could not look to others to see how they interpreted a situation. In their **experiment** the participant discussed a topic with others via an intercom. They thought the others were close by and were told the intercom helped to avoid embarrassment during the discussion. Early in the discussion one of the others casually mentioned that he sometimes had seizures and later in the discussion it appeared that he was having a seizure. How did participants respond?

SOCIAL

Results showed that of the participants who thought they were the only person listening most of them went for help very quickly, and when they thought someone else was listening over half the participants went for help, but only one-third went to help when they thought there were four others listening. This is called **diffusion of responsibility**, which is the belief that someone else will help. The more 'others' that are present, the greater the diffusion of responsibility (or the less likely one person is to help).

Others as models

If someone else goes to help, does that encourage others to follow their example? The answer appears to be yes. A study by J. Bryan and M. Test (1967) took place at the side of a motorway. They arranged for a woman (a confederate) to stand beside a car with a flat tyre – this was the test condition. In the experimental condition a 'helping situation' was set up one quarter of a mile *before* the parked car. In the helping situation a woman was stood beside a car watching a man change the tyre – he provided the model for helping.

LEARNING

Results showed that of the many cars which passed during the experiment, more stopped to help when they had passed the 'helping situation' then when there was no helping situation. We can **conclude** that people are more likely to help others when they have seen someone else model helping behaviour.

These factors were amongst several which were tested in a **field** experiment devised by Irving Piliavin and his colleagues. The details are given on page 275.

Piliavin's subway experiment shows when there is no ambiguity (the bystanders were face-to-face with the 'victims') then helping behaviour occurs; even though there were many bystanders there was no evidence of less helping (diffusion of responsibility). In addition, as soon as one person made a move to help, several others followed. This is further evidence to show that

Piliavin, Rodin & Piliavin (1969)

The **aim** of the study was to investigate the effect that the type of victim, the race of the victim and the presence of a model has on helping behaviour.

The **sample** comprised approximately 4,500 males and female participants, approximately 45% were black and 55% white. They were people who were travelling on the New York subway when the various conditions of the experiment occurred, so they were **opportunity sampled**.

The **procedure** was that two male confederates played a 'victim' who collapsed and a helper who came to his aid. The conditions varied – sometimes the victim was white, sometimes black, sometimes carrying a cane, sometimes appearing to be drunk and sometimes apparently bleeding from the mouth. Sometimes the helper waited one minute before helping, other times he waited two and a half minutes. Two observers noted information such as the characteristics of the participants who helped, how long it took and what comments were made.

The **results** showed that the 'cane' victim was helped immediately in almost every trial. When the victim was drunk or bleeding he was helped 50% of the time before the 'helper' intervened. Bystanders helped the 'cane' victim regardless of his race, but there was more same-race helping of the drunk victim. Several people helped and men were much more likely to help than women.

The researchers **concluded** that people do help in an emergency to a greater degree than laboratory experiments would suggest. The high level of helping of the 'cane' victim could have been because there was less risk than helping the 'drunk' victim, whose condition and possible reaction were unknown.

LEARNING

people are more likely to help when they see someone else model helping behaviour.

The research evidence just described suggests that situations which make a bystander more likely to help in an emergency include:

- when there is no ambiguity about the situation
- when the bystander is the only one who knows of the emergency
- when the bystander is face-to-face with the victim
- when it is fairly easy to help the victim
- when someone models helping behaviour.

PERSONAL FACTORS AFFECTING BYSTANDER INTERVENTION

Psychologists have proposed a number of personal factors affecting bystander behaviour. This is known as the decision model of bystander intervention, because the following five factors affect the bystander's decision to help

Attention

COGNITION

In order to help someone, you need to notice that they may need help. Your attention might be drawn to something because:

- it is so close you cannot fail to notice it, as in the subway experiment
- it is **distinctive** or **unusual** such as the sound of breaking glass, a cry for help, groceries scattered on the pavement, the smell of smoke
- it is **schema-related** so you are primed to notice it. For example a nurse or doctor is more likely to notice someone who is very ill.
- it is **self-related**, for example it involves someone similar (the same age, gender or race).

If you do not notice that help is needed, you will not act.

Interpretation

COGNITION

Once you have noticed an event, the next stage is how you **interpret** what you see – what does it mean? Are those three children just playing or is the little one frightened? Is the person running towards you a shop-lifter on the run or is he about to miss his bus? Are that man and woman who are arguing having a lovers' quarrel or is she about to be attacked? Is that old man who has collapsed drunk or ill? When is an event an emergency? The way we interpret or define a situation will affect whether we intervene or not.

SOCIAL

When we are uncertain we look to other people for more information, but research has shown that other people may also *change* our own interpretation, as Latané & Rodin's study with the 'injured' researcher shows. If this happens then we take no action, which is an example of **pluralistic ignorance**. One of the reasons why a **model** may affect helping is because the model has defined the situation as an emergency for other bystanders.

Personal responsibility

The likelihood that someone will step in to help is related to how much they feel personal responsibility. This is increased by:

SOCIAL

- thinking you are the only one who knows of the emergency. The more bystanders there are, the greater the **diffusion of responsibility**. This is related to **social loafing** (see p. 103), which occurs when many other people are doing the same task, so the individual puts in less effort.

FIGURE 18.3 Is this an emergency?

- the **immediacy** of the emergency – in Piliavin's subway study the 'victim' was in front of the participants, it was hard to escape what was happening so witnesses felt greater personal responsibility. If the 'victim' is not very close then other people may be nearer to offer help so the individual feels less personal responsibility; they can also pretend they have not seen the emergency.
- the **explicitness** of the responsibility – when we are asked *specifically* to take responsibility for something, we are much more likely to show helping behaviour. Tom Moriarty (1975) conducted an **experiment** on a beach, where a confederate left some belongings on a towel. In the experimental condition he asked someone nearby to keep an eye on his belongings whilst he went away for a few minutes. In the control condition no-one was asked. In his absence a 'thief' stole his portable radio. The researchers found that 95% of those who were asked to take responsibility gave chase, but in the control condition only 20% of bystanders gave chase.

Perceived similarity

The work we have seen so far has involved people who are strangers to the bystanders. What about those who are similar or familiar to us? Greater similarity seens to be related to higher empathy and therefore altruism. Jane Piliavin and her colleagues (1969) have proposed that seeing others in distress does create arousal. However, it is only if we see the distressed person as similar to ourselves that we label our feeling as empathy.

This could explain the results of Piliavin's subway experiment – there was more helping from male than female victims because all the victims were male, and those of the same race were more likely to help the 'drunk'. This suggests that the more similar we are to the person in distress, the more likely we are to intervene. Research shows that even a warm smile or very brief conversation with someone will make us more likely to help. We are also more likely to help those we know, whether relatives or someone we have met recently. This may because we become more emotionally aroused when someone we know, or who is similar, needs help.

Knowing how to help

The final factor which affects whether bystanders will help or not is if they feel that they are competent to help. A study which arranged for students and nurses to witness an accident showed that the nurses were more likely to help and the students held back. However, when there was not a nurse present, students helped as readily as the nurses had before.

SOCIAL

This suggests bystanders are making some calculations as to how useful they can be before they act, perhaps because they fear evaluation by others. If you know what to do, the presence of others may encourage you to help. If you do not, you will be reluctant to appear incompetent in front of others. This is an example of **social facilitation** (see p. 105), and is explained below in the Arousal: Cost-reward model of helping.

METHODS

The research we have looked at has focused on behaviour. Social psychologists are interested in human behaviour in a social setting, so they are particularly keen to use a 'natural' social setting rather than the artificial laboratory setting for their research. This is called a **field experiment**, examples of which are Piliavin's subway experiment and Moriarty's beach experiment. Some of the advantages and disadvantages of field experiments are listed below in Box 18.1.

This decision model of helping behaviour has been criticised because it explains why people do not help, rather than why they do. Research shows that even though people take personal responsibility there are many circumstances and reasons why they do not take personal action, and this model does not deal with them adequately. An alternative model which takes account of these factors is described below.

THE AROUSAL: COST-REWARD MODEL OF HELPING

This model has been proposed by Jane Piliavin and her colleagues (1969). It identifies various factors which help explain why bystander intervention takes

18.1 ADVANTAGES AND DISADVANTAGES OF FIELD EXPERIMENTS

Advantages:
- whatever is being studied occurs in a natural setting, so behaviour will not be affected by an artificial laboratory setting
- if the participants are unaware they are taking part in an experiment, their behaviour will not be affected by demand characteristics
- because the experimenter has *some* control, for example over the independent variable and the time and place the experiment occurs, it is possible to draw tentative conclusions about what causes behaviour: this would not be possible for example in an observational study.

Disadvantages:
- the experimenter is unable to control many of the other variables and these may affect the results: for example in the subway experiment most of the participants may have been from the same socio-economic class or of similar ages. Because the experimenter cannot select the participants they are unlikely to be a representative sample of the population.
- when there are many participants the observers may be unable to note everything which everbody does
- it may be impossible to keep to ethical guidelines, for example participants in the subway study did not consent to participate; witnesses of the 'emergency' may have experienced distress but it was not possible to debrief them.

place, and starts by noting two basic influences on helping behaviour – arousal and cost-reward calculations:

INBORN

- **arousal** – we saw earlier in the chapter that arousal is an emotional response to the distress of others, and it can be reduced if the bystander relieves the distress of the victim. This is why people are motivated to help.

COGNITION

- **cost-reward** calculations are made by weighing up the costs of helping with the rewards of helping. If the rewards are greater than the costs, the bystander will help. This part of the model is based on the same principle as social exchange theory (see p. 101).

The model says that bystanders will act to reduce arousal, but also explains why they take the action they do – it is whatever involves lowest costs and greatest rewards. What is costly varies from individual to individual. We saw above that a nurse was more likely to help than a student: the student's costs would include fear of doing the wrong thing, but to the nurse this is unlikely to be a cost.

Cost also varies for the same individual from situation to situation: the nurse may stop to help if she is going in to work, but is less likely to stop if she is

FIGURE 18.4 Could you explain this picture using some of the ideas from research into bystander intervention?

hurrying to catch the last train home. The Arousal: Cost-reward model is valuable because it brings together the notion of arousal and cognition, and can be used to explain helping behaviour by a variety of individuals and in a variety of situations.

How may social norms affect pro-social behaviour?

SOCIAL

We have looked at how others may affect our behaviour in an emergency, but what about more general situations when we help one another? One way of explaining pro-social behaviour is to say that people do what society expects of them. These unspoken rules and expectations about how we should behave are called the **social norms**.

They operate at a lower level of helping than we have looked at earlier under **altruism**, because these norms are about what society expects us to do, whereas altruistic behaviour is *more* than we would normally be expected to do. These norms exert pressure on us as to how we should behave in particular circumstances. We will look at four of them below.

THE NORM OF SOCIAL RESPONSIBILITY

SOCIAL

Social responsibility relates to the idea that we should help those who are more disadvantaged than us – like the teenager giving her seat to an old lady. You might lend your notes to a fellow student who had missed classes because of illness, but not if you thought she was just lazy. If we feel a moral obligation to help then we have internalised the norm of social responsibility. We are more likely to be influenced by this norm when:

● the other person is not responsible for their need
● the other person obviously needs help
● it does not cost us much to help.

THE NORM OF EQUALITY

SOCIAL

This norm requires that when help is given it should be shared out equally, for example a teacher should spend an equal amount of time with every member of the class. In a family, the parent should treat all of the children the same. Most children complain at some time 'it's not fair!', which shows they understand the norm of equality at an early age.

THE NORM OF EQUITY

SOCIAL

Equity means that help is given in proportion to what is deserved. In contrast to the norm of equality, this social norm is an expectation that, for example, the teacher should help students in proportion to the amount of effort the student makes. This norm is related to something called 'belief in a just world', which is the idea that people get what they deserve, so they should receive less help if they are responsible for the situation they are in.

THE NORM OF RECIPROCITY

SOCIAL

This means that we help others when we ourselves have been helped, or expect to be helped. If you lend your class notes to a friend who misses class, you expect her to do you a favour in the future if you asked her to. It is related to feelings of indebtedness or gratitude, and research suggests that the greater the help given, the greater the help which is returned. This underlines that we have a sense of balance about how much help we 'owe' someone. However we are less likely to be influenced by this norm if:

● the other person is forced to help us
● the other person did not intend to help us
● the help is at very low cost to the giver.

The last two of these social norms include the notion of exchange, but cross-cultural research of helping behaviour shows that the emphasis on exchange is a Western trait which may be related to our more individualist cultures. In collectivist cultures there appears to be a universal norm to help, regardless of perceived need or closeness of relationship.

Whatever the social norms are, research in the West suggests that the degree to which we *conform* to social norms varies. There are many reasons for this – for example, some of these norms conflict, it depends how strongly we have **internalised** them, how much our social group influences our behaviour, we may not apply them to those we see as in the 'out-group' (see p. 118), it depends on the level and strength of our **moral development** (see p. 264). Social norms are only a very general guide to who will help, why they do so, who they will help and in what circumstances.

Summary

This chapter has looked at several kinds of helping behaviour. We looked at empathy, as a major factor in altruism and moved on to consider research on altruistic behaviour. Our review of research on why people help, and do not help, in emergencies has pointed up several situational and personal factors. These have been linked with the notion of arousal in Piliavin's model, which explains why and predicts when people will perform particular types of helping behaviour. We finished by considering helping behaviour which we perform in order to conform to social norms – we do it because it is expected.

Exercises

1 What is empathy?
2 Describe the stages in a child's development of empathy.
3 How does empathy develop?
4 What is altruism?
5 Describe one psychological study of altruism.
6 How might someone affect an individual's altruistic behaviour?
7 From what you have learned in psychology, describe two situations in which a bystander is likely to help another person.
8 From what you have learned in psychology, explain one reason why a bystander might decide to help another person.
9 Give an example of one way in which a social norm may affect pro-social behaviour.
10 Explain why social norms affect pro-social behaviour.

Construction of Social 'Reality'

19

Have you ever compared your view of someone with a friend and found that you 'saw' him differently? You think he is cold, your friend thinks he is shy. We often 'see' the world differently from others, we put our own interpretation on it, we have our own construction of it. At the same time, our view is more *real* for us than anyone else's view. So we construct our own social 'reality'. In this chapter we are going to look at some ways in which we construct our own reality. We will consider how we form impressions of people when we first meet them and how our mental processes may affect what we notice and what we ignore. Finally we will look at how this 'reality' can be influenced by others.

Forming impressions of others

COGNITION

We form impressions of others constantly and rapidly, often based on only one or two items of information about them. How do we choose this information, how accurate are the impressions and how long do they last? To answer these question psychologists have studied how we **select** information, **organise** it and what **inferences** we make from it. You can see from the three explanations which follow that each of these features are present.

PRIMACY AND RECENCY EFFECTS

DEFINITION

Imagine a new student joins your class. She seems pleasant and outgoing but after a couple of weeks she starts to demand a lot of the teacher's time. If someone asked you what you thought of her, you would probably say something like 'She seems O.K.' That is, your first impression (which was pleasant) was stronger than the more recent one (unpleasant). The evidence that first impressions are more influential than later ones is very strong, and this is called the **primacy effect**. We will look first at the primacy effect before considering the circumstances in which the last, or most recent, information is more powerful – the **recency effect**.

The primacy effect

A. Luchins (1957) tested primacy and recency by giving information about an imaginary person called Jim to four groups of participants. The information was in two parts: one part described Jim as outgoing, the other as shy. Each group read a different version of this information: one read a description in which Jim was outgoing but was then described as shy; a second group read the description in which he was shy but then outgoing. The other two groups received only one piece of information, that he was either shy or outgoing. All participants then rated Jim for personality characteristics, including friendliness. Here are some of the results.

Description	Percentage rating Jim as friendly
Friendly description only	95%
Friendly first – unfriendly last	78%
Unfriendly first – friendly last	18%
Unfriendly description only	3%

TABLE 19.1 Percentage of participants rating Jim as friendly

Results showed that in the two groups receiving *both* types of information, what the participants read *first* determined their judgement of Jim's personality: this is evidence of the **primacy effect**. Participants also rated Jim more positively when the outgoing information was given first – he was thought to be more likeable and good looking. This shows that participants **inferred** other, positive characteristics as a result of their first impression.

COGNITION

Another study of the primacy effect involved participants watching a confederate solve difficult problems – he always got 15 of the 30 problems right. When he got most of the *early* problems right participants estimated an average of 20 out of 30 correct, but when he got most of the later problems right they estimated 12 out of 30 were correct. When asked the reasons for their judgements, those who saw the confederate's early right answers replied that the later wrong answers were due to tiredness or boredom, whereas if the early problems were wrong, his later success was due to luck or guesswork.

Luchins found that the primacy effect is strongest when we are given information about someone we do not know. This could be because:

COGNITION

● we give more weight to the first information we receive, particularly when meeting people for the first time. As we know nothing about them, this first information is not modified by previous knowledge.

COGNITION

● our early information affects the meaning of later information – we *alter* the later information to make it consistent with our first impression and we may pay less attention to it (see the reasons for the problem-solver's abilities given above)

FIGURE 19.1 First impressions count

The Recency Effect

DEFINITION

Under certain circumstances we do take more account of the *last* information we receive – the **recency effect**. It occurs when:

● we are careful not to make a judgement too early on, which is particularly important when interviewing others or hearing evidence as a member of a jury
● there is a period of time between receiving the two lots of information
● information is about people we already know
● the first information we receive is positive but it is followed by *negative* information. For example if I describe a friend as sociable and reliable and having being drunk last night then you are more likely to remember the last item, and your impression will be negative.

Primacy and recency effects are important in our lives and primacy is particularly powerful because we interpret subsequent information in the light of these first impressions. For example research has shown the effect primacy and recency can have on the way jurors understand and think about the testimony of witnesses in court.

CENTRAL AND PERIPHERAL TRAITS

COGNITION

Research has suggested that some information about people is more important than others – the important information is **central** to our judgement of that person. These central traits will influence the impression we form of them. Solomon Asch (1946) proposed that one central trait was how warm or cold the person was. He gave two groups of participants an identical list of personality traits which he said described someone. The traits were:

intelligent skilful industrious – – – – determined practical cautious

COGNITION

The difference between them was that one group saw 'warm' as the trait in the blank space, and the other group saw 'cold'. They were then given a list of additional traits (such as generous, wise, happy, good-natured, reliable) and asked to choose which of them this person would have. Asch's **results** showed that participants reading the 'warm' list gave more positive additional characteristics than those reading the 'cold' list. In other words, participants **inferred** these positive qualities simply because the person was described as warm.

In another study Asch substituted the traits 'polite' or 'blunt' for the 'warm' or 'cold' traits. He found that these new traits had little impact on participants' impressions of the imaginary person, because they chose the additional traits in roughly equal percentages for 'polite' or 'blunt'. These **results** have been compiled in Table 19.2 below.

Additional traits	Traits inserted into description					
	Warm	or	cold	Polite	or	blunt
Generous	91		8	56		58
Humorous	77		13	71		48
Altruistic	69		18	29		46

TABLE 19.2 Table showing percentage of participants assigning additional traits to an imaginary figure

Asch **concluded** from these results that certain traits are central to the impression we have of others. They even influence our perception of other (peripheral) traits. However, there have been criticisms of this study, some of which have extended our understanding of central traits, for example:

● Harold Kelley (1950) argued that participants in Asch's research only had to imagine the person. In a study of real-life impression formation he gave students information on a new teacher which included the words either 'rather warm' or 'rather cold'. After they had all been in the same class with this new teacher, Kelley found that students reading the 'warm' information rated the teacher more highly (and interacted more with him) than those reading 'cold'. This supports the idea that warm/cold *are* examples of central traits, because on the basis of one word participants perceived the same person differently, and behaved differently towards him.

● S. Rosenberg (1968) argued that if someone is already described as helpful then warm does not add much more information. It was the **distinctiveness** of the information which created the effect Asch found, because the warm/cold trait was a social one but all the other traits were *intellectual* ones. Rosenberg proposed that there are two major dimensions which underlie our assessment of others. One is the **social/interpersonal** dimension (which applies to warm/cold) and the other is the **intellectual/competence** dimension (which applies to intellectual abilities). Traits relating to social *and* intellectual dimensions are central traits.

COGNITION

IMPLICIT PERSONALITY THEORIES

These are our own theories about people. We think that certain personality traits go together like a package, so these theories relate to the way we organise information. When we see someone we do not know, we identify *one* of their features and then apply the whole personality package. From this limited information we make inferences about people we do not know. We are not usually aware of the judgements we make, nor do we test them, which is why they are called 'implicit' theories. We will look at the halo effect and stereotyping.

COGNITION

The Halo effect

This refers to the way we generate information about a person based on one known factor which is either positive or negative. The most vivid example of the halo effect comes from how we judge a physically attractive person. Karen Dion (1972) found that attractive people in photographs were thought to be more sensitive, kind and interesting than less attractive people. Other research shows that attractive people are treated more leniently – whether they are writing poor essays or being tried in court.

DEFINITION

One study looked at teachers' judgements of 11 year old children. The teacher was provided with a small photograph of each child and information about them. Although this information was identical for each child, teachers rated the more attractive children as being more intelligent and socially adjusted than the less attractive children.

FIGURE 19.2 The attractiveness of this woman will affect the judgements that others make of her

When participants are asked for their impressions of people who are described with a negative, unpleasant trait, they infer that they have have other negative traits – so the halo effect can occur with both positive *and* negative features.

COGNITION

The halo effect appears to happen when attention focusses on a particular feature. For example, in the teacher study, the teachers could compare the appearance of the children. In everyday life we are less likely to make such a direct comparison if we have other information about the person, but if a person strikes us as *particularly* attractive, or *particularly* bad-tempered, then we are likely to take that feature as typical of that person's overall personality. We are likely to make some inaccurate inferences about how good, or bad, their qualities are.

Stereotyping

COGNITION

A stereotype is a rigid, generalised and simplified set of ideas about others. These ideas are culturally shared and are applied to others simply because they belong to a particular group or because of a particular feature they have. So, on the basis of one feature, we categorise someone and infer they have a whole range of characteristics and abilities which we assume all members of that group have (see p. 31). Stereotypes can be:

- **group** stereotypes – a rigid set of shared beliefs about all members of a group, groups being based on social or physical features such as age, race, disability, sex, clothing, nationality or accent. Once we classify a person as belonging to that group we infer he or she has the traits we apply to all members of that group. Examples of stereotypes are that the elderly are timid, black people are good athletes, women are dependent.

FIGURE 19.3 Evelyn Glennie a world-famous percussionist. She is also deaf. Does she fit your stereotype of a deaf person?

- **individual** stereotypes – which are based on more individual features, for example redheads are hot-tempered or people wearing glasses are intelligent. In a study which examined name stereotypes, teachers were asked to mark children's work. Each piece of work was identical, the only thing that was manipulated was the child's name – for example either David or Hubert. Work which teachers thought was produced by a 'David' got higher marks than work by a 'Hubert'. This is evidence that stereotyping influences our judgements and behaviour.

When we stereotype we tend to look for information which confirms our stereotype, and ignore information which contradicts it, so we do not see the *individual*, only a stereotyped distortion. This is demonstrated in a study where participants were given a description of an imaginary person, including information that she went out on dates and never had a steady boyfriend in high school. Afterwards participants were given additional information: some were told she married, others were told she adopted a lesbian lifestyle. **Results** showed that participants later recalled more of the original information which conformed with their stereotype: those who were told she got married remembered her dates, those who thought she was lesbian remembered she never had a steady boyfriend.

Due to the self-fulling prophecy (see p. 220) our stereotypes may provide evidence that our assumptions about others are right because we treat people as we *expect* them to be. When they behave in accordance with our expectations, this confirms what we thought originally, so our stereotype is strengthened.

Constructing social 'reality'

The debate over what 'reality' is has been raging for centuries. To what extent is there an objective, accurate truth about our experience of the world or do we all construct our own version of 'reality'? We can look at this from two perspectives:

COGNITION

SOCIAL

- the **personal** – how do we, as individuals, make sense of the information we receive?
- the **social** – what information do we receive? how is it shaped to create a particular version of events?

Whichever perspective we take, psychological research has shown that the massive amount of information which is available to us about 'the world' has to be reduced in order that we can manage it. It may be reduced by others, who therefore act as **social filters** of information, or by ourselves through our personal filters.

The effect of personal filters on the construction of social reality

In our waking lives we are constantly bombarded with information which we have to reduce or we would become overwhelmed by it, so we filter this information. On what basis do we filter it? How does the filtering process work? What effect does it have on our construction of social reality? We will look at the answers to these questions in relation to three personal filters – attention, personal constructs and scripts.

ATTENTION

COGNITION

Attention helps us to select particular information from the vast array of information which is available to us at any time. We have already seen in the section on impression formation that we select information such as a physical feature, a central trait, the first information. Psychologists who are interested in how we process information have proposed that we are more likely to attend to information which has one of the following characteristics:

- **Distinctiveness** (or saliency) – we notice information which is unusual or distinctive, for instance someone who is very tall, who behaves in an unusual way, who is 'the odd one out' in a group (see Figure 19.4). Research shows that someone who is distinctive seems to have more influence on group discussion and decisions than the others. If you remember earlier when we looked at central and peripheral traits, Rosenberg argued that 'warm' was influential because it was so different from any of the other traits described.
- **Vividness** – information which is emotionally engaging, or perceptually bright (for example a colour photograph as opposed to a black and white one) is more likely to be attended to. We attend to something vivid at the expense of other information, as Elizabeth Loftus and her colleagues found when participants were shown an incident in which a character produced a knife. They were not able to recall *other* details of the situation such as the person's appearance.
- **Pertinence** – you are more likely to attend to information which is relevant to you, so you will hear your name amongst a lot of background chatter, but miss what your friend is saying to you; if you are weight-watching you will notice what people eat but fail to register other information

FIGURE 19.4 An example of distinctiveness

about them; if you are unsure about something you will attend to information which makes you more confident.

- **Accessibility** (or priming) – some information will be more easily picked up because it fits in to a schema which we have readily available (we are 'primed' to pick up this information). The schema may be available because it has recently been used: if a friend has just described a great new film you are more likely to notice advertisements for it or what other people say about it. Your friend's description has primed you. The schema may be accessible because it is frequently used – for example those who gender stereotype will notice information related to gender.

D. Norman and T. Shallice (1980) have proposed that some of our attention is completely automatic so we are not aware of what we notice. But if our attention is drawn to certain things, we are less able to pay attention to others, so this information may be filtered out and lost to us. Thus we can see that what we attend to and what we 'lose' in turn determines how we construct social 'reality'.

PERSONAL CONSTRUCTS

COGNITION

We all try to make sense of our world, to understand and predict events. George Kelly (1955) proposed that through experience we develop our *own* theories about what the world is like. He called these theories **personal constructs**, and each construct comprises a pair of opposite words, for example, one person might have the construct 'friendly – unfriendly', but another's might be 'friendly – shy'. Because the 'opposite' word is different, this shows that 'friendly' has a different meaning for each of these people.

Kelly maintained that we have between three and six of these constructs: they represent the way we view the world, particularly other people and their behaviour. One person may have the friendly–shy construct and another have *no* construct related to these characteristics; it depends on what is important to us. We are not usually aware of our constructs, but Kelly devised the Rep Grid technique which reveals them. We use our **personal constructs** to:

- organise information about our social world. We perceive others, and their behaviour, through our constructs. Imagine two men who meet the same person for the first time – she is very quiet. The man with the friendly-shy construct sees this quiet woman as shy. But the other man has 'interesting-boring' as one of his constructs and therefore sees her as boring. They perceive the same woman in a different way, indeed they will view most aspects of their social experiences in a different way so they construct their own social reality.
- act as a guide for our own actions and responses. We respond to others in

accordance with the way we perceive them. The man with the friendly-shy construct may encourage the quiet woman to talk more, the other man may simply ignore her.

● we test our personal constructs (which are theories of what the world is like) against what we see or experience. Our concern is *not* for objective truth but that things have meaning only as they fit our personal construction of the world. We are constantly checking these constructs against our experiences and we adapt them where necessary to fit new information.

So our personal constructs filter information, and that filter is based on our own, individual, perceptions of the social world. They are ways of organising social information and explaining the world to ourselves.

COGNITION

SCRIPTS

COGNITION

A **script** is a sequence of events and behaviours in a social setting which are linked together. It is a way of organising and representing our social knowledge (see p. 28). Scripts:

● help us to act in the appropriate way, for example you have a script for what happens each time you go to psychology class. There may be noisy chatter, students sitting on desks, but once the teacher arrives you settle in to your places. Chatter will continue until the teacher shows, in some way, that formal lessons have begun. Each teacher may show this in a different way, but the basic script is the same.

● include the roles which people perform, so they enable each participant to play the appropriate role at the right time. You play your student role once the teacher arrives just as your teacher plays his or her teacher role on entering the classroom.

● help us interpret the actions of others and predict what they will do. You expect your teacher to assert the teacher role soon after entering the classroom. If she sits down and starts reading then she is not conforming to the script. Scripts provide us with social rules: when to speak, how to address someone, whether to act casually or formally, who has power. They help us to predict what will happen and are triggered spontaneously at the start of a script 'sequence'.

How do we learn **scripts**? Initially we learn them from others – what they tell us, and what we see others doing. Through this we develop a simple schema for an event. The more we see these situations being acted out, the more complex our schema becomes. Scripts are also known as **event schemas** because they are a way of organising our experiences (see p. 28). If we are able to participate in a script this provides even more detail.

In a study of the 'dating' scripts of American students, researchers found that those who dated a lot had rich and complex scripts, and could identify behaviour as belonging to a script very easily. Those who dated less had more simple scripts. So although scripts are socially shared experiences, to some extent they are personal, depending on our experience and interests.

We are constantly learning new scripts – the five year old learns the 'going to school' script, the teenager learns the 'dating' script, the hospital patient learns the 'being a patient' script and the unemployed learn the 'claiming benefit' script. Once the script is under way we notice and interpret things in terms of the script, because they:

COGNITION

- direct our **attention** to material which is relevant to the schema. We notice what we expect to notice but may 'miss' something we are not looking for. In your first psychology class you may have watched everything the teacher did when he or she entered the room. Once you have learned the script, you only attend to information which is relevant, such as when formal teaching is about to start.
- enable us to **interpret** ambiguous information, so you interpret the teacher's polite coughing as the start of the class in a different way from coughing whilst the class is under way.
- lead us to **infer** information which we do not actually experience, for

FIGURE 19.5 These teenagers going to their sixth form prom are learning a special kind of dating script

example in a study in which participants watched an 'eating in a restaurant' script, they reported seeing incidents such as paying the bill when they did not actually happen.

● act as a guide to future action because they represent our accumulated knowledge of what people or situations are like, and we use this knowledge to predict what they will be like, so we expect certain behaviours. From your psychology class script you will know the sign that the class is to start, and you will know what it means, so it is a guide to your own actions.

To summarise, we have noted how attention, personal constructs and scripts act as filters of information from the real world. Our tendency to generate information from very little, to select only certain aspects of our environment and to be influenced by our own needs will distort the way we see the world, the way we construct our own social reality. As we discover next, this distortion is increased by the information we receive through social channels of communication.

The effect of social filters on the construction of social reality

If your friend describes the events of the previous evening, her description will not be an exact replica. She will summarise what happened, mention certain details but omit others. She may add information which she did not see or hear, but which she assumes from everything else she experienced.

This is a simple example of how information is filtered by others, whether by a friend, a teacher, a politician, or the director of a TV programme. During the process of filtering, the information is changed in some way. First we will consider the media, which is an important social filter, then we will look at a number of other social filters, sometimes known as gatekeepers.

THE MEDIA AS A SOCIAL FILTER

The media has to filter information in order to pass it on to the public. It has to do this because there is just too much but also because, for example, a magazine wants to create certain impressions, to appeal to a certain type of reader, or to get across a particular message.

Manipulating information using cognitive processes

COGNITION   The earlier section on **attention** identified several reasons why we select certain information to attend to, and in the process ignore other information.

The media can do this for us – it can manipulate the way information is presented so that we attend to certain aspects and ignore others. For example:

● **Distinctiveness** – information which is unusual is more likely to be covered in the news, which is why charities and pressure groups try to gain media attention through publicity stunts. Air crashes (because they are more unusual) receive more prominence than car crashes, leading to the assumption that air travel is much more dangerous. In fact the opposite is true – so the media has helped create a false social 'reality'.

● **Vividness** – material which has a high emotional content (which creates anger, excitement or empathy) is more likely to gain attention, for example broadcasting violent films or reporting news items with a violent bias. Research showed that in the 1980s fights between striking miners and police were more likely to be broadcast than peaceful strike action. Such broadcasts create the impression that violence and aggression are more common than they actually are.

● **Inference** – attitudes do not have to be stated, they can be inferred. For example, **ethnocentrism** is promoted by statements such as '350 die in air crash, no Britons were aboard', the inference being that British people are

FIGURE 19.6 Distinctiveness is one way to gain the attention of the media and the public

the most important. If two things are unusual and they appear close together, we infer that they are associated, so if a news item reports that an Asian man was charged with a crime we are likely to infer that Asians are more likely to be criminals than members of other ethnic groups. This false relationship is called an **illusory correlation** and affects our perception of reality.

- **Primacy** – as we saw at the start of this chapter we are more likely to attend to the first information we receive – the **primacy effect**. Later information is filtered through, and therefore affected by our first impression. The media can influence the way we understand information by determining the order in which information is presented.

Presenting biased information

People receive a considerable amount of information about the world through the media, how others behave, what happens in certain circumstances and so on. When this information is biased, it can affect people's perceptions, as the following examples show.

SOCIAL

- The 'public interest' and 'public opinion' are presented as though they are something concrete, so when the media uses these terms it gives the individual the impression that others have this view, and so contributes to the creation of **social norms**. This is particularly likely to happen when people are uncertain because they look to others for information.

COGNITION

- **Stereotypes** can be triggered by the language used – the viewer or reader understands 'terrorist' in a different way from 'freedom fighter'. The choice of label may trigger a stereotype which will in turn affect the way any additional information is processed. The media therefore provides the filter for us.

COGNITION

- Stereotyped information may have considerable influence on children because their knowledge is limited and uncertain. For example, research shows that white children with little everyday contact with black people formed most of their views from the way in which black people were portrayed on television.

LEARNING

- The media is a valuable source of information relating to **roles** and **scripts**. Through observational learning we can discover what people do in all kinds of circumstances, such as going to hospital after an accident, going for an interview, being arrested, checking in at an airport, attending a funeral, going to a restaurant. However the information may be biased because these events are usually shown for dramatic reasons and are therefore made more exciting, the actors' behaviours are more extreme. Research has shown that scripts for resolving problems frequently contain aggressive behaviour, possibly learned through observation from television.

We have seen some examples of the way in which the media can select and present information and so affect the way we interpret reality. Additional examples are covered elsewhere in this book under gender stereotyping (see p. 201) and prejudice (see p. 128).

GATEKEEPERS AS SOCIAL FILTERS

Gatekeepers are those who are in a position to control the flow of information to others. They are people who have information which others may want or need or should have. They are in a position to control how much is released and in what way – it may be reduced, condensed, biased, supressed, invented, highlighted. By controlling it in this way, gatekeepers contribute to the construction of social 'reality'. For example:

COGNITION

- **Politicians** are gatekeepers. What they consider important, the information they choose to use in support of their arguments, they way they present policies, the people they choose as **scapegoats** for problems, the issues they talk about or ignore are aimed at influencing the way we think and, just before a general election, the way we vote.

COGNITION

- **Experts** act as gatekeepers, because of their detailed knowedge. Scientists, doctors, economists for example, when asked to give advice or information, must assess what is relevant and provide it in a way which is understandable to the questioner. Experts may be advising government ministers and civil servants, they may be answering questions put by a radio interviewer or debating the topic with others on a television programme, or talking to a patient in a hospital. What they say and do not say contributes to the construction of social reality.

- The **media** – people such as newspaper editors and the producers of television programmes are in a position to decide whether or not to publish or broadcast information (the private lives of public people, environmental incidents), how important it appears to be (front page or bottom of page 11), how it is portrayed (does it show 3,000 peaceful demonstrators or the one scuffle which occurred?), what bias or spin to put on it (are striking health workers 'protesting at the government' or 'concerned about patients' wellbeing'), the time information is broadcast (will that documentary on a miscarriage of justice go out at 8.00 pm. or 11.30 pm.?). The decisions these gatekeepers make affect what information we receive and how we understand it.

- **Censors** – official censors decide whether material (such as books or films) are suitable for public use. They can restrict audiences for films and prevent publication of books. The film 'A Clockwork Orange' is a recent example of a film which has been released nearly 30 years after its production.

Social filters of information are therefore in a position to shape the reality of the world for us. They are particularly influential in areas that we know little about, perhaps because they are new or require expertise to understand.

Summary

This chapter has described several ways in which our perception of the 'real' world can be constructed. It shows how cognitive factors such as what we attend to or how we organise information can in turn affect what we notice and use, and equally why we do not notice other information. We have seen a number of examples of our tendency to generate information from one small fact, and how that too may prevent us from noticing other aspects of our world. We have noted reasons why one person might select information differently from another person and seen how we rely on others to interpret or provide us with information, particularly those who have considerable knowledge which has to be reduced or simplified in order to be transmitted to us. With greater awareness of how information is filtered, we might be less inclined to thoughtlessly accept someone else's version of of social 'reality'.

Exercises

1 Explain how central traits influence our overall impression of a person.
2 When forming impressions of others, what is the primacy effect?
3 Explain how an implicit personality theory might create an impressions of someone when we meet them for the first time.
4 How do personal constructs act as a personal filter of information?
5 From your study of psychology, describe one way in which one person might select information differently from another person.
6 How does attention act as a personal filter of information?
7 From your study of psychology, describe how different people might think about information in different ways.
8 Give an example of a social filter and explain how it influences the information we receive.
9 Describe one way in which the media can act as a social filter of information.
10 Describe the ways in which the media can influence people's thinking about what happens in the world.

Further Reading

Argyle, M. (1994) *Psychology of Interpersonal Behaviour* (5th ed), London: Penguin

Association for the Teaching of Psychology (1992) *Ethics in Psychological Research*. (This is provided as Appendix A in the Syllabus Support Material book which is produced by the Southern Examining Group for GCSE Psychology)

Baron, R. & Byrne, D. (1997) *Social Psychology* (8th ed), Needham Heights, Mass: Allyn & Bacon

Bee, H. (1992) *The Developing Child* (6th ed), New York: Harper Collins

Coolican, H. (1995) *Introduction to Research Methods and Statistics in Psychology*, London: Hodder & Stoughton Educational

Deaux, K., Dane, F. & Wrightsman, L. (1993) *Social Psychology in the 90s* (6th ed), Pacific Grove, Calif: Brooks/Cole

Golombok, S. & Fivush, R. (1994) *Gender Development*, Cambridge University Press: Cambridge

Gross, R. (1999) *Key Studies in Psychology* (3rd ed), London: Hodder & Stoughton Educational

Gross, R. (1996) *Psychology: The Science of Mind and Behaviour* (3rd ed), London: Hodder & Stoughton Educational

Hayes, N. (1998) *Foundations of Psychology* (2nd ed), Middlesex: Thomas Nelson & Sons Ltd

Hewstone, M., Manstead, A. & Stroebe, W. (1997) *The Blackwell Reader in Social Psychology*, Oxford: Blackwell Publishers

Meadows, S. (1993) *The Child as Thinker: the Development and Acquisition of Cognition in Childhood*, London: Routledge

Nicholson, J. (1984) *Men & Women – How Different Are They?* Oxford: Oxford University Press

Rutter, M. (1981) *Maternal Deprivation Reassessed* (2nd ed), Harmondsworth, Middx: Penguin

Sabini, J. (1995) *Social Psychology* (2nd ed), New York: W. W. Norton & Co. Inc.

Sampson, E. (1991) *Social Worlds – Personal Lives: an Introduction to Social Psychology*, Orlando: Harcourt Brace Jovanovich

Glossary

accommodation modifying a schema or creating a new one in order to cope with new information (Piaget) (p. 233)

affiliation the need to be in contact with others (p. 19)

altruism behaviour which puts someone's well-being before your own, perhaps in a way which is damaging to oneself, without thought of reward (p. 269)

assimilation using a schema to act on the environment (Piaget) (p. 232)

attachment a close emotional bond felt by one person towards another (p. 75)

attention the process by which we notice or attend to information (p. 290)

autonomous morality morals based on one's own rules and taking account of intent (Piaget) (p. 255)

bar chart a way of showing amounts or number of times something occurs (p. 61)

behaviourist relating to the view that behaviour can be best understood by studying only that which can be observed (p 13)

bystander intervention the way in which people behave who witness an incident (p. 273)

case study a detailed study of an individual (or a small group) (p. 39)

categorisation grouping things together on the basis of some similarity (p. 117)

child rearing style the way parents bring up children, relating particularly to affection and discipline (p. 142)

classical conditioning learning which occurs when an automatic response becomes associated with a previously unrelated stimulus (p. 11)

concept an abstract idea, a way of grouping things (p. 31)

conclusions ideas which can be drawn from the results of a study (p. 66)

concrete operational stage third stage of cognitive development (Piaget) (p. 229)

conditional response the response which occurs when the conditioned stimulus is presented (p. 11)

conditional stimulus the stimulus which is presented with the unconditional stimulus (p. 11)

conditions   the experiences which different groups of participants undergo (p. 52)

confederate   someone who appears to be a subject but who is actually following the researcher's instructions, so is part of the study (p. 107)

cognition   anything to do with mental processes such as remembering or thinking (p. 52)

conformity   following the ideas or behaviour of others rather than one's own (p. 107)

confounding variables   any variables which may distort results (p. 59)

conscience   the part of the superego which stops us from doing things we know to be wrong (Freud) (p. 153)

conservation   the understanding that somethings stays the same even though the appearance changes (Piaget) (p. 230)

control condition/control group   the group of participants who do not experience the IV (p. 52)

counterbalancing   giving half the participants the experimental condition first and the other participants the control condition first (p. 53)

correlational study   a study to discover if there is a relationship between two variables (p. 44)

cross-cultural study   a study which compares people from different cultures (p. 46)

cross-sectional study   a way of investigating change by studying people at different ages or stages at the same time (p. 46)

debrief   giving a general explanation of the study to participants when they have finished and ensuring their wellbeing (p. 70)

decentre   to be able to take into account more than one aspect of a situation at a time (Piaget) (p. 230)

defence mechanisms   unconscious strategies to reduce anxiety (Freud) (p. 154)

deindividuation   a state in which the individual becomes less aware of themselves and has less control over their own behaviour (p. 109)

demand characteristics   the clues in an experiment which lead the subject to think they know what the researcher is looking for (p. 43)

dependent variable   the outcome of manipulation of the independent variable – the results (p. 42)

deprivation   in attachment, being separated from an attachment figure (p. 89)

discrimination   treating people differently on the basis of their membership of a group (p. 122)

distress syndrome   the pattern of protest, despair and detachment shown by children upon separation (p. 82)

dizygotic twins   twins from two eggs – fraternal or non-identical (p. 8)

ego   the part of personality in touch with reality (Freud) (p. 153)

ego ideal   the part of the superego that represents what we would like to be (Freud) (p. 153)

egocentrism   seeing the world only from one's own perspective, understanding the world as an extension of oneself (Piaget) (p. 229)

empathy   a response to someone else's emotions which is very similar in emotional tone (p. 267)

enrichment   something which stimulates cognitive development (p. 182)

environment   our surroundings and experiences (p. 23)

equilibration   restructuring schemas into new structures (Piaget) (p. 233)

ethics   desirable standards of behaviour towards others (p. 68)

ethnocentrism   viewing other cultures through your own cultural lens and using it as a standard for judging any other culture (p. 119)

ethology   the study of animals in their natural environment (p. 133)

experiment   a research method in which all variables are controlled except one, the IV, so that the effect of that variable can be measured (p. 41)

experimental condition/experimental group   the group of participants who experience the IV (p. 52)

extinction   when a response to a stimulus is no longer seen (p. 12)

formal operational stage   fourth stage of cognitive development (Piaget) (p. 231)

frustration-aggression hypothesis   the proposal that frustration always leads to aggression (p. 136)

gatekeeper   someone who is able to control the flow of information (p. 298)

gender   the psychological or cultural aspects of maleness or femaleness (p. 187)

gender concept   a full understanding of gender, including its permanence (p. 188)

gender constancy   the understanding that one stays the same sex despite changes in appearance (p. 194)

gender identity   the knowledge of one's own and others' gender label (p. 188)

gender stability   the understanding that one stays the same sex throughout life (p. 193)

generalise   applying information from one situation to other similar situations (pp. 12, 39)

genetic   due to the action of genes (p. 8)

graph   a way of representing data to show change over time (p. 61)

halo effect   the tendency to assume that someone with an attractive quality has other positive qualities (p. 287)

heredity   anything we inherit through our genes (p. 7)

heteronomous morality   moral standards imposed from outside the individual and based on the consequences of actions (Piaget) (p. 255)

hypothesis   a prediction of what will happen, an expectation (p. 51)

id   part of personality which contains our instincts and desires (Freud) (p. 153)

identification   the process by which the child comes to take in the ideas and behaviours of the same sex parent (Freud) (p. 156)

impression formation   making inferences about people on the basis of little information (p. 283)

imitation   copying behaviour (p. 16)

inborn   any characteristic we are born with (p. 3)

independent measures   an experimental design which has different participants in each group (p. 53)

independent variable   what the researcher manipulates in an experiment (p. 41)

inference   filling in the gaps in information, an assumption (p. 28)

ingroup-outgroup   the division of people into two groups, the ingroup is the group to which we belong, the outgroup is all the others (p. 117)

information processing   viewing cognition by looking at the processes and strategies we use in cognitive activity (p. 26)

instinct   an inborn need and the drive to satisfy that need (p. 2)

internalise   to feel that a behaviour or idea is part of us, that we own it (p. 16)

IQ   intelligence quotient, a person's score on an intelligence test (p. 169)

labelling   identifying people as different in a certain way, and then treating them accordingly (p. 216)

learning   a relatively permanent change in behaviour which is due to experience (p. 10)

libido   the life instinct (Freud) (p. 155)

longitudinal study   a study which follows the same participants over an extended period of time (p. 45)

matched pairs   an experimental design in which each condition has different participants but they are paired on the basis of their similarity in several characteristics (p. 54)

maternal deprivation   having no attachment, or a damaged attachment, to the mother (Bowlby) (p. 82)

maturation   a genetically programmed sequence of change towards full development (p. 5)

mean   average (p. 64)

model   someone whose behaviour is imitated (p. 16)

monozygotic twins   twins from the same egg – identical (p. 8)

nature or nurture debate   the discussion as to whether differences in human abilities and characteristics are inborn or the result of experience (p. 7)

negative correlation   a relationship between two variables in which as one increases the other decreases (p. 64)

negative reinforcement   anything which stops an unpleasant experience (p. 14)

norms   the beliefs or expectations which members of a group share (p. 107)

object permanence   a child's understanding that although it can no longer see an object, the object still exists (Piaget) (p. 228)

observation   research which involves watching and recording behaviour (p. 37)

observational learning   human learning which takes place by observing others, social learning (p. 16)

operant conditioning   learning which occurs as a result of reward or punishment (p. 12)

opportunity sampling   selecting whoever is available as a participant (p. 56)

partial reinforcement   reinforcement which only follows some responses (p. 13)

perception   the process of interpreting, organising and elaborating on sensory information (p. 236)

personal construct   the individual patterns we have for interpreting our experiences (p. 292)

personality   the pattern of individual characteristics which combine to make each person unique (p. 151)

phallic stage   the stage of psychosexual development when the libido is focussed on the genitals (Freud) (p. 156)

pie chart   a way of showing data by proportions (p. 62)

positive correlation   a relationship between two variables in which as one increases the other increases (p. 63)

positive reinforcement   anything which is rewarding to the learner (p. 13)

practice effect   when subjects do better on a task the second time they do it, occurs in a repeated measures design of study (p. 53)

prejudice   an extreme attitude for or against a group, or a member of the group (p. 113)

pre-operational stage second stage of cognitive development (Piaget) (p. 229)

primacy effect   the disproportionate influence of first impressions (p. 284)

primary reinforcer   anything which satisfies basic instincts (p. 13)

privation   never having formed an attachment (p. 88)

pro-social behaviour   behaviour which helps others (p. 267)

psychoanalytic theory   theory based on the idea that behaviour is caused by unconscious forces (Freud) (p. 152)

psychometric tests   standardised tests which measure characteristics such as intelligence, personality or attitude (p. 43)

punishment   anything which weakens behaviour, makes a behaviour less likely to happen (p. 15)

quota sampling   calculating what proportion of particular characteristics there are in the target population and selecting participants in the same proportions (p. 56)

random sampling   selecting participants on the basis that all members of the target population have an equal chance of being selected (p. 55)

range   the difference between the highest and lowest scores (p. 65)

recency   effect where later information has more influence than earlier information (p. 285)

reflex   an automatic physical response (p. 4)

reinforcement   any consequence which strengthens behaviour, makes a response more likely to happen (p. 13)

repeated measures   an experimental design in which the same participants are in each condition (p. 53)

role-taking   in a social setting, the ability to take the perspective of someone else (p. 269)

sampling   the method by which participants are selected for research (p. 55)

scapegoating   the process of blaming someone else for your problems (p. 116)

scattergram   a way of showing the degree to which two variables are related (p. 62)

schema   a mental framework for organising, interpreting and recalling information (pp. 29–30, 232)

script   the sequence of events, in a social setting, which go together (p. 28)

secondary reinforcer   anything which strengthens behaviour but does not satisfy basic instincts (p. 13)

self-concept   the set of views, beliefs and feelings which we have about ourselves (p. 207)

self-efficacy   expectations and feelings of competence about one's abilities (p. 162)

self-esteem   how we feel about ourselves (p. 208)

self-fulfilling prophecy   the process by which a person's expectations about someone else may come true, because they treat this other person according to their expectations of them and so bring about the expected response (p. 220)

self-image   what we know about ourselves (p. 208)

self-perception theory   the idea that we discover what our feelings are by watching our own behaviour (p. 207)

self-selected sample   a sample of people who have offered to be participants (p. 57)

sensitive period   the time when an aspect of development is particularly responsive to certain experiences or influences (p. 6)

sensory motor stage   first stage of cognitive development (Piaget) (p. 225)

separation distress   unhappy response shown by a child when an attached figure leaves (p. 76)

social categorisation   classifying people as members of either the in-group or the out-group (p. 28)

social cognition   how people understand and make sense of others and themselves (p. 225)

social conformity   following the actions and opinions of others rather than one's own (p. 107)

social exchange theory   the idea that we consider our interactions with others on the basis of rewards and costs (p. 101)

social identity theory   the sense of who we are which is gained from membership of a group (p. 118)

social learning   human learning which takes place by observing others, observational learning (p. 16)

social norms   society's unspoken rules about what is acceptable and unacceptable (p. 21)

social role   the part played by an individual which involves expectations from others and obligations towards others (p. 22)

standardise   to make consistent so that results are comparable (p. 172)

standardised instructions   the identical instructions given to each subject in a study (p. 59)

stereotype   an organised set of beliefs and assumptions about the characteristics of all members of a group (p. 31)

stereotyping   categorising someone as a member of a particular group and assuming they have the characteristics which all members of that group are thought to have (p. 288)

stranger fear   distress shown by a child when a stranger approaches (p. 76)

superego   the part of personality related to morals, to what we know is wrong and to the kind of person we want to be (Freud) (p. 153)

survey   a way of gathering information by asking many people to answer questions (p. 40)

temperament   the individual's style of responding to his or her environment, which is generally thought to be innate and to persist over time (p. 163)

thanatos   human instinct for self-destruction (Freud) (p. 134)

trial   a rehearsal or practice (p. 11)

unconditional response   automatic behaviour, over which one has no control, e.g. a reflex (p. 11)

unconditional stimulus   anything which causes an automatic response (p. 11)

valid   to measure or test what is supposed to be measured (p. 174)

vicarious reinforcement   learning from the way others are reinforced or punished (p. 16)

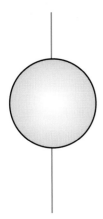

Index